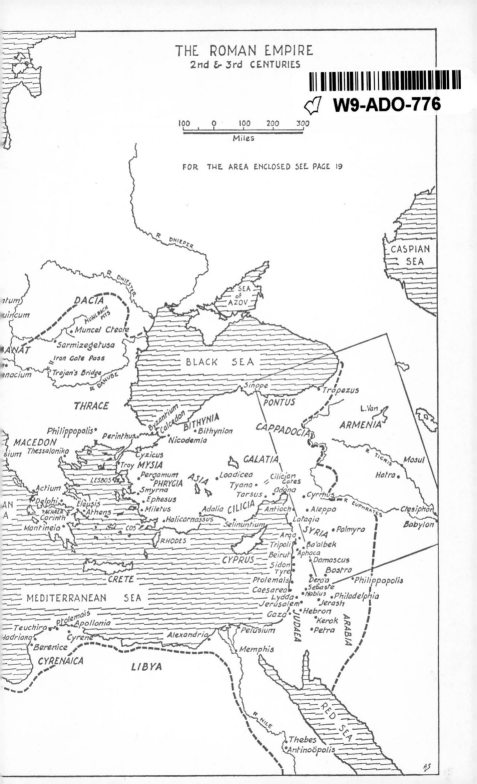

THE ROMAN EMPIRE
2nd & 3rd CENTURIES

W9-ADO-776

100   0   100   200   300
Miles

FOR THE AREA ENCLOSED SEE PAGE 19

CASPIAN SEA

R. DNIEPER

R. DNIESTER

SEA of AZOV

atum

uincum

ANAT

anacium

DACIA

MUHLBACH MTS

Muncel Cleole

Sarmizegetusa

Iron Gate Pass

Trojan's Bridge

R. DANUBE

BLACK SEA

Sinope

Trapezus

PONTUS

L. Van

ARMENIA

R. TIGRIS

Mosul

THRACE

Byzantium

Calcedon

BITHYNIA

Bithynion

CAPPADOCIA

Hatra

MACEDON

sium

Thessalonika

Philippopolis

Perinthus

Nicodemia

Cyzicus

MYSIA

Troy

LESBOS

Pergamum

PHRYGIA

Smyrna

ASIA

GALATIA

Loadicea

Tyana

Tarsus

Cilician Gates

Adana

Cyrrhus

R. EUPHRATES

Ctesiphon

Actium

Delphi

TACHAEA

Corinth

Elausis

Athens

Ephesus

Miletus

Adalia

CILICIA

Antioch

Aleppo

Babylon

Mantineia

COS

Halicarnassus

Selinuntium

Lataqia

SYRIA

Palmyra

RHODES

Arqa

Tripoli

Beirut

Ba'albek

Aphaca

Damascus

CYPRUS

Sidon

Tyre

Bostra

Philippopolis

Ptolemais

Deroa

Sebaste

Caesarea

Lydda

Noblus

Philadelphia

MEDITERRANEAN   SEA

CRETE

Jerusalem

Jerash

Gaza

Hebron

Kerak

Petra

ARABIA

JUDAEA

Teuchira

Ptolemais

Apollonia

Hadriano

Cyrene

Berenice

Alexandria

Pelusium

CYRENAICA

LIBYA

Memphis

R. NILE

RED SEA

Thebes

Antinoöpolis

AS

CAESARS AND SAINTS
The Evolution of the Christian State
AD 180–313

CAESARS AND SAINTS

by

Stewart Perowne
M.A., F.S.A.

W · W · NORTON & COMPANY · INC · New York

To
my godson
PAUL FOOT

CONTENTS

LIST OF ILLUSTRATIONS

MAPS

Acknowledgements to illustrations

[1] German Archeological Institute, Rome

[2] Bibliotheca Bodmeriana, Geneva

[3] National Museum, Damascus

[4] Cambridge University Press

[5] De Liberali

[6] The Cyprus Museum, Nicosia

[7] Ny Carlsberg Glyptotek, Copenhagen

[8] Anderson

[9] Fototeca Unione

[10] Crown Copyright Reserved. Photo: J. K. St. Joseph

[11] Alinari

[12] Commendatore Salvatore Aurigemma

[13] Bibliothèque Nationale, Paris

[14] British Museum

[15] Lenbachhaus, Munich. Photo: Grete Eckert

[16] The Warburg Institute, London

[17] Acropolis Museum, Athens. Photo: Nik. Stouvnaras

[18] Institut Archéologique Français, Beirut

[19] Yugoslav National Tourist Office

[20] Corpus Christi College, Cambridge. Photo: Edward Leigh

[21] Italian State Tourist Office

INTRODUCTION

THE death of Marcus Aurelius, like that of Queen Victoria, marked the passing not only of a sovereign, but of an age and an empire as well. In each case, the shock was its own anaesthetic: it was only later that men realized what had gone from them. The name "Antonine", like the word "Victorian", was to stand for later generations as a synonym for stable bliss, just as the Romans ascribed to Augustus, the English to Elizabeth I, the foundation of the splendid fortune they now saw to be declining. The psychological parallel is close; but history never repeats itself, and the story of the twentieth century is wholly different from that of the third.

The history of the third century is of interest for two reasons. The first is that it is, in many aspects, obscure: it tempts us with problems of interpretation such as few others present. For the scantiness of our written annals, see *Sources*: the secular record of the greater part of the century hangs solely on the frayed thread of the *Augustan History*. One has only to read the twelfth and final volume of the *Cambridge Ancient History* to appreciate the difficulty in which the editors found themselves. It was, admittedly, aggravated by the threat of war, and the impossibility of communicating with certain of the European scholars who contributed to the book. Even so, it is a groping, uncertain work. "Believing where we cannot prove" might well have been its motto, there is so much in it of conjecture, of hypothesis, even of confessed contradiction. Unsolved enigmas always attract.

The second reason why the third century is crucial is that it saw the rise of a force which was to transform society, namely the Christian faith.

But how did a pagan monarchy centred in Rome become transmuted into a Christian theocracy directed from Constantinople? And in the space of a century and a half? Gibbon, whose mountainous genius still casts a shadow over any discussion of the question, settled the matter with characteristic confidence. The Christian faith was the source of Rome's troubles. The more Christianity rose, therefore, the more Rome declined. The two were as logically linked as two buckets on the same rope: the harder men hauled to raise the one, the more surely sank the other. This theory, which shocked the orthodox, failed to convince the impious. Gibbon's buckets do not hold water.

The Cambridge historians tried a new line. They fully appreciated the nature, force and achievement of the Christian faith. They treat of it with all fairness and sympathy. And yet they entitle their volume "Crisis and Recovery", the inference being that the fabric of the state, gravely imperilled as it had been, was restored, put back to its original form, maintained, and that this was the work of a series of remarkable soldiers and administrators drawn chiefly from what is now Jugoslavia.

To this exposition, brilliantly and modestly as it is portrayed, there are two objections. The first is that there was not a restoration. Crisis, yes, continual crisis. But the original state was not restored. If it had been, the rise of the Byzantine empire could be explained only by a sort of *coup de théâtre*, a transformation scene. History does not proceed like that. There have been many "restorations" in history, but the last state has never been the same as the first. England in 1660 was not the England of 1649, nor France in 1815 that of 1789.

The second objection is that the Illyrian emperors, as they are called, good soldiers though they were, came from a part of the empire that was intellectually and spiritually barren. They could not and did not promote or regulate the spiritual development of the age. And the age must have developed spiritually, for on no other hypothesis is the triumph of Christianity explicable. The Sower was at work; but some at least of the seed must fall on good ground. Who had prepared it? It was hard for European scholars, born in the nineteenth century, to picture an age when Europe was not the hearth and centre of light and leading. It was easier for them to believe in the efficacy of Illyria than in that of the Levant. For us, it is far easier to find the clue. If we cast our eyes over the list of the later Roman emperors (see Table I), we are bewildered at the disorder of the times. Where do we find any "dynasty" such as the "Julio-Claudians", the "Flavians" or the "Antonines"? On the contrary, we note that between the years 235 and 285, nearly twenty emperors were proclaimed—and this does not include several successful usurpers who, in Britain and in the Levant, maintained their authority for longer than many of the "official" rulers. This half-century was one of chaos: to the extent that Diocletian arrested it, he is entitled to be called a "restorer". But what immediately preceded this welter of dynasts?

In the year 193, Septimius Severus becomes emperor: with the exception of one year, members of his family will rule until 235. Thus, for forty years, the domestic fabric is renewed. But with two basically important differences. The first is that, after 193, it was the army which, quite openly, made the emperors. The second is that this family were not Romans at all, they were Semites, sprung from the union of Punic with Syrian.

Both these aspects of the new régime will be treated in some detail. Here it is only desired to make the point that in the Severan dynasty we have the key to the problem which has baffled so many for so long—the means by which the transformation of the pagan to the Christian, the western to the eastern, may be seen as a logical, organic process. It was a development, an evolution, not an explosion or a "new departure".

That in the secular sphere there had been change and decay is unquestionable; but in the spiritual domain there was continual progress. In the last of the Severans, the authors of the *Augustan History* saw the ideal ruler: they give him more space and more praise than any other of their subjects. It is easy to see why: to *them* he was the ideal pagan: to *us* he is the forerunner of Constantine.

In the following chapters an attempt will be made to show three things: first, why the material world of Rome was in decline, secondly, how it was saved from dissolution as much by Semitic as by Italic enterprise, and thirdly, how natural, and indeed inevitable, it was that Christianity should become the basis of a new order.

The sources, both ancient and modern, on which this attempt is based are described in the appendix.

Chapter I

ROMAN SUMMER

"IF a man," says Gibbon in a famous sentence, "were called to fix the period in the history of the world during which the condition of the human race was most happy and prosperous, he would, without hesitation, name that which elapsed from the death of Domitian to the accession of Commodus." That is to say from AD 96 to the year 180.

In the year 96, on the assassination of Domitian, the senate had invested a respected and honest Roman called Nerva—whose busts bear a striking resemblance to those of the Duke of Wellington—with the purple. He in his turn had named a victorious and popular young general as his adopted son and successor. His name was Trajan. He became emperor in 98; and in a series of brilliant military campaigns carried Rome's frontier to the widest limits it was ever to know. Trajan was a colonial from Spain; and he in his turn adopted his cousin, also Spanish-born, called Hadrian. When Trajan died on active service in 117, Hadrian became emperor. He was to rule for twenty-one years. He left an assured succession by adoption, so that he was followed by Antoninus Pius, who gave his name to the age, and Antoninus by Marcus Aurelius, the "philosopher-emperor".

The later Romans looked back upon the Antonine age as an apogee of glory. Just as we regard two epochs, the Elizabethan and the Victorian, as the twin peaks of English greatness, so did the Romans regard the ages of Augustus and the Antonines, to such an extent in the case of the latter that emperors of the third century, who had no blood relationship with Antoninus, assumed his name and his putative ancestry. Generally speaking, it was the half-century that preceded the year 180—the years when Hadrian had done his work, and the era he bequeathed to his successors—that may be accounted the "golden age" of Rome.

What had he achieved, this "universal genius", as H. A. L. Fisher was to call him?

Trajan had inherited the direction of a vast empire. During a period of nearly three centuries, Rome had made herself mistress of the whole of the Mediterranean littoral, of Spain and Gaul, even of Britain. Her European frontier was furnished by two rivers, the Rhine and the Danube. The whole northern coast of Africa was now Roman; Egypt, so ancient, so august, an appanage of the Caesars. Palestine, Syria, Asia Minor, Greece itself—all these ancient lands, the cradles of civilizations far older than that of Rome—all now obeyed the master of the Capitol.

The empire thus created was primarily a land empire. Almost every province was accessible from some other by land, and the crossings which separated Asia, Africa or Britain were then as now little more than ferry-services. Rome therefore was never a predominantly maritime power, such as for instance Holland and England were to become. Fleets she did have, but in imperial times, when both pirates and rivals had alike been overcome, they were little more than transport commands, one based on Misenum near Naples, and another in the Adriatic. The corn trade was largely in the hands of Greek and Phoenician shipowners. It was a Greek, Hippalus, who, in the days of Augustus, had discovered the secret of the monsoon, and so had opened up the Red Sea and the Indian Ocean to Roman shipping. This throve, and a fleet of over a hundred sail went to the Yemen, Abyssinia and India every year. Navigation was slow; three weeks from Egypt to Italy was the average. And shipwreck was a much commoner hazard then than now.

It was on the roads rather than ships, on soldiers not sailors, that Rome depended for the diffusion of her power, even if for long-distance transport in bulk the sea must still be used, as it had been in ages gone by, and would be again, when an empire was no longer one "monolithic" unit, but consisted of territories separated one from the other by oceans.

This vast and opulent patrimony had not been assembled without Rome's encountering and overcoming opponents. Sometimes, as in the case of the Britons and most of the Africans, these had been mere tribes of no highly organized polity or culture. Others had represented rival civilizations. There were three cultures in particular which had opposed Rome. They are of abiding importance for this reason: in each case Rome claimed that she had vanquished them, and in each case, on the spiritual plane, the rival was to prove superior to the mistress. The three powers were Carthage, Greece and Persia. In the case of Greece it is a commonplace to say that the arts of Hellas had conquered Rome. The Romans said it themselves. They spoke Greek, and wrote Greek, and were proud to be esteemed Greek. For Hadrian, as for many of his countrymen, Athens was the city of his soul. But it was not the Athens of Pericles. The classics were still read, still discussed, still admired, but it was a barren

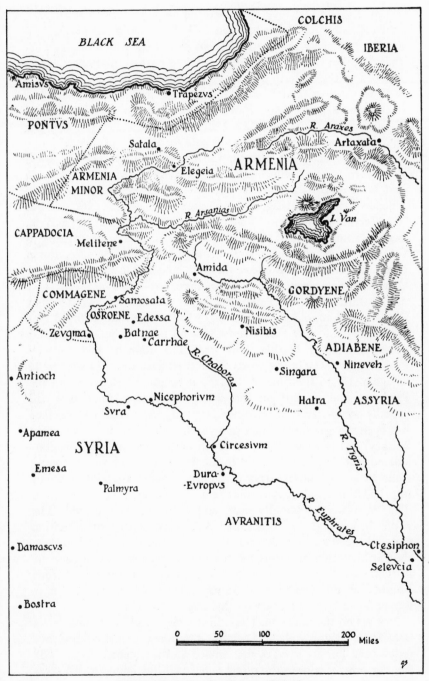

COLCHIS

BLACK SEA

IBERIA

Amisvs

Trapezvs

PONTVS

R. Araxes

Satala

Artaxata

Elegeia

ARMENIA

ARMENIA
MINOR

R. Arsanias

L. Van

CAPPADOCIA

Melitene

Amida

GORDYENE

COMMAGENE

Samosata

OSROENE

Edessa

Nisibis

ADIABENE

Zevgma

Batnae

Carrhae

Nineveh

R. Chaboras

Antioch

Singara

ASSYRIA

Nicephorivm

Hatra

Svra

R. Tigris

Apamea

SYRIA

Circesivm

Emesa

Dura-
-Evropvs

Palmyra

AVRANITIS

R. Euphrates

Damascvs

Ctesiphon

Selevcia

Bostra

0   50   100   200   Miles

Map to illustrate the Eastern Question.

antiquarianism that they nourished, no more a vivifying spirit. And when the spirit of Hellas had gone, all of her had gone; because the Greeks had never been serious rivals of Roman armed might, since that day, more than two hundred years ago, when the Roman legion had beaten the hitherto invincible Macedonian phalanx.

With Carthage and Persia the case is far different. Carthage had been Rome's first enemy. It was only after a century of strife that Rome had conquered her. As a writer of the Antonine age was to put it, "With other states, it was a struggle for the independence of one or the other state, but with the Carthaginians it was one for world dominion" (Aulus Gellius, *Attic Nights* X, xxvii). In 146 BC Carthage had been destroyed, and the site ploughed over, and it was held officially that the Carthaginian or Punic spirit had been extinguished. The Carthaginians were of Phoenician, that is Semitic stock; and the Semitic strain is one of the toughest there is. It is not surprising to find, therefore, that in a later century this same Semitic, Punic strain, despite all that Rome could do to hold that it was dead, was to shew itself once again as very much alive.

The third power was Perśia. Persian civilization was as old as that of Greece, if not older. Persian might had at one time matched that of Greece, and now that Greece was no longer a military power, Persia, or rather Parthia, still was. The Romans had suffered ignominious defeat at the hands of the Parthians, and they were to do so again. Up to the time of Trajan, although the Romans and the Parthians had clashed on the eastern frontier, neither side had actually occupied any of the other's territory. An uneasy co-existence had been the rule for two hundred years, with Armenia (now eastern Turkey) a shuttlecock state, to which both Rome and Parthia considered that they had the right to nominate kings. This compromise came to an end in the days of Trajan, whose expansionist policy impelled him to reduce Armenia to the status of an imperial province. The Parthians he soundly beat, and occupied their capital. The royal throne and the king's daughter were carried off. Hadrian restored the status quo in Armenia; but he was determined to shew the Parthians that they were inferior to the Romans; he sent back the daughter but kept the throne. So did his successor, Antoninus. This haughty attitude was to start the whole cycle all over again. There was never to be stable peace on this eastern frontier.

Nor yet on the northern. Here, in the bleak and mysterious lands beyond the Rhine and the Danube, it was not a rival culture, but jealous and hungry savages that envied and threatened Rome. The frontier provinces were the direct concern of the emperor, who was represented in them by legates of his own choosing, who were also in command of the troops. They held office at Caesar's pleasure. Their selection was of the first importance, because an army commander could and often did turn against his master, and make a bid for the supreme power. The older provinces, which required no military garrison or frontier forces, were ruled by ex-consuls, chosen by the senate. Only in Africa did a proconsul, as these officers were called during their provincial appointments, have any troops under his command. Egypt was ruled by a prefect appointed by Caesar. Third-class provinces, such as Judaea in the days of Jesus of Nazareth, were ruled by procurators, who might have a few auxiliary troops at their disposal, but no regulars. The regular army consisted of thirty legions, amounting in all to about 150,000 men, considerably less than the combined allied armies at Waterloo. This number astounds us by its smallness. How could so insignificant an army defend so great an empire, even with the support of locally raised auxiliaries, which perhaps doubled the total number of effectives?

That question states the dilemma of the empire. If these troops were spread out along the frontiers, from Britain to Palestine, they would be too thin on the ground at vital spots, such as the Danube or the Euphrates. If, on the other hand, they were concentrated, so as to provide at least the semblance of a non-existent strategic reserve, not only would sensitive frontier areas be left bare, but it was open to their commander to make a bid for control of the whole. Vespasian had become emperor by those means. Hadrian placed the seal on his adoption by the same method. In the days of Marcus Aurelius, the holder of the eastern command, Avidius Cassius, made an unsuccessful attempt on the throne. In the following century such bids became a commonplace of Roman politics. Meanwhile, as the pressures of the barbarians in the north and in Africa, and of the Parthians in the east became ever more violent and menacing, Roman arms became ever less able to defend Roman property. The pay was augmented, the term of service was increased to twenty-five years, recruitment spread its net ever wider, until the army, originally enlisted in Italy or southern France, became a consortium of territorial forces; but all to no effect: the best days of the Roman army were over. Trajan was its last great commander. Hadrian, who tried to keep it up to strength if not to enlarge it, failed to do either; but such was his address, his activity and personal ascendancy that by a series of imperial tours, unprecedented and unrepeated, he succeeded in maintaining the empire inviolate, and the army loyal.

Within this precarious framework, the empire, most of whose citizens little realized how dangerously they lived, flourished in a secure tranquillity. The rule of Rome has sometimes been pictured as oppressive. There had been, it is true, in the latter days of the Republic, greedy governors who had regarded their provinces as estates to be exploited, just as in the early days of British colonial rule a class of nabobs and slave-owners was later to do. Cicero and Burke have made us familiar with them. But under the early empire, provincial government had progressively improved. Rome ruled with a light rein, maintaining wherever possible local forms of government. This was the outcome less of policy than of necessity: there were simply not enough Romans to go round. Many governors, such as Agricola, Tacitus' father-in-law who ruled Britain, or Pliny, the friend of Trajan who governed Bithynia, were men of great ability and integrity. Antoninus himself had been a successful governor of Asia. By the age of the Antonines, the senatorial class, from which the majority of the governors was still drawn, had ceased to be predominantly Roman, or even Italian. A governor of Asia might have been born in Africa, and his chief assistants would consist of his personal friends and clients from the same region. The rest of the staff was, perforce, of local origin. The maintenance of local, traditional forms of government was thus the only possible method of maintaining an administration at all. In the eastern provinces, and in the older, more civilized portions of the western empire, this was not difficult. There had been city-states in the Hellenic world from time immemorial; and in Spain and southern Gaul Roman institutions founded upon Greek models had flourished in the days of the Roman Republic. It was harder to institute stable government among tribes such as the Britons and the Africans; and Rome, outside her own "white" settlements, never really came to terms with them. That Rome never attempted to advance her frontier to the Elbe is often attributed to the terrible defeat inflicted by a German tribal confederation on a Roman army in the days of Augustus, a disaster that haunted the emperor during the night-season to the end of his days; but the fact that there was no existing structure on which to base an administration was also a contributory reason. Only where there was the over-riding attraction of gold, as in Dacia, did the prudent Hadrian maintain Trajan's northern expansion.

This *laissez-faire* attitude towards local administrations did not imply a liberal attitude towards sectional patriotisms. The Roman empire had no place whatever for what we should call the development of subject peoples, or "trustee territories". On the contrary, its political direction was clean contrary to it: in the words of Tacitus, "Rome made even kings the instruments of servitude". A border kingdom might be suffered to exist as an "ally", but only until such time as Rome was ready to take it over as a province. Any people, therefore, which aspired to national existence, peoples such as the Jews or the Britons, felt the full rigours of Roman repression. *Politically* speaking, for Rome the only good province was a dead province.

Its life was, in Roman eyes, only to be lived economically. It is in its economic aspect that the empire appears most attractive. The basic reason for this is the same that made the United States of America so prosperous during the nineteenth and twentieth centuries: the empire was the largest single trading-area, without customs barriers or frontiers, and lapped in "the immense majesty of the Roman peace", that the world had ever known. It holds a strong nostalgic appeal for our own era, when Europe, at least—and the Roman dominion was at least twice as large—is once again striving for economic unity. Not that capitalism as we understand it then existed: the idea of the joint stock company was unknown. The prosperity was based on two factors: agriculture and urban trade, of which agriculture predominated. Rich men there certainly were; men who dealt in the export of olive oil for instance, the ancient equivalent not only of edible fats, but of soap and electric light as well. There was, too, a class of merchants, generally banded into guilds, which grew rich on the import of corn and other necessities for the requirements of Italy, of the Roman armies throughout Rome's dominions, and of the Roman circus, which meant the purveyors of savage and rare beasts. How lucrative this odious commerce was may be judged from the palace, almost a small town in itself, that a retired contractor built at Piazza Armerina in Sicily, its sumptuous chambers decorated with mosaics portraying the capture and transport of these living wares.

In general, the social structure of the provinces must have resembled that which we see in the pictures of the Brueghels, or of the Dutch masters of the seventeenth century, where a busy countryside nourishes a well-to-do commercial bourgeoisie. Under the early empire, prosperity and comfort increased and expanded. Nowhere, for instance, is it more marked than in the "marginal" regions of north Africa, where the sown invaded the desert with increasing assurance. Some of the finest mosaics of the first century come from smart villas built on the coast of Tripolitania, as it now is, and these mosaics are largely devoted to the illustration of the agricultural cycle.

Even here, there was a fatal flaw in the imperial fabric. Roman society, at peace and prospering, increasingly craved imported luxuries. They came from the east, and they were paid for in gold and silver. Nothing was exported in return. There was no balance of trade, no "invisible exports". This meant that Roman bullion, which came from the mines controlled by Rome—except when a successful campaign brought home a booty of precious metals, and with the stabilization of the frontiers such windfalls grew ever rarer—dwindled as time went on: not even the retention of Dacia (p. 22) could arrest the drain. It was this economic exhaustion which was largely responsible for the domestic strife of the third century.

Economic laws were understood even less in those days than in our own. "The method of improving the financial management of the Empire which its rulers adopted proved fatal", says Rostovtzeff (*The Social and Economic History of the Roman Empire*, 2nd Ed., p. 391). "With one hand they endeavoured to create a healthy middle class and establish new centres of civilized life, and with the other they destroyed their own work by retaining the baneful system of compulsory labour, of requisitions, and of supplementary levies . . . As the regular income of the state was not adequate to meet emergency needs, the emperors, instead of prudently increasing the taxes, which they disliked doing, resorted to far worse expedients by attacking not income, as before, but capital. The result was disastrous."

Turning finally to the spiritual plane, we survey no brighter prospect. Virgil, in one of the best-known passages of the *Aeneid*, had foretold what he—and he was the noblest Roman of them all—thought should be the destiny of Rome:

> Let others better mold the running Mass
> Of mettals, and inform the breathing Brass;
> And soften into Flesh a Marble Face:
> Plead better at the Bar; describe the Skies,
> And when the Stars descend and when they rise.
> But, *Rome*, 'tis thine alone, with awful sway,
> To rule Mankind, and make the World obey;
> Disposing Peace, and War, thy own Majestic Way,
> To tame the Proud, the fetter'd Slave to free;
> These are Imperial Arts, and worthy thee.
> (*Aeneid* VI, 847–53, tr. Dryden, 1697)

Even though a governing nation is no longer such an exalted model as it used to be, the proposed division of talents might, even in this age, be accepted as fair, provided it existed. The fallacy in Virgil's

review is that it never did. Rome ruled, but the arts were not cultivated on any comparable scale. Architecture, it is true, continued to
flourish, and some of the most majestic buildings ever erected were
produced by imperial Rome. But of philosophy, poetry, drama,
music the empire was to produce nothing that was new, and very
little that was old. As for "freeing the fetter'd slave", the Roman
bent was to acquire more of them, and to go on doing it. There was,
it is true, a glimmer of hope, of a growing humanity among the best
spirits of the age. Almost pathetic is the phrase that occurs more than
once in some imperial rescript counselling clemency, or forbidding
brutality: "This is not in accordance with the spirit of the age." But
against the gloom of a slave society, such a vague aspiration was no
more than a will-o'-the-wisp. The actual status of the slave had, it is
true, progressively improved, as more and more official posts had
been entrusted to the lower, servile members of the imperial household, and thus more and more slaves had eventually become freed-
men. Actual brutality had been increasingly repressed. Slaves might
not be sold to gladiators or brothels, exposed children adopted by
their finders might not be classed as servile, the examination of slaves
in judicial investigations became more humane. But these measures,
which must have mitigated the harshness of the slaves' lot to such an
extent that Christianity in its early days did not attempt to combat it
(it had many other far more evil things to fight), did not touch the
institution of slavery itself. That is to say, they did not alter the bad
effects of slavery on *society*. For once it has become a recognized
institution, slavery invariably corrupts the master far more ruinously
than it frustrates the slave. This sad truth was to be proved in other
continents in later centuries.

Slavery induces an idleness of spirit which leads to stagnation.
Why should a man worry himself to harness the powers of nature,
when so much manpower was available? It is this basic sloth of
intellect that is the true bane of the slave-owning society. Moreover,
whatever may have been the amelioration of the domestic slave's lot,
it amounted to little when set against the beastly exhibitions of the
amphitheatre, in which the citizens of Rome assembled to witness the
slaughter not only of animals, but of their fellow-men, mostly slaves
or captives, "butchered to make a Roman holiday".

Only in the east shone the star of hope. For a century and more the
ancient genius of the Orient for furnishing the souls of men and
women with a zest for life had attracted more and more western
adherents. Of these religious systems there were many, of which much
will be said in the course of this study. Two in particular had proved

magnetic: they were the only two which still to-day are the guiding principle of millions, Judaism and Christianity. At the end of the first century, Judaism was about to enter on a period of eclipse, Christianity on an epoch of expansion. But Rome as yet reckoned little of either.

Such was the background of the "golden age" of the empire. It was an age of security, of tranquillity, an age of commerce and comfort. But within and without it was menaced by dangers, physical, economic and spiritual. Socially it lived for itself. Spiritually it lived on, and largely in, the past. To posterity it recognized no debt; and it was to discover, this proud and complacent empire, as other empires have discovered since, that posterity is the most relentless of creditors.

Chapter II

PEACE, PERFECT PEACE

IT is given to few men to rule from the grave; yet it might almost be said of Hadrian that he succeeded in doing it. Viewed in retrospect, the period covered by the reigns of Trajan, Hadrian, Antoninus and Marcus Aurelius is not so much four reigns of almost identical span—an average of just over twenty years each—as a single majestic cantilever of time, with Hadrian as the central pillar. For forty years after his death, the régime he had created was to endure.

Antoninus was fifty-one when he became emperor. His ancestors came from Nîmes in southern Gaul; but during the last two generations, running parallel with the Trajan-Hadrian clan from Spain, the family had risen to eminence in Rome. The colonial, or rather what we should now call Dominion, origin of the two houses was a bond between them. Unlike Hadrian, who never really became acclimatized to Italy, Antoninus was very much at home there—too much, as events were to prove. On both sides of his family he was the heir to great estates. He owned land in Latium, in Etruria, in Picenum and Campania. These together with numerous legacies from relations made him one of the richest men in Rome. They also made him more inclined to live at one or other of his villas—for an Italian villa was as desirable a retreat then as now—than to face the discomforts of foreign travel and the cares of official life. Of both he had had his fill; he had been one of the four circuit judges whom Hadrian had appointed to supervise matters of personal status in Italy. The link between him and Hadrian was reinforced by his marriage with Faustina, whose brother, Annius Verus, was Hadrian's first choice as successor, probably because he was in reality a natural son of Hadrian and father of Marcus Aurelius, whom at Hadrian's bidding Antoninus himself adopted. In the year 134, that is after the interval which constitutional custom required, Antoninus became governor of Asia, as his grandfather had been sixty years earlier. Here he had seen enough of turbulence and travel. Never would he forget, for instance, the night he had reached Smyrna at the end of a long journey to find that the "notable" with whom he had hoped to stay had not received his message and was away. He moved into the house, only to be turned out in the middle of the night when its owner returned and found that his home had been commandeered and he himself excluded from it by the governor's sentries. Through the tact of Hadrian, the two men had afterwards become friends and they used to joke about the episode. But Antoninus did not want any more of that sort of thing, not at his age.

Then too there was the senate. Antoninus had had to deal with it when he was acting for Hadrian during the last days, and the dying and mentally deranged emperor was ordering executions right and left, which Antoninus would try to countermand. He did in fact save many senators, but not Servianus, Hadrian's brother-in-law, who had been compelled to commit suicide despite his ninety years, together with his eighteen-year-old grandson. This rankled.

When Hadrian died, the senate had wished to withhold from him the title *Divus* and even to annul all his acts. It took Antoninus all his talent for persuasion and accommodation to cajole the senate into acquiescence. If they annulled Hadrian's acts, he pointed out, they would annul his own adoption, and then where would anybody be? He "removed none of the men whom Hadrian had appointed to office" knowing that they had been well chosen. He earned the title *Pius* by the dutiful way in which he laid Hadrian's body to rest in the new and splendid mausoleum which we know as Castel Sant' Angelo, and built in his honour the magnificent temple of which part survives to this day in the fabric of the Rome Bourse—the only ancient temple still to resound with the cries of the Roman populace. He also built a temple at Pozzuoli, where in a villa which had once been Cicero's, Hadrian had first of all, in view of the senate's opposition, been buried; and he founded a confraternity of priests to honour the dead emperor, on the lines of those which already served chantries for the Augustan, Claudian and Flavian houses.

All this had been wearing. What Antoninus wanted now was peace and quiet, specially in his relations with the senate. He therefore decided to do nothing without their advice, which meant that he could be vacillating when he should have been firm. For his decision not to leave Italy, he gave as his excuse that royal progresses were a burden to the provinces, and that by staying at the centre of the empire he was able to receive messages from all quarters with equal speed, rather like a modern telephone operator.

So there he stayed, this good, rich, respected and rather idle man. He was affable to his friends, simple in his habits, generous to his dependants; in fact the picture of him given in the *Augustan History* reads like an expanded epitaph of so many eighteenth-century Englishmen.

For the rest, there were Hadrian's public works to be finished at home (and finished they were, which shewed that as always with Hadrian, they had been designed for public amenity not personal ostentation), and the ravages of fire and earthquake to be repaired, the former in Rome and Carthage, Antioch and Narbonne—so common was this disaster in Roman times—and the latter in Rhodes and Cos, Bithynia, Lesbos, Smyrna and Ephesus—for then as now the region was perpetually liable to seismic disaster. The prestige which Trajan and Hadrian had built up was enough to avoid war in the east. Indeed, one king from the Caucasus who had refused to visit Hadrian now paid a state visit with his queen. Antoninus appointed another as far afield as the eastern shore of the Black Sea.

Hearing that King Vologases III of Parthia was preparing to reopen the Armenian question, and even contemplating an invasion of Syria, Antoninus induced him to abandon the idea simply by writing to him, in the style of modern east–west exchanges between heads of state. In the region of the Black Sea, the Crimea, and southwestern Russia the new emperor was active diplomatically, and even, through his generals, militarily, when it was a question of protecting Greek settlements in the region. In the latter years of his reign, that is after 152, the Antonine peace was broken by local insurrections. The Jews, who had suffered terribly for the folly of their revolt in 133, nevertheless found the punitive restrictions imposed by Hadrian and maintained by his successor intolerable. They were excluded from their Holy City, or rather from the new Roman town which had arisen on its ruins. Posts were placed at Bethlehem, Emmaus and what is now Beit Liqya, among others, to prevent access to it, and, so St Justin tells us, "no Jew was allowed to live in Jerusalem, and those who were caught trying to get there were killed". As if that were not enough, the Jews were subject to forced labour, even on the Sabbath (from which they had long been officially exempt), they were forbidden to conduct schools or hold services, nor were they permitted to circumcise their children. It is not to be wondered at that Jews were willing to face death rather than suffer this wholesale negation of Jewish life. It was, as usual, in Galilee that the revolt broke out, headed by survivors of the earlier revolt. As a result, the Jews, but they only, that is to say no proselytes, were allowed to resume the rite of circumcision. Any others who practised it were liable, we learn from the *Digest*, to the penalty of those who performed castration, that is, death.

This concession was to win a unique fame in Jewish legend for Antoninus, who was even said to have been circumcised himself, and to have studied the Law with the great Rabbi Judah. There is no doubt a confusion here with Elagabalus, who was circumcised and did call himself Antoninus, and with his successor Severus Alexander who favoured both Jews and Christians (see Chapter XVI).

There were also risings in Achaea, and in remote frontier areas, as far apart as the Red Sea and the Dnieper. The Britons, as usual, were restive. Ever since the days of Boadicea, they had despised the Romans. This disgusting woman—the atrocities which she and her Britons committed are unprintable—had become a legend of barbarous ferocity, so that even in Dio's day she was still a by-word for savage individualism. "She was very tall"—the type has persisted—"ugly to look at, with a terrifying glance, and a grating voice. A great mat of flaxen hair fell to her waist. She wore a large gold necklace, and a tunic of different colours, with a thick mantle, done up with a brooch over it. She never wore anything else." Dio makes her deliver a long harangue—of particular interest in view of the speech of Aristides which will be quoted shortly—the gist of which is that, in no circumstances, could there be peace between Briton and Roman. They could never come to terms with these men, she says, "if indeed we really can call them 'men' who have hot baths, eat made dishes, drink neat wines, use scent, sleep on soft beds, with boys, and boys past their prime, just as they are slaves to a harper [Nero], and a bad one at that". This speech, the confection of a Roman senator at the end of the third century, suggests that even by then, the British were not Romanized. Despite all the retrospective piety of modern classical scholars, it is not possible to claim that the Britons ever accepted a Latin destiny.

Antoninus had to deal with them. He did so, and he was able to reinforce the famous wall of Hadrian by a secondary rampart made of turf between the Forth and the Clyde (Plate 10).

There was trouble, too, in north Africa, in Dacia. None of these peripheral disturbances was of the first importance in itself; but with our hindsight we are able to see that they were, taken as a whole, the first symptoms of that universal storm which was to assail the still complacent empire within the century. The most serious outbreak from Antoninus' own point of view was one in Egypt. In 152–3 the fellahin raised a tumult which seriously imperilled the corn supply of Rome. The citizens of the capital rioted, and would have stoned the emperor had he not issued a largesse of flour, oil and wine from his own resources.

Empty flattery Antoninus despised, and he refused to accept various compliments, the most important of which from our point of view was that the months of September and October should be called Antoninus and Faustinus after him and his wife, just as our July and August commemorate to this day the first two Caesars. From the point of view of his contemporaries, his remission of the "coronation money" was more relevant. This was a contribution, originally voluntary, but later compulsory, towards providing gold wreaths (in imitation of laurel) for a triumphing general. Augustus remitted it, but none of his successors appears to have done so until Trajan. Like Hadrian on his accession, so Antoninus, when the tribute was offered him on his adoption, remitted the whole of Italy's share and half the provincial quotas. He followed up this precedent by refusing legacies from those who had children of their own.

To this august and genial court, there came in the year 145 a polished Greek orator. He had come from Smyrna, by land, along the Via Egnatia, in just under three weeks—an astonishingly rapid transit given the terrain and the distances. He arrived in Rome for the birthday of the city, which was, and still is, celebrated on the 21st April. For nine hundred years, short of only two, Rome had stood. Aristides had come to praise the eternal city. His oration is the finest and most famous of its kind. There is, naturally enough, a great deal of flattery, a great deal of verbiage in the speech. Nevertheless, it does leave on the reader, even to-day, an impression of majesty and amplitude. Rome, says Aristides, is unique, both in power and size. To look at the empire, and reflect what a small area rules the whole world, is to be amazed at the city; but to look at the city itself is to cease to wonder that the world is ruled by so great a creation. To Rome, the whole world sends its products: it is the universal emporium. "What the Mediterranean used to mean to the Persians, the Atlantic means to you." But how different is Rome from Persia! (And here we have a reflection of the contemporary preoccupation with east–west relations.) The Persians ruled "as the result of a curse rather than in answer to a prayer. A child's beauty was a terror to its parents, a wife's to her husband." How different is Rome. Better not only than the Persians, but even than the old Greek polities, which, whatever their virtue in resisting Persian aggression, shewed themselves incapable of rule. Rome is a partnership, not a despotism. "Neither sea nor intervening continent are bars to citizenship, nor are Asia and Europe treated differently in regard to it. In your empire all paths are open to all. No one worthy of rule or responsibility remains an alien, but a civil community of the world has been established as a free republic under one man, the best, the ruler and teacher of order."

Rome has encircled the whole empire with a living wall of devoted and disciplined legions. Within this circle "cities gleam with radiance and charm, and the whole earth has been adorned like a garden". In fact, concludes Aristides, to praise Rome aright is beyond anyone's power, "for it would require just about as much time as is allotted to the empire, and that would be all eternity".

The eternal city: it was a delightful vision. Eternal, Rome was to become, but not through the faith which sustained Antoninus, or Aristides.

Antoninus died as he had lived, in tranquillity and dignity. Death came to him in his seventy-fifth year, at his country seat just north of Rome, Lorium, where he had so often attended the vintage-feast and entertained his friends at pleasant house-parties. One evening he felt ill and lapsed into a fever. Realizing that his end had come, he gave orders that the golden statue of Fortune, which the emperors always kept in their bedchambers as a sort of talisman, should be committed to his adopted son and son-in-law Marcus Aurelius, as a symbol of his succession. When the officer of the day asked him for the watchword, "Equanimity," said Antoninus, "and so turning as if he would sleep, he ceased to breathe".

Chapter III

THE PHILOSOPHER SOLDIER

OF all the Roman emperors, Marcus Aurelius is the most pathetic and paradoxical. In him, posterity has chosen to see all that is best in the "pagan" character—although the very word was unknown while he lived. In him is fixed all that is highest, in "the high Roman fashion"; and yet it was Marcus who was to be the harbinger of Rome's dissolution, he, the one and only philosopher king to adorn a throne, was to demonstrate how vain is philosophy, how transient a throne.

Marcus had been born lucky. His family, the Annii Veri, were "old" Spanish, and so when Marcus entered the world in 121, it was natural enough that he should be brought up in the circle of Hadrian's friends. When only six years old, he had been admitted by the "Spanish" emperor to the Salian priesthood, a clear sign that even thus young he was marked out for high advancement, even as Hadrian himself had been; for this was, in the Roman era, the high noon of successful favouritism, just as the eighteenth century was to be for Britain. It gave Rome an Aurelius, and was to give England a Wellington.

The boy's upbringing was disastrous. No less than twenty tutors were engaged to sharpen his wits. Of only two have we any direct record. Fronto was a professional don. He was also a mental eunuch, a minikin creature who doted on royalty—the ancient equivalent of the Fellows of a now bygone age, who lived on those awful little jokes which they hoped that no one other than their own stuffy côterie would understand. Pedant, and suppressed pederast, Fronto could write to Marcus in terms which make Shakespeare's sonnets sound hearty. He could warn him of the perils and dangers of being associated with an "older man"—other than himself—and then write: "When you see the must fermenting in the cask, let it remind you that my longing for you wells up the same way and foams in my breast."

The second tutor who is more than a mere name was Herodes Atticus, a delightful Athenian extrovert. He was raffish, saucy and enormously rich. He wore odd hats, and was always ready with advice, wit and cash. Marcus and he became close friends, and many are the stories of how the philosopher emperor would put up with his friend's eccentricities. Herodes was a loyal realist. When Avidius Cassius (see page 40) raised his rebellion Herod wrote the shortest letter of which ancient history has record: "Dear Cassius, You're mad. Yours Herod."

In his love of learning, and his feeling for Hellenism, Marcus resembled Hadrian; but unlike Hadrian he had a real feeling for "divine philosophy". Unfortunately, the race of philosophers was extinct. The sophists of whom we have record were empty prigs, who spent their time and talent on unbelievably vain disputations. Had the lofty stoic Marcus ever heard of the Psalms of David, his favourite would have been the forty-second: he really was as the hart which desireth the water-brooks; but alas! he lived in a barren and dry land where no water is.

Thus it came about that his life was a tortured contradiction. Marcus would go to the theatre: he would shew his contempt for the bestiality which he had to attend by reading or writing during the performance, and would then look up to see that a poor rope-dancer had fallen and injured himself. He gave orders that in future, tight-rope-walking acts must only be given over a mattress, or a net—Marcus' legacy to the circus of today. He hated bloodshed, but was compelled to provide animals by the hundred for slaughter. He could write, in his intimate diary, that to hunt down Sarmatians was mere robbery, and yet go on hunting them down in his capacity as emperor. In the same record he could pride himself on his restraint in having touched "neither Benedicta nor Theodotus"—an abstinence which Marcus cites as a testimony to his chastity, but which, as Dean Inge pointed out, is a damning exposure of the moral standards of the age, which could equate, even in ethics, the natural with the unnatural. This enquiring spirit thought that an intelligent man of forty had seen all that life has to show us.

The most tragic contradiction of all lay in the terrible events which Marcus had to attempt to control, for he, the philosopher, was destined to spend the rest of his active life as a soldier. Antoninus, on his death-bed, had murmured of "the state and the kings he was angry with". No sooner was he dead, than the tempest broke. The years of ease and neglect were now to exact a humiliating penalty. Yet another disastrous flood of the Tiber—a frequently recurring calamity—and a famine in Asia which spread misery throughout the province, these were as nothing to the wars which were to shatter the security of the empire. To start with there was Vologases of Parthia. His patience was exhausted. He declared war in due form, and sent

34

his General Osroes into Armenia to place a Persian on the throne. The governor of Cappadocia was killed in battle, and the Parthians, easily routing the Syrian legions who had become demoralized by the delights of the Levant, occupied the province, which was one of the most fertile and most populous in the whole empire. It was exactly two hundred years since any Parthian had been seen west of the Euphrates except as a suppliant, a prisoner or a hostage. Now the Parthians were there as conquerors.

Clearly the situation must be restored. But it was not only in the east that there was trouble: war threatened in Germany and Rhaetia, and once again the fretful Britons were afoot. Marcus, who dreaded the possibility of a war on two fronts, dare not leave the capital. To take command on the eastern front he therefore sent his adoptive brother, Lucius Verus. Lucius was ten years his junior, but had been chosen by Hadrian to be one of the eventual successors, probably because Lucius' father, Aelius, whom he had first selected, was a natural son. When Aelius died, his son Lucius was placed in the succession as co-heir with Marcus, whose daughter he married. The two "brothers" were, in fact, consuls at the time of Antoninus' death, which had made the succession all the easier. Unfortunately, Lucius was a man of a very different stamp from Marcus. He was a tough, handsome lowbrow, with a great mop of curly blond hair, on which he used to sprinkle gold-dust to heighten the effect. He gambled, was an ardent backer of the Greens—one of the four racing syndicates—and had a gold statue made of his favourite horse, called Speedbird, which he carried about with him. He was notoriously unchaste, both with women and boys.

He was now thirty-one. As co-ruler with Marcus, he had every right to command; but it must have been with a feeling of relief that the temperate and modest Marcus saw him set out. He went with him as far as Capua. Verus was in no hurry; he knew that the troops which had been summoned from Bonn could not reach Syria until the following spring. Others had to come from the Danube, from Africa and from Egypt. Verus dallied at Athens, where he had himself initiated into the Eleusinian mysteries, and visited his old tutor Herodes Atticus. Dawdling by way of all the best spas and casinos in Asia Minor, he reached Antioch in the spring of 163, to find that the army had been reorganized by a cold but capable martinet called Avidius Cassius, himself of Syrian origin. Verus spent most of the next three years revelling at Lataqia, Antioch, and in the beautiful park of Daphne near by, where two centuries earlier Mark Antony had had his headquarters. The actual direction of the war fell to

Marcus, who was responsible for the overall strategy, and to a band of capable generals, with Avidius Cassius as generalissimo. The war lasted three years, and ended with an overwhelming Roman victory. It was Trajan over again. The Parthian capital of Seleucia on the Tigris, just south of modern Baghdad, was captured and destroyed, as well as its twin city Ctesiphon. The king of Parthia took to flight. A Roman nominee, a senator from Emesa, modern Homs, called Suheim, was placed on the Armenian throne. This name is Semitic, and had been borne by members of the family of priest-kings who ruled Emesa, which suggests that the present Suheim was of that dynasty: it means "Little Arrow", and is used by Arabs to-day. This was not the first time Armenians had been given a Semite as king: two members of the Herodian house had ruled in Armenia and Lesser Armenia. The house of Homs was to reach the imperial throne within a generation: this advancement may well have been a first step in its promotion. (See page 51.)

Parthicus Maximus, Medicus, Father of his Country—the farced titles reigned thick on Verus, and perforce on Marcus too, who would have preferred to be without them. On the 12th October, 166, the two Augusti celebrated their joint triumph. It was the very day on which the first Augustus, on his return from Syria, had consecrated the altar of Fortune Returned.

Alas! It was not only victory that Verus had brought with him from Syria. His army had become infected with the plague. The pestilence raged for some years, and it spread even as far as the Rhine. It was a disaster of the first magnitude. Just as the Black Death altered the aspect of England, so now did this scourge from the east afflict the Roman empire. Rome never really got over it. It is only necessary to look at the works of art, from statues to gems, that were produced in the next quarter of a century to realize what irreparable damage the plague had wrought.

One of its first effects had been to halt Verus' campaign at its climax. The Parthian question remained unsolved, just as it had after Trajan's campaigns, and as it was later to remain after those of Septimius. In fact, it never was solved.

Meanwhile, there was the German menace to be met. Even while the Parthian campaign was in progress, the Marcomanni were causing trouble, which was met by diplomatic appeasement. War was inevitable; and here, as in the east five years before, it started with a major disaster. With one interval of two years, it was to last for the next thirteen. The drafts for the Mesopotamian campaign and the plague had seriously enfeebled the armies of the north. When, in the summer of 167, a horde forced its way across the Danube, it engulfed a Roman army 20,000 strong by sheer weight of numbers. There was now nothing to stand in its way. It was all very well for Aristides to laud the legions guarding the frontiers; but once they were overcome —or simply not there—then there was no second line of defence. So it was now. The invaders moved over the Alps and down into the plain of the Veneto. They even reached Verona. The frontier had collapsed.

Would Marcus be able to restore it?

Chapter IV

"AND WE ARE FOR THE DARK"

WITH amazing resolution, Marcus set about the task. In the awful days after Cannae, Rome had enlisted even slaves for service. They had been called *volones*. Marcus did the same now, and called them *volunteers*, reviving a good old republican word. Brigands were enrolled in the militia, Germans dwelling within the pale of the empire enlisted to oppose their brethren from without it. The Greek police were armed. Most remarkable of all, two new legions, IInd, Loyal, and IIIrd, Harmony, were raised. To pay for this national defence effort, Marcus sold the imperial art collections. The palaces were ransacked for plate and pictures. Hadrian's collection of gems and even the empress's wardrobe were auctioned to replenish the treasury, for the plague had so impoverished the empire that Marcus was unable to collect current taxes and reluctant to impose new ones. Under the threat of invasion, road-blocks were erected on the Alps, cities as remote as Philippopolis in Thrace, and Spalato on the Adriatic were fortified. The catalogue of precautions inevitably reminds the reader of those which were adopted by a later empire in the face of a threatened German invasion.

By the spring of 168, all was ready. Marcus entrusted the east to Avidius Cassius—a step which was to have disastrous consequences —and set out, together with his brother. He dared not send him alone, nor leave him behind. Since his return from the east, Verus had behaved even more outrageously. Despite the plague and the economic collapse, he gave extravagant and lascivious banquets. His association with a Syrian mime called Memphius, whom he nick-named Joy-Boy, and the troop of Levantine jugglers and mounte-banks he had brought back with him, led the wits of Rome to say that he seemed to have spent his time in the east chasing not Par-thians but actors.

The Germans were driven from Italian soil, but only after the prefect of the guard had been killed, among a long list of casualties. Verus wanted to break off the campaign. Marcus knew how fatal it would be, but he yielded to the unmanly pressure and headed south. In January 169, as the two Augusti were driving together at Altino, in Venetia, Verus was seized with apoplexy. He died three days later.

Marcus, who had borne Verus' behaviour with dignity and patience, carried the body back to Rome, buried it in the family mausoleum, and had Verus deified.

The tale of family grief and public misfortune still mounted. Marcus' little six-year-old son died in September. Apart from the German war, there were to be insurrections in Egypt, and even an invasion of Andalusia by raiders from Africa during the following years. There would be war in Britain, troubles in Armenia and Pontus. If these disturbances did not affect the central problem, if they were in fact met with effective resolution by the local commanders, they nevertheless demonstrate the extent to which the imperial fabric had already decayed, how far it had declined from the great days of only a decade before.

The defeat of an embattled German army is always a long task. It was to take Marcus six years, and even then was broken off owing to troubles in the east before the work was completed. But the frontier was restored, the intruders humbled. The campaign is also remarkable for two extraneous reasons. The first is that it was amid the rigours of army life, in the damps and dusks of the penumbra and the periphery of empire, that Marcus composed the *Meditations* on which his fame as a philosopher will for ever rest. The man who by day had to be the leader, the man of action, the lord of men, retired at night to become the self-questioner, the almost morbid analyst of his own soul. Cold, bleak, negative—that Marcus' creed may be. But there was no evil in it, much compassion and much pathos. In the words of Rand (CAH XII, 59), "He rendered unto Caesar the things that are Caesar's and unto the Infinite the things that are the Infinite's, preparing his soul as conscientiously for its extinction, as a Christian prepares his for immortality." The following passage, from Book IV, sums up Marcus' attitude to public and private life:

"The names of those much belauded heroes of old are in a way as out of date as obsolete expressions: Camillus, Caeso, Volesus, Denttatus, or a bit later on Scipio and Cato, then Augustus, even Hadrian and Antoninus. Everything fades, and swiftly passes into legend, until oblivion builds her cairn over them. And I am talking of those who shone in the world, admirably: for the rest, as soon as they cease to breathe it is 'Out of sight, out of mind.' What then is of everlasting remembrance? Just this: equity in thought, unselfishness in action, a tongue that cannot lie, and a disposition ready to welcome whatever befalls as necessary, and known, as flowing from one and the same origin and source."

This is scarcely the panoply of a happy warrior.

The second episode concerns a so-called miracle. The Quadi, in the campaign of 174, had ambushed a Roman detachment, which included the VIth legion, known as the "Thunderbolts". The Romans were surrounded, and the enemy stayed their assault, thinking that the legion, now in extremity and fighting with locked shields, must surrender, worn down by heat and thirst, cut off as they were from any water supply. As they stood there, tortured with wounds, fatigue and the sun which blazed from an unclouded sky, unable to fight or to retreat, suddenly the heavens were overcast and a thunderstorm burst over the field. Down came the rain. Catching it in their shields and helmets, the Romans revived both themselves and their horses. Seeing them thus occupied, the enemy charged; but hail and thunderbolts struck the barbarian ranks. Their rout was complete. The campaign was over. Marcus triumphed for the seventh time, the empress was hailed as Mother of the Camp.

It happened that the legion in question, which came from Cappadocia, was composed of Christians. This is the first mention we have of Christian soldiers being victorious as such. That the outcome of the battle should be attributed to miraculous intervention is in accord with the spirit of the times. That it was really due to the constancy of the Christians, who, as so often, were reday to face death rather than betray their faith and loyalty be it to Caesar or to Christ, is the underlying truth of the matter. Raised in the east, this legion now proved in the far west that a new spirit was abroad and at work. The incident itself made such an impression that it is represented on Marcus' column in Rome. The rain-god is shewn succouring the hard-pressed troops, the showers descending from his outstretched arms (Plate 2(b)).

Marcus was robbed of the full fruits of his victory by yet further insurrection in the Levant. Here, Avidius Cassius the Syrian had governed Syria for the last eight years, and for the last six he had been to all intents and purposes viceroy of the east. Rome was remote, Rome was weak; of Rome's rulers, the one they did not know, Marcus, was too busy to care, the other whom they did know, Verus, had proved himself to be beneath contempt; for it is a rule of race relations that the lower the moral standards of the governed are the higher they expect those of their governors to be. The memory of the Parthian invasion was still fresh. It had been defeated, but it had shewn that Rome was not invulnerable. Besides, was not the east in reality greater, more vital, than the west? Could not a Syrian aspire to the purple itself? It was rumoured that the empress Faustina had agreed to marry Cassius. She despaired of Marcus' health, and the prospect of the elevation of Commodus, his son, was alarming. Faustina was known to have had a weakness for gladiators, and Commodus had already given symptoms of a hereditary predisposition for the arena. The prospect of such a creature as emperor, coming on top of Verus, was too much.

It seemed therefore that the time had come for the rule of the earth to return to the east, whence it had sprung. Two other emperors, Vespasian and Hadrian, had owed their elevation to the fact that they had been in command of the army of Syria. Might not a native Syrian achieve empire through the same means? Cassius was proclaimed emperor; he appointed a commander of the guard, and other officers. Cilicia and Syria were his from the start. Egypt went over to him, and thus he was able to threaten the food-supply of Rome, just as Vespasian had done.

To the challenge of this crisis Marcus rose as he had risen to that of earlier ones. Disdaining "alien" assistance, Marcus prepared to defend his legitimate rights. Fortunately for him, the usurper met his end by assassination, only three months and six days after his elevation. His head was brought to Marcus, who ordered that it be buried: he only regretted that he would have no opportunity to shew mercy to his rival. He did, however, treat Cassius' relations with marked clemency. The situation in the east had been saved by the firmness of the governor of Cappadocia, but Marcus felt that the prestige of the empire demanded his own presence in the east, if only to efface the memory both of Lucius and of Cassius. The latter proved the more permanent. It was the custom of the Romans that when an emperor or an usurper had been disowned by the senate, his memory was "damned", and his name was completely obliterated, hacked out from all the inscriptions in which it occurred. There are scores of extant examples of this. It is significant, as Abel points out, that in the case of Cassius, his name in inscriptions in his own country has received no more than a formal working over: it is everywhere clearly legible. He was, ominously, even in death Syria's favourite son.

Marcus progressed by way of Asia Minor. With him were Faustina and Commodus. Faustina died at the foot of the Taurus in the winter of 175: perhaps, as Dio hints, she felt she could not face those whom her own intrigues had ruined. It was now made a rule that no man should be appointed governor of the region from which he had sprung. Otherwise there were no punitive measures, no reprisals. Marcus declined to visit Cyyrhus, Cassius' birthplace, and for a time forbade public assemblies in Antioch, where he would have been liable to insult. With Commodus, now fifteen, and his sister, Verus' widow, now remarried to Pompeianus, Marcus went down through Palestine to Egypt. The local Jews had fallen into such pitiful penury that Marcus is recorded to have cried out "O Marcomanni, Quadi, Sarmatians [his German foes] at last I have discovered people more squalid than you." The province of Palestine, as it had been called since the first Jewish revolt a century before, now reverted to its ancient name of Judaea. Marcus had abandoned the excellent system of succession by adoption. Since he had a legitimate, even if not actual, son of his own, it would have been difficult to maintain it. If only, for instance, he could have nominated his excellent son-in-law Pompeianus. But with ruinous indulgence he now elevated his son to the rank of Augustus, declared the fifteen-year-old boy the *Father of his Country*, and made him consul. A firmer character than Commodus might have been debauched by such mockery of authority.

The German war still continued, when in March 180 Marcus died in Rome, apparently of the plague, for he adjured those who stood about him "to think not of him but of the plague and the death which is common to all". And he sent Commodus from his death-bed, "for fear he would catch the disease".

With the death of Marcus, the Old Rome came to an end. This philosopher, who had ten times been hailed as *Imperator*, this contemplative who had spent all his official life in action, he it is who mirrors for after ages the setting sun of Rome. He had done his utmost to be a restorer. He had failed. No longer is Rome to be the inviolate mistress of the world, no longer Italy the central domain of an empire irradiated by "the immeasurable majesty of the Roman peace". Already, the old gods are leaving the Capitol. Already, a son of the east has made a bid for the supreme power, soldiers nurtured in an eastern faith proved that they can be faithful unto death.

Dio Cassius is not much given to phrases. Yet the words with which he ends the last book of his history which deals with Marcus Aurelius (LXXII) sound in our ears like a passing-bell: "Our history now descends from a kingdom of gold to one of iron and rust, as affairs did for the Romans of that day."

Marcus, despite his nobility, his policy, his devotion, had failed. "And we are for the dark." Already men are scanning the eastern sky for the glimmer of a new dawn.

Chapter V

CHANGE AND DECAY

IF Marcus had felt able to continue the adoptive principle which had produced a succession of Rome's finest rulers, including himself, history would have been different. Instead of choosing his son-in-law, Pompeianus, he allowed his son Commodus to succeed him. Pompeianus was an easterner, a native of Antioch, whose merits had so attracted Marcus that he insisted on his marrying the widow of Lucius Verus, Lucilla, his own daughter. He was therefore, whatever Faustina and Lucilla might say—and they said a good deal—well within the aura of the purple.

Once Commodus was acclaimed emperor, Pompeianus prudently returned to his estates. Prudently? However much we may admire the character of a man who had been a successful general—he had repelled the Germans from Italy—and had been twice consul, we are nevertheless shocked at the utter lack of spirit in the Romans of the period, even of the best of them. The old fire of freedom had long been extinct. No longer would there be a Cincinnatus, nor even a Cicero, to risk his life, to stake his reputation on the maintenance of principle. Of this "masterful negation and collapse of all that makes me man", the historian Dio Cassius is himself a damning example. He mentions in passing (LXXIII, 4, 2) that he is now, that is about the year 180, writing not as before on the authority of others, but from his own observation. He then goes on to relate some of the disgusting pranks of the emperor. Whether Commodus really was the son of a gladiator, and his adulterous mother was known to have a liking for them, whether, as Dio says, he was just a simple lout, the victim of corruption, or whether, as the *Augustan History* says, he was lewd and cruel from his earliest years, is irrelevant. What is important is that he was a thoroughly evil man and a bad ruler. Politically, he was listless, and shewed a complaisance which is always fatal when dealing with the Germans. In Britain there was a rebellion and then a mutiny. The rebellion was quelled by a soldier of resolution and ability: Commodus took the credit and the title *Britannicus*. The mutineers had the effrontery to send a delegation 1,500 strong to Rome: Commodus allowed them to butcher the distinguished general who censured them. His private life, if such it can be called,

43

because it was the talk of Rome, was repulsively lascivious. He had a large collection of women and boys. He appeared in the Circus as a charioteer or a gladiator. He murdered almost every eminent man in Rome, either through jealousy, or, if he were rich, through greed. In fact it was said that Pertinax, who was to succeed him, Pompeianus and one other were the only ones who escaped.

In the face of this behaviour, what did the noble Romans do? The answer is that they did nothing—for thirteen years they did nothing at all, if we except one feeble plot to get rid of the brute. The language which Dio uses in recording events in which he, as a senator, took part makes the modern reader gasp—and it must be remembered that Dio was a very eminent man, who was to be twice consul, once as the colleague of an emperor, and held important provincial appointments. Yet he can write: "We always used to shout out whatever we were told to, particularly, over and over again, 'You are the Lord, you are the Leader, you are the most fortunate man in the world. You are conquering, and you will go on conquering. Always, Amazonian, you have been conquering.'" This was the way in which the senate acclaimed a man who had killed many of their number, and had threatened many more, the man who had said that Rome was to be called "Commodiana", who had altered the names of the months to his own assumed titles. And here is Dio's account of a pleasant afternoon in the theatre: "Commodus had killed an ostrich. He cut off its head, and then came up to where we were sitting, with the head in his left hand, and his still dripping sword in his right. He said nothing, but grinned and wagged his head, as much as to say he would treat us in the same way. As a matter of fact, a good many would have died there and then for laughing at him (because it was laughter more than indignation that took hold of us), had I not chewed some laurel leaves, which I had picked from my garland, and persuaded those who were sitting near me to do the same, so that the regular movement of our jaws would hide the fact that we were laughing."

Such was Rome in the days of Commodus, such its senators, and such the use to which the laurel, the symbol of imperial dignity, was degraded. There they sat, and trembled, while the imperial buffoon squandered the material and the spiritual patrimony of the Eternal City.

Not once does Dio reprobate the absence of practical indignation. "I should make my history very tedious, if I gave a detailed account of all the people who were put to death by Commodus." Wholesale murder for this refined Bithynian is "tedious". Well, he could at

44

least say, like the Abbé Sieyès in comparable circumstances, "I have survived."

Only after thirteen years was Commodus despatched. In the last year of his life, 192, there had occurred an event which to the superstitious emperor—and most Romans were pathologically superstitious—might have been an omen of change. A fire swept the city, destroying the record-office and a large part of the palace. One of its first victims was the Temple of Peace, which Vespasian had built after the destruction of Jerusalem, and in which he had reposited the Temple spoils. It also contained a number of Galen's manuscripts. All were now destroyed, except the famous *Menorah*, or seven-branched lamp, which was to resume its travels in the fifth century.

Commodus was only thirty-one when he was assassinated at the instigation of the officer commanding the household brigade, the Praetorian Guard, and Marcia, the emperor's concubine. It happened that one afternoon, when Commodus had finished his siesta and had gone off to seek some exercise, his little page ran out of the bedroom holding in his hand Commodus' bedside memorandum-tablet. In the corridor, he chanced to meet Marcia, who, recognizing the tablet, took it from the child, and saw to her horror that it contained a list of people who were marked for death, including herself and the prefect. She summoned him at once. They tried to poison Commodus, and when that failed, they had him strangled in his bath by an athlete. Commodus' death was of more than passing importance. It not only rid Rome of an individual tyrant: it imposed upon her a tyrant in mortmain: from this day forth for as long as Rome remained an imperial capital it was the soldiers who ruled it. In a sense, ever since the days of Marius, more than two hundred years before, the army had taken, or could assume, a decisive role in politics. Of the year 68, "the year of the four emperors", Tacitus had written that "the great secret had been divulged, that emperors could be made elsewhere than in Rome", that is, by the army, as Vespasian had been. But the power of the troops, the iron hand of Rome, had hitherto been veiled in the velvet glove of the senate. Now the glove was off.

The soldiers' choice fell on Pertinax, a general of sixty-six, who had been governor of Syria and Moesia. Pertinax would have liked Pompeianus to don the purple, but he refused: what was done was done. The elevation of this capable and modest man gave general satisfaction both in Rome and in the provinces. He had a wife and son, whom the senate had proclaimed as Augusta and Caesar. On the 6th March, 193, three months after his accession, the prefect of Egypt invited the Alexandrines to offer sacrifice for the new family, and to

45

wear garlands for a fortnight. Damascus and Gaza struck coins in his honour: Jerash put up a statue to him. But Pertinax had forgotten something—the army. True, he was faced with a financial crisis. Four years before, the plague had again ravaged Italy. Two thousand a day died in Rome, says Dio, adding the curious fact that throughout the empire many people were killed by means of needles infected with poison. He records the same thing in the reign of Domitian, whôm Commodus resembled. The inference is that, as the Arab proverb says, "the fish stinks from the head"—where the emperor is murderous, the subjects will be encouraged to murder.

Pertinax did what he could to replenish the almost empty treasury. Commodus' collection of women and boys was sold, and fetched handsome prices (though many of them were soon back in the palace). So were a number of Commodus' other treasures, including what must be accounted the forerunner of the modern taxi-cab "carriages that measured the road, and shewed the time". Out of the proceeds, Pertinax managed to pay the Praetorians the bribe he had promised them; but he proved to be not only mean, but tactless.

The soldiers who had raised Pertinax to the throne decided to get rid of him; after a reign of less than three months he was murdered in the palace. The supreme power was then, quite literally, put up to auction by the guard. Sulpicianus was inside the praetorian camp (which was a little to the north of what is now the railway station) and a rich man of Milanese origin, Didius Julianus, outside it. After spirited bidding, Didius won. Down he went to the senate-house, where the cowed assembly, including Dio, were constrained to acknowledge him. He then crossed the forum and went up to the Palatine, in time to be offered the frugal dinner which had been prepared for Pertinax.

The soldiers had made Didius ruler; but the people who had seen in Pertinax a saviour, were angry, and shewed their anger by shouting, storming the reserved seats in the theatre, and stone-throwing. They knew, too, that there were other candidates in the field. There were three of them—Albinus in Britain, Niger in Syria, and Septimius Severus in Pannonia. Severus won the race for Rome. A new age was to begin. Severus was Punic, his wife Syrian. Both were Semites.

Chapter VI

THE EASTERN WEST

IN order to understand the profound and lasting influence which the emperor Severus and his Augusta were to have on the future of the Roman world, it is essential to know something of their backgrounds and upbringing.

Septimius Severus was born in the year 146, at Lepcis Magna, a splendid and prosperous city on the coast of north Africa, just to the east of the modern Tripoli. His ancestors had been made knights, two of his great-uncles had been consuls. At first sight, the history of Lepcis seems much the same as that of many another Graeco-Roman city. By the end of the second century BC, it had become the "friend and ally" of the Roman people—the usual preliminary to absorption by Rome, which in this case occurred in the year 47 BC, when Julius Caesar reduced the town to "stipendiary", that is, subject status. The secret of Roman rule at its best was that, if it demanded tribute, in cash or kind, it also produced the conditions in which that tribute could be provided. Lepcis, together with the other two cities, Oea and Sabratha, which gave the region its name of *Tripolitania*, or Land of Three Cities, throve. Three times towards the end of the first century AD marauders from the parched and hungry south were repelled. The cities were rewarded by being made "colonies", that is they acquired Roman citizenship, which was still a coveted honour in the provinces. Lepcis was thus elevated in the year 109, when Trajan was emperor, and was officially styled "the faithful"—*Colonia Ulpia Traiana Fidelis Lepcis Magna*.

There is nothing in this development which might not have come from a score of other cities throughout the enipire: it is as true to type as a *Times* obituary of a civil servant. A visit to Lepcis discloses a very different story.

At first view, the city, or what is left of it, astonishes by its size. It covers more than three hundred acres, about the area of the state of Monaco. And what profusion! There are streets, triumphal arches, porticoes, temples, forums, baths, gymnasium, basilica, theatre, amphitheatre, hippodrome, a great barrage to ensure a copious water supply and a large harbour, complete with quays and lighthouse. At first, the effect is overwhelming, but when the visitor starts to sort out impressions, to "place" the various buildings, their date and style, he is impressed by two arresting facts. The first is that the people who built and dwelt in this city were above all a maritime folk. They lived between the desert and the deep sea. The olive groves that gave them a substantial part of their wealth form but a fringe between their civilization and the barren wilderness beyond. It was to the sea they looked for life. Their city is built on the shore, almost on the beach itself. Even in their theatres and their hippodrome, above the voices of the actors, above the shouts of the charioteers and their backers, there was to be heard the boom and rattle of the sea as it broke upon their frontier. Secondly, as we examine the monuments, we observe that the inscriptions are carved not only in Latin, but in another, unfamiliar script. It is neo-Punic. Then we notice that many of the names, even in the Latin inscriptions, are reminiscent of the days of Hannibal. Annobal Rufus gave the theatre and the market; and his munificence is recorded both in Latin and in Punic. Iddibal Caphada gave a portico. Another bilingual inscription records that G'y ben Hanno embellished a colonnade. The very decoration itself is reminiscent of the east, of Syria or Mesopotamia, both in the themes employed—the vine, for instance, which figured in Herod's Temple, and is still to be admired in its successor the Dome of the Rock—and in the intricacy of the execution, wholly foreign to the plain straightforward Roman work. This is particularly true, significantly enough, of the portion of the town which arose under the patronage of its most famous son, Septimius Severus.

The fact is that Carthage, which was deemed to have ceased to exist, officially, in 146 BC, was still very much alive. The Carthaginians were Phoenicians, they had come from the Levant, they brought with them the gods and the ideas of the Semitic littoral in which they had lived. Originally these traders from Tyre and Sidon had been content to make periodical voyages, to traffic for the slaves, the gold, and the ivory which the caravans brought to the coast from the depths of unknown Africa. Gradually, the trading-posts became settlements. Of these, the greatest was Carthage, "the new city", sited on that proud promontory, which now shelters the modern Tunis between the two harbours, the western of which is not only one of the safest, but also one of the most beautiful in the whole Mediterranean. Carthage grew rich on its maritime traffic, and enforced her monopoly of the carrying-trade not only on her dependencies, such as Lepcis, but even on Rome itself, this being recognized in a treaty as early as 507 BC. But a clash, one of the most famous in history, was inevitable. Carthage precipitated it by occupying Messina in Sicily. That was in 264 BC. It was to take Rome more than a century, and three campaigns, to reduce Carthage. Carthage was destroyed, but the Carthaginians were not. They left a deep impression on the Roman mind. Dido, as the embodiment of the alien city, is presented in Virgil's *Aeneid*, less as a forlorn woman (though she tries to make herself out to be one) than as an imperial menace, Aeneas not as a cad for deserting her, but as a dutiful Roman for eluding her. Cleopatra was regarded as a second Dido: Berenice as a third. The old fear still lived.

And with reason. Punic was still not only spoken but written; Punic art, as a visit to the Tripoli museum confirms, is far superior to the intrusive Roman, in its coins with their lively horses, and in its elegant glass. They had a taste for imported Greek and Etruscan wares, too. Unfortunately, with the Romans they shared a taste for cruelty. Among the mosaics preserved in the Tripoli museum are some from Abu Qumeira. They are exquisitely done, fishing scenes, birds and other rural themes. But among them is one which depicts "sport". This shews a man tied to a stake, in a push-cart, being thrust forward by an attendant towards a waiting lion, while a band of music plays to drown his screams (Plate 13).

Such was the land and culture from which Septimius sprang. Outwardly it wore a Graeco-Roman veneer, and Septimius spoke both languages, though with a Punic accent. Basically, he was a Semite, proud of his ancestry and his culture, so much older and stronger than that of Rome.

The impact of such a man on Rome—the first non-Italian ever to rule it, for though Trajan and Hadrian were born in Spain, they were of Italian stock—must have been deep in any case; but it was more than redoubled by his union with Julia Domna, his second wife; and before resuming the narrative of events, it will be useful to explain why. His first wife, Marciana, died when he was in his thirties—we know nothing of her, except that Septimius did not mention her in his autobiography, but did erect statues in her memory. In the year 185 he was thirty-nine, and already well advanced on a successful and ambitious career. As a young man, he had come to Rome to continue his education and had attracted the favour of Marcus Aurelius, who granted him senatorial rank. He was appointed quaestor, and then governor of Baetica, the province from which Hadrian had sprung. As an aspiring provincial, we are not surprised to learn that Severus had a high regard for Hadrian. He was transferred to Sardinia, then to his native Africa, where he made it plain that he was a legate of Rome, and not the local boy who had made good. He was named tribune of the people by Marcus Aurelius, and when only thirty-two became praetor. After service in northern Spain, he visited Athens, whose citizens did not take to this intellectual Semite, any more than they had to an earlier one, Paul of Tarsus. Septimius was not only sensitive, but vindictive, and had his own back on the conceited Hellenes when he became emperor. Finally, he was sent as governor to the important province of southern Gaul, of which the capital was Lyons.

It was here that he decided to marry again. A man so high in official favour, for Commodus had continued his father's patronage of the capable African, could have chosen a bride from many of the first families of Rome. Instead, he decided to marry the daughter of a Syrian prince-priest. One of the imperial ladies herself prepared the marriage chamber "in the temple of Venus near the palace", which shews that the union had official blessing. And who was this Julia Domna, Septimius' second wife, destined to be the wife of an emperor, the mother of two others, and the great-aunt of two more? (See Table II.)

She came from Emesa, the modern Homs, in Syria, a town which dominates the plain, tawny and fertile in contrast to the pallid grit of the desert to the east and south, through which flows the infant Orontes, pausing on its way to nourish the lake which in antiquity, as now, formed the reservoir of an elaborate irrigation system. The chief importance of Homs, however, was and still is, that it forms a staging-post between Palmyra to the east and the gap in the mountain chain which gives access to the Phoenician littoral. Its material prosperity, in antiquity, fluctuated, as Seyrig has pointed out, with that of Palmyra. To-day, one may meet in Homs the most mixed, and least cosmopolitan, throng in all Syria; for it is still the meeting-place of tribesman and townsman, of farmer and nomad, of all the multitudinous types that constitute the population of Syria. The railway-junction and the oil-refinery seem extra-territorial, irrelevant. Emesa of old had something of the same quality: it was in the Roman province of Syria, but not of it. It led its own cultural life—and to what exquisite heights its arts were raised may be gauged from the helmet and other treasures, rings, gold ornaments and seals, preserved in the Damascus Museum (see Plate 1(b)). But its eminence was due primarily to religion. Emesa was a holy city, ruled by a dynasty of prince-priests dedicated to the service of the sun-god. In truth, the setting is apt for such a cult, because the acropolis of Homs, a rocky outcrop from the plain, stands up in the light of day like the gnomon of a sundial.

The princes of Emesa first enter Roman history in the days of Pompey in 64 BC and the entry they make is dignified and important. The then ruling prince was called Sampsigeramus, a name meaning, probably, "The sun hath established" (the first syllable is certainly the Semitic *shams*, meaning sun). Pompey became such friends with him, that Cicero, in writing to his friend Atticus, more than once calls Pompey "Sampsigeramus", hoping that the courier would not know to whom he was referring.

The dynasty was continued in authority and prestige by Rome. In AD 44, King Agrippa I of Judaea, when he summoned a conference of kings at his new capital of Tiberias, included the then prince of Emesa, a later Sampsigeramus, in the list of guests. His brother Aristoboulos had, in fact, married the daughter of an earlier prince, called Suheim. In 52, Agrippa's own daughter Drusilla married the then ruler of Emesa, 'Aziz. These alliances between the Herods and the ruling family of Emesa are very significant: they shew that the Herods (who were very proud of being royal) regarded the Emesans as being "good enough", and also as having some claim, however vague, to be regarded as "monotheists"—a fact which was later to emerge into the first political importance (cf. page 36).

The family continued to rule, as we know from several inscriptions —it was in fact still ruling in Emesa after it had ceased to rule Rome.

That Septimius now chose to ally himself with Julia Domna is the clearest possible indication that he intended that his authority should depend on his own race—on that, and on the soldiers. Rome had defeated Carthage, Rome had dominated Syria. Now, Carthage would unite with Syria to dominate Rome.

Septimius, a successful and popular governor of Gaul, was appointed consul by Commodus, and later governed Pannonia and Sicily. He was back in Pannonia as commander-in-chief when Commodus was assassinated. Septimius acted with vigour and resource. There were other aspirants in the field: Didius Julianus (see page 46), Niger in Syria, and Albinus in Britain. Didius offered to share his authority with Pompeianus, but Pompeianus—the only man in the whole history of Rome who was once denied the purple and twice refused it—had no intention of leaning on a broken reed. Septimius at once appointed Albinus as his Caesar, and moved on Rome. He outwitted, disarmed and disbanded the guard, replacing it with a corps of his own trusted legionaries, 15,000 strong. Didius was soon liquidated. Septimius took the cognomen of Pertinax, whose avenger he claimed to be. This was to please the senate. At the gates of Rome, he dismounted, changed into civilian clothes, and made an entry accompanied by his whole army in review order, which Dio says was the most brilliant spectacle he ever saw. He shortly afterwards held a magnificent memorial service for Pertinax. Niger in the east, Albinus in the north, each was in turn defeated and killed. Septimius announced that he was adopted into the Antonine family, and hailed Commodus as his "brother" (see Plate 6). This was not quite as ridiculous as it might sound: both Marcus Aurelius and Commodus had shewn him marked favour as a young man, as had at least one princess (see page 50). If Hadrian, whom Septimius admired so much, had been adopted only on the death-bed of his predecessor, could not Septimius carry the principle one step farther, and assume a posthumous adoption?

So was the empire transformed: technically, an Antonine, approved by the senate, now ruled Rome. In fact, it was a Semite of the west, allied to a Semite of the east, and supported by arms, who now dominated the empire. Materially, the east had risen again to primacy. Would that resurgence be accompanied by a resurgence of the east in the realm of the spirit? It would. And would not in the end the most vital and viable of the religions of the east emulate and ally itself with an eastern executive? It would, and it did. This is logic, not paradox. It will now be well to examine its development.

Chapter VII

THE MANY AND THE ONE

THE triumph of Christianity in the early years of the fourth century has for long been regarded as the outcome of a straight fight between paganism and the Faith. In fact, the process was far more subtle, far more complex, the final stage in an evolution during which Christianity was to profit doubly, from its reactions to heresies within, and from its contests with rivals without, by whom the heretics were often influenced.

To start with, there was no such thing as "paganism", as a creed. The word can be used in a negative sense only, to indicate what a man did not believe, not what he did. In fact the word pagan means simply one who lives in a village, just as the word heathen means one who dwells on a heath; that is, remote from civilization, at a time when that had been assimilated to the Christian Church.

To put the growth of Christianity in its right setting and perspective it is necessary to go back to Alexander the Great. His ultimate aim had been the creation of a multi-racial society, and despite his early death, he had gone a long way towards achieving it. His marriage, and that of so many of his soldiers, with Persian brides was a literal allegory of the union of Greek and Persian which he hoped to bring about. The process was carried farther by his successors, the Seleucids and the Ptolemies. These two Greek dynasties ruled in Syria and Egypt respectively, and thereby brought about a fusion of Hellenic with Syrian and Egyptian ideas which was of the greatest importance for mankind. The achievement is not easy for a modern mind to grasp. We live in an age of almost feverish physical development, the bewildered heirs of the powers bequeathed to us, in dazzling accumulation, by steam, by electricity, by the internal combustion engine, by nuclear energy. In the physical domain, the post-Alexandrine age knew no such activity. It was utterly stagnant. The only motive power that man knew was the one he had always known, the muscles of his kind and of certain animals, supplemented on the sea by the winds. The only chemical agent was fire. There had been no technological development for centuries. Opposed to this technical inertia, the spiritual vigour of the age is all the more striking. It represented what would be called in the scientific jargon of to-day "a major break-through". Hitherto, religions had been national. Jahweh was a national god; Rimmon was another, Dagon a third. Assyria had its gods, and Egypt had yet others.

The Alexandrine system did away with this narrow religious nationalism for ever. Henceforth religion was to know no frontiers, no nationality. This idea, which sounds so modern, so "Christian", in fact antedates Christianity by three centuries.

Once the barriers were down, the Mediterranean world was flooded by a host of new cults, and all of them came from the east. They may be divided into three main classes, geographically. First there were the religions of Asia Minor. That is only natural. Asia Minor had been "Greek" for centuries; but it was also the heir, political and spiritual, of Persia. The very countryside, with its lush meadows and perennial streams nestling between the great, gaunt uplands and the blue sea, is quite unlike that of Hellas. Next came the deities of Egypt, tailored by the Ptolemies for western society. Third and finally were the gods of Syria. Could, then, the west produce no new faith of its own? Yes, one: and that was an eastern importation, too. The cult of the deified emperors, which was to become the official religion of Rome, was modelled on the divine honours paid by oriental subjects to their sovereigns: it was even in the eastern parts of the empire that it received its first manifestations, so paramount had the east become in the realm of the spirit.

The Asian cults reached Rome during the Punic Wars. The Sybil had promised that the Great Mother, Cybele, would bring victory to the Romans against the defeated but still formidable Hannibal who had sought asylum in Asia. In the form of a black aerolith, kindly supplied by king Attalus, she made a formal entry into Rome, where many of the first families, remembering their Trojan origin, were delighted to do her honour. In the same year, 202, Scipio defeated Hannibal at Zama. Cybele had arrived, soon to be followed by her consort, Attis. These deities, originally Thracian, were celebrated by ceremonies which included frenzied "possession" culminating in self-castration. The cult, despite its un-Roman nature, flourished at Rome, as did later importations from the same source. It was to their votaries that the word "fanatic" was first applied; but they appealed to the emotions, and they stayed on. The death and resurrection of Attis, represented by a decorated tree rather like our Christmas trees, was commemorated hard by the imperial palace itself, and the cult of Cybele, the Great Mother, spread to Spain, Britain, Africa and Gaul. The image of the goddess was transported on a chariot, amid the acclamations of the faithful, in a manner which seems to prefigure the veneration paid to the statue of Our Lady in the streets of contemporary Seville during Holy Week. In both cases, the processions enjoy official patronage. It was, moreover, from the cult of Cybele that the adherents of Mithras were to borrow the disgusting ceremony of the *taurobolium*, or baptism in the blood of a slaughtered bull, the neophyte cringing in a pit wherein, through perforated boards, he was drenched by the steaming blood of the victim.

The Egyptian contribution to international religion was very different in origin and expression. The first Ptolemy realized two things: first, that the traditional religion of Egypt, ancient and august as it was, would not appeal to his Greek subjects, secondly, that the overwhelming prestige of the ancestral cults must nevertheless be exploited. Hence came into being the synthetic cult of Sarapis. Sarapis himself is of uncertain origin: perhaps he came from Sinope, on the Black Sea coast of Asia Minor, perhaps from Babylon; but the name seems to be undoubtedly derived from *Osiris-Apis* (Usur-api) the protective deity of the Memphis necropolis. The great statue in the Sarapeum in Alexandria, the mother-church of the cult, was the work of Bryaxis the Athenian, a contemporary of Scopas. It was one of the last expressions of the Greek genius for representing godhead, recalling as it did, in the features of the deity, his double character of ruler of the abundant earth, and monarch of the kingdom of the dead. With Sarapis was associated Isis, the sister-wife of Osiris, and Horus, their son. Of this triad, it was Isis who attracted the greatest multitude of votaries. Both Isis and Sarapis were early installed in Rome, and throughout the Mediterranean. Their appeal was twofold: the magnificence of the ritual of their ceremonies, and the sense of certainty they bestowed. The former was to influence even the practice of the Catholic Church. When the veneration of the Virgin as the Theotokos, or Mother of God, was introduced (about the time of the destruction of the Sarapeum in 391) devotees of Isis were able to continue their worship of the mother-goddess merely by changing her name. In many cases the statues of Isis served as those of her successor-deity. The practice of suspending *ex voto* representations of various parts of the human body, in gratitude for cures, the ceremonial burning of candles, even the monastic tonsure may all have been taken over from the earlier faith. The peace of mind which the Sarapis religion bestowed was its second outstanding advocate. Alexandria was a hotbed of "philosophy", just as Athens and many another hellenized city were later to become. Men and women argued endlessly "about it and about": Sarapis promised endless felicity. No wonder therefore that his religion became so widely popular. In Rome, it was soon to enjoy court favour. The Flavians, the Antonines, the Severans all patronized it. The arch-hellenist, Hadrian, constructed a Sarapeum in his great "villa" at Tibur which to this day remains one of its most imposing features. In the empire the Egyptian religion reached its apogee at the beginning of the third century AD. Thereafter, it yielded the primacy to the religions of Syria, and to the Persian Mithras.

This was partly due to the patronage of the Semitic Severans, and their connexion with the sun god of Homs. But even without this official favour the Syrian religions would have won adherents. In fact, they had been doing so for some time. They spread all over the empire. In Italy, in Spain, even in Britain inscriptions have come to light honouring the gods of Syria. Generally speaking, the Syrian deities were connected with the sun, or were regarded as being one with it. Thus, they were well on the road to monotheism. They had another advantage: they made a serious attempt to work out a systematic and scientific theology. This they owed to the Persians. It was Persian astronomers who had plotted the courses of the stars, and who had established that certain stars returned to certain portions of the heavens at regular intervals. They were undimmed, timeless. Therefore, *a fortiori*, must not the power who had made them be omnipotent and eternal? These speculations had a profound effect on religion, even on Judaism itself. Before the Captivity, the Jews believed in a *sheol*, or underworld, as gloomy and feeble as that of Homer. But Judaism returned from "beyond the river" with a sense of heaven, a place of bliss beyond the stars—a projection of the after-life which became almost universally adopted by every religion, and has lasted in popular imagery down to our own age. It came from Persia. In Cumont's words: "Chaldaean astrology, of which the Syrian priests were the convinced disciples, had supplied them with the elements of a scientific theology. It had led them to the idea of a god enthroned far away from the earth, above the zone of the stars, almighty, universal and eternal, everything here below being regulated by the revolutions of the heavens during infinite cycles of years, and it had at the same time taught them to adore the sun, the radiant source of earthly life and of human reason."

In its final form, therefore, Roman religion was a good deal farther removed from the old pieties that Augustus had sought to restore, than it was from Christianity. The rivals were all bent on attaining the same goal—eternal bliss. By isolating the supreme being who dwelt in the distant heavens from the boundaries of a sublunar world,

Syro-Persian religion had started on the path which would end in Christian monotheism. Gradually, the religious and mystical spirit of the east was to impose itself on the whole of society. It was this spirit which prepared all nations to unite within the bosom of a single, universal Church.

In this field of competitors, already so crowded—and the foregoing sketch has of necessity been compressed to the point of desiccation—was it possible that yet another religion could hope to compete? And so late a starter as Christianity? On the face of it, the idea seems absurd. But Christianity had three supreme advantages.

The first was its Jewish origin. Its Founder had been a Jew, his first disciples had been Jews. As such, they were the heirs of by far the most sublime religious philosophy that had yet appeared. And not only philosophy. In Matthew Arnold's words: "Conduct is three-fourths of life." The Ten Commandments are unique: there is nothing like them in any of the competing religions. Far from it: the religions of Asia Minor and of Egypt, like certain of their Syrian competitors, not only countenanced but encouraged sexual excesses. In Rome itself there were recurrent scandals involving the hierophants of one or other of the alien gods. We can still read with pleasure not untinged with awe the description of the splendours of the ceremonies which accompanied the conversion and initiation of Lucius into the religion of Isis. At the same time it does not escape us that this "conversion" was a passing, superficial thrill: it imposed no permanent sanctions. Judaism was wholly different: its moral code was strict, implacable and permanent. Christianity took it over in its entirety. That was its first advantage.

The second advantage was that, whereas no one had ever *seen* Isis, or Atargatis or Mithras or the rest, thousands *had* seen and known Jesus of Nazareth. He had lived in one of the most crowded regions of the whole empire: he was always on the move: he was famous. Men and women remembered his words, recited his deeds. It was possible for his first disciples to appeal to the memory of their auditors—and they did. As St Luke, one of the first non-Jewish adherents of the new way, said—or makes St Paul say: it was an accepted literary convention—"these things were not done in a corner". And the first apologist of whom we have record appeals, in the days of Hadrian, to the testimony of those whom Jesus had healed, many of whom had lived to within his own lifetime.

The third advantage which Christianity possessed is one which has never been explained: its organization. From the very beginning, from the days of Peter and of Paul, it had been governed by an efficient and adaptable system. Its first martyr, Stephen, was a member of the administrative branch. No other faith had anything remotely resembling this organization. Jews, it is true, corresponded with each other all over the world. The Temple dues had been collected, so long as the Temple stood, and transmitted in bullion or specie to Jerusalem from all the Jewries of the Diaspora. Jews, too, owing to their trustworthiness, had established a primitive banking system, whereby letters of credit issued in Alexandria would be honoured in Rome. But nothing approaching the administrative unity of the Catholic Church had ever existed before—except in the Roman state. To-day, when the Roman empire is but "the shadow of a great name", the Roman Catholic Church stands as the most efficient administrative machine in the world.

Such were the advantages of Christianity. So great were they that, in retrospect, it is easy to see that its triumph was inevitable. Why was it so long delayed?

The answer to that question is to be found not on the religious, but on the political plane. The new Faith had one tremendous drawback: its Founder had been executed as a rebel against Rome.

Those Jews! Everybody knew how seditious they were: they had actually dared to rebel against Rome, an unheard-of outrage, and not only once, but three times. No wonder that Hadrian had forbidden the propagation of their faith, and that later emperors had followed his example. Yet here were these Christians, as they called themselves, going about worshipping a Jew, whom they claimed to be the Son of God, and persuading large numbers of other people to do the same, having cleverly evaded the imperial proscription by making it plain that a man could become a Christian without first becoming a Jew. True, these Christians were good, upright folk. But, in an empire which was evolving more and more into an autocracy, was there room for such a sect?

That was the problem. It was not a religious one at all: it was political. These Christians, this organized, international society, was it to be the rival, or the ally, of the state?

Chapter VIII

BORN OF THE SPIRIT

"THAT which is born of the flesh is flesh; and that which is born of the Spirit is spirit. Marvel not that I said unto thee, Ye must be born again. The wind bloweth where it listeth, and thou hearest the sound thereof, but canst not tell whence it cometh and whither it goeth: so is every one that is born of the Spirit." The words of Jesus to Nicodemus (John iii, 6) are his own definition of what Christian conversion meant, and how it operated. It was a new birth; but how that birth came about remained a secret between God and man.

In comparing Christianity with other religions, and in trying to determine why it proved superior to its rivals, men have spent much time and ingenuity. But when it comes to defining just what happened inside a soul which resulted in that soul's becoming Christian, we have no knowledge. The most famous conversion of all, that of Saul of Tarsus, still remains a mystery. We have his own account of the experience, told in no less than three different versions in The Acts, and in yet a fourth in his letter to the Galatians. Still the mystery remains. "I conferred not with flesh and blood", St Paul tells his Galatian converts: and not in terms of flesh and blood can his experience be explained even by himself.

It is the same with other eminent converts: St Justin, St Cyprian, Tertullian, St Hilary of Poitiers among them. And if these saints and doctors have been unable to explain the process by which they became Christian, how much less can we hope to know of the paths which led countless poor and ignorant men and women to find salvation and power in the faith of Christ?

Nevertheless, despite our ignorance of the method by which a soul is reborn, it is possible to form some idea of what led men and women to *desire* rebirth. Three main motives may be distinguished. The first is the desire for truth, the second is the hope of deliverance from fate and from sin, and the third is the quest for holiness of mind and soul.

The history of St Augustine's conversion, although it is so fully documented, is in a category by itself. He did not have to discover the Faith; he was brought up in it. He was for long seduced by Manichaeism, one of the toughest of Christian heresies, but a Christian heresy none the less: in the end he found rest in the Catholic Church. But what had started him on this long, and successful, journey? The very same motive as had animated so many others, whether born in Jewish, pagan or Christian surroundings: the search for truth. St Augustine was nineteen years of age, he tells us, when for the first time he was charmed by a treatise of philosophy, the *Hortensius* of Cicero—for which the Church must always be grateful to Cicero. The love of truth which Augustine drew from this work sent him first of all to the Manichees, a heretical sect which sought to combine Christian monotheism with Persian dualism, together with much else, and succeeded in so doing to the comfort and satisfaction of many. But not of Augustine. "They kept on saying to me: 'truth, truth', but it was not in them", he tells us early on in his *Confessions* (III, viii, 10). "They served out errors, not only about you who are the Truth, but also about the elements of this world, which is your work . . . Truth, truth, how much even then, and from the bottom of my soul I sighed for thee!"

Later, it was truth that he found in the Catholic faith: "I have seen many people out to deceive others: never anyone who wanted to be deceived. Then where did they get this idea of the happy life from, if not from the same source as that from which they took the idea of truth?" (*Ibid* X, xxiii, 33.)

This desire for the truth had actuated many before Augustine. "It seems", says Bardy (page 122), "that the ancient world, even more than our own, was, at least at certain epochs, tortured by intellectual restlessness." (Had not even Pilate, weak and superficial though he was, had not even he, in a famous self-question, asked, "What is truth?") Of this disquiet there is evidence in the last letters of St Paul himself. He warns the young church of Colossi against bogus philosophies and pretended revelations of esoteric truth, worship of angels and such-like trumperies. There was, as always, a supply to meet the demand of the credulous, in the form of *gnosis*, or knowledge. The Gnostics assembled a fantastic gallimaufry of every conceivable mumbo-jumbo, based on stars, planets, numbers, and abracadabra of every sort. The idea of being an initiate, of knowing something that the rest do not know, has always made an appeal to man's self-importance. But for the Christian this was out of the question: the light that lighteth *every man*, not only some favoured men, had come into the world once and for all with Jesus the Divine Word. As Tertullian was to put it (see p. 92): "The first article of our faith is this: that there is nothing beyond this that we need believe."

60

Anything short of, or beyond, that was "knowledge [*gnosis*] falsely so called". But it was a major threat to the Catholic faith, and will be further considered in its place (see page 64). On the other hand, as with many contemporary and later heresies, down to those of our own day, Gnosticism was to serve for some as a side-entrance, as it were, a sort of postern, to the Catholic Church.

We come now to the second motive for conversion: the hope of deliverance from fate and from sin. It is hard for a modern reader to conceive the terror in which the ancients lived: they were tied and bound by fate at every turn. Human slavery was bad enough—and it might overtake large sections of society through foreign conquest, debt or crime—but added to it was the awful, enervating slavery to the unseen and unknown. Long after the old deities had ceased to charm or elevate the Roman mind, the sanctions of omens, of birds' livers, of stars, monsters, poltergeists and demons haunted and stunted it. To be liberated from this slavery was to enter a new life— it was indeed to be born again. As Jesus said to those who heard him in the Temple: "The truth shall make you free" (John viii). In that one sentence he sums up the first and the second motives of the Christian decision. And in the Christian Church it was literally true. Seneca might prate that the slave was the equal of the free man, but he never treated him as such: the Christians did. The freedom from sin struck deeper. It depended not on prohibition, but on consecration, an active, not a passive decision. There the Christian was maintaining the old Jewish conception of religion, that it was an interior state, not an exterior badge (as the majority of its rivals were), but without the cramping and irrelevant externals which Judaism had conserved as vestiges from its remote ancestors—the coelacanths, as it were, of the new creation. This renunciation of the flesh and of its lures was the hall-mark of the "reborn". St Justin, in his apology, was on sure ground when he claims that it was the example given by the Christians in their private life and conduct which made them respected, and in many cases imitated, by the pagans among whom they lived.

Thus, the Christian, or the would-be Christian, was logically prepared by the desire for truth, and the desire for deliverance from fate and sin, for the final and positive desire: the living of a holy life—in a word, for salvation. *Salus*, means health; but in the Christian context it had come to mean the health of the soul, its inner, unstunted growth. Other cults, it is true, had, as we have seen, offered a mode of "salvation"; but it was Christianity's superior conception of what it really meant, drawn from the matchless example and precept of its

Founder, that made it pre-eminent. In the Roman world, the acceptance of this way of life was not easy. The Christian was carried forward and upward by the intense consciousness of his new worth, his new relationship with God, bound by the chain of love. Equally, he was conscious that a large part of the secular life of the society in which he moved could be his no more; and that was to be one of the factors that made for the suspicion and hostility with which an increasingly autocratic state was to treat the faithful. The more a man rendered to God, the less he was able to render to a Caesar who increasingly came to regard himself, and to be regarded by others, as himself a god.

It was ultimately by the austerity of its demands, as much as by the amplitude of its gifts, that Christianity triumphed. Only one other of its rivals can be compared with it in this respect, and that is Mithraism. To start with, Persian moral standards were much higher than those of the Mediterranean world, a fact which may come as a shock to those who have been brought up to believe that "orientals" do not possess "our outlook on these matters". The Persians had always—we have Xenophon's testimony for it—had the highest regard for truth, whereas the Greeks took a far laxer view of it, and the moral obligation to stick to it. When Euripides' Hippolytus says: "My tongue has sworn, my mind remains unsworn" he propounds a view of perjury which few Greeks would have found unduly lax. To a Persian, such an attitude was sinful. For them, an oath was binding and irrefragable. Next, among the "commandments" of Mithras, was continence. The gods and goddesses of Asia and Egypt all had a sensual side. Sarapis is the brother-husband of Isis, Attis is the lover of Cybele, every Syrian Baal enjoyed a female counterpart. Mithras was alone, chaste and holy. "For the adoration of a bountiful nature, he substituted", in Cumont's words, "a new reverence for continence."

Then, too, Mithraism instilled a sense of fraternity, or rather of camaraderie, for it was more militant and brusque than the brotherly love of the Christians. The initiates were called "soldiers", and were actuated rather by an *esprit de corps* than by pity for individual neighbours.

"If Christianity", said Renan, "had been halted in its growth by some fatal disease, the world would have been Mithraic." Hardly— for one thing Mithras made no appeal to women. But in its elevation of moral outlook, its certainty of deliverance, and its promise of salvation to its initiates, this latest newcomer from the east, this proponent of the Unconquerable Sun as the supreme deity, was bound to win many disciples—specially among soldiers. Then who more likely to favour it, as against its rival, Christianity, than a soldier-emperor, married to the daughter of one of the sun god's most eminent hierophants?

Chapter IX

CHOICE AND OBEDIENCE

HERESY is a splendid tonic—except for heretics: it is the orthodox who profit by it, not those who would be their own guides. The word heresy means nothing more wicked than "choice"; but, for a society which depends for its existence on obedience, nothing can be more wicked than choice. It is that society's reaction to the would-be dissidents that braces it, or dooms it to dissolution.

The Catholic Church had to face the threat of heresy very early in its life; and by the ways in which it overcame the threat, it took to itself new vigour for the struggle with paganism. The infant Church was threatened by three forms of heresy. First, there was Gnosticism (which, as we have seen, had preceded the new faith); next, the heresy of Marcion; third that of Montanus. Each of these three "tendencies" had a different origin and direction, each called for a different remedy, and so each contributed individually to the consolidation of the Church.

As related in the last chapter, Gnosticism had arisen in the post-Alexandrine period, and had been fortified by Persian speculation. The lower forms of Gnosticism were vulgar magic, in a region where, as in the north, belief in spells and compulsion is still not extinct. In the Levant, no less than in Italy, the evil eye is still a real menace; and cases of attempted witchcraft still occur from time to time in the United Kingdom. It is a commonplace of magic, that its spells are drawn from the repertory of older religions than that professed by the majority; Egypt, therefore, where religion had such a long history, and Persia, where its ancestry was if anything longer, were the natural breeding-grounds for magical systems. The danger which such popular, and ancient, practices held for the new religion was very great; the contest of Simon Magus with Peter at Samaria (Acts viii) and that of Paul with Bar-Jesus in Cyprus (*ibid* xiii) shew us how early it had to be faced.

But the real crisis came later on, in the second century, when Christianity had spread not only horizontally, far and wide, but perpendicularly too, and had invaded the most polished and influential circles of society, where there was now a genuine interest in the Faith and its tenets. Once this had occurred, it was inevitable that different ideas should appeal to different folk. As Origen, the greatest of all the apologists, was to put it in his answer to Celsus:

"Since Christianity appeared to men as something worthy of serious attention, not only to people of the lower classes as Celsus thinks, but also to many scholars among the Greeks, sects inevitably came to exist, not at all on account of factions and love of strife, but because several learned men made a serious attempt to understand the doctrines of Christianity" (*Against Celsus* iii, 12). The last sentence explains the whole appeal, and the whole danger, of later Gnosticism.

The problem which agitated these later Gnostics was a familiar one—the origin of evil. Basilides, who taught in the days of Hadrian, solved the question by the simple proposition that all evil is the result of personal sin. True, there is an élite, composed of people who discern by intuition, and that is the meaning of faith. For Valentinus, a later exponent, it is the ordinary folk who live by faith, the "perfect" by gnosis, or knowledge. But for both, mere faith is no longer what Clement of Alexandria, in refuting Basilides, calls "the natural disposition of a free soul".

A great stimulus to these speculations was given by the dualist religion of Persia. Already in the first century Plutarch, describing the religion of Zoroaster, in his *Isis and Osiris*, introduces the rival gods, Hormuzd the god of light and Ahriman the god of darkness. Once godhead is so divided, the path lies open to endless speculation. The earth is the work of a sort of under-god, the Demiurge. Wisdom and Power are the first-born angels: they make the first heaven, their children make the second, and so on until there are 365 heavens, which is why there are 365 days in the year. There is a whole series of spiritual emanations of godhead, a Pleroma, or "fulfilment", Eons or "ages", linked in groups of eight, or ten, or twelve—the whole phantasmagoria is so bewildering that it is not surprising that its promoters considered it was only the true initiate who could be expected to grasp it. There were, in fact, for the Gnostic, three classes of man: the spiritual, the "psychic" and the material. Only the true Gnostic could attain to the first class.

From the foregoing brief survey of Gnostic teaching—and there were many systems, each with its own theories of numbers and spirits—it is clear that, by the Gnostic, God is no longer to be regarded as One: the Father-God, the supreme first cause, is parted by an infinite distance from the Creator-God, that is, the one who made the world and inspired the legislation of the Old Testament. Between the True God and creation a complicated chain of beings is interposed.

Our world originated in a catastrophe, and is evil, material. Jesus came to rescue those who are capable of redemption. But, matter being accursed, the incarnation could not have been a real union of divinity and humanity: it was only an apparent phenomenon. It follows that neither the passion nor the resurrection of Jesus was "real".

This magical fantasy had no cohesion: it was as divided as the dim sects that inhabit the Protestant underworld of our own day, from flat-earthers to Pyramid-inchers, with whom, indeed, it had much in common. But a man was not lacking to reduce the crude mass into a neat, simple unity, into the creed of a Church, in fact. That man was Marcion.

Marcion came from Sinope, a flourishing seaport on the Black Sea coast of what is now Turkey. His father was a bishop, and he himself had made a fortune as a shipowner. He came to Rome, and there set about founding his church. His theology was drastic and simple. The God of the Old Testament could not be the God of the New. This was shewn in a book of *Antitheses*. For instance, Isaiah makes his God say "I make peace, and create evil", whereas Christ has told us that a good tree can bear only good fruit. If the Creator is the bad tree which bears bad fruits, we must recognize another god, the good tree which bears good fruits. The Old Testament says "an eye for an eye, a tooth for a tooth": Christ said "turn the other cheek". Elisha sets a bear on the children who mocked him: Christ says "suffer the little children to come unto me". Moses spread out his hands on the mountain, so that Israel should wipe out its enemies: Christ spread out his hands on the cross to save sinners. Joshua halts the sun so that carnage may continue: Christ says "let not the sun go down upon your wrath".

Clearly, for the bluff shipping magnate, what was wanted was a new Bible, and Marcion proceeded to make one. He scrapped the whole of the Old Testament, and much of the New as well, keeping only the Gospel of Luke (who was a Gentile), except for the first two chapters and bits here and there which did not fit in with his "theology", and ten Letters of St Paul, discarding the Pastoral Epistles and the Epistle to the Hebrews. In the letters he retained, he cut out anything which showed a "judaizing" tendency: this was obviously interpolated by "false apostles". Marcion's breezy methods prefigured much German scholarship of the nineteenth century.

For the rest, Marcion accepted and taught the Gnostic dualism, with the Demiurge and the rest. The third chapter of St Luke's Gospel, now promoted to be the first, opens with the words: "Now in the fifteenth year of the reign of Tiberius Caesar". For Marcion, this was the beginning of the Gospel: "In the fifteenth year of Tiberius Caesar, in the days of Pontius Pilate, Jesus descended from heaven at Capernaum, a town of Galilee, and he taught in the synagogue."

The Demiurge had made this world, this wicked world, and had promised through the prophets that a Messiah would come. In the event, it was not the Demiurge, but the True God who sent his Son, as the Messiah. That is how, said the Marcionites, God had revealed himself: not by creating the world. The apostles, they claimed, had been taken in by the Demiurge, and had preached him; whereupon the Saviour had raised up St Paul to continue his work, which St Paul alone did, preaching salvation by faith: it is enough to believe and to love.

Marcion insisted on a rigid asceticism, which Tertullian was to castigate as inconsistent: "Why impose on a flesh so weak and unworthy a sanctity so heavy and glorious?" He organized his followers in churches which were to multiply and to endure until the third century, when they were either reclaimed by the Catholic Church or engrossed by the Manichaeans.

Montanism, the third primitive heresy, was quite different from the other two. Gnosticism was an infiltration of ideas from without, many of which antedated Christianity by some centuries. Marcionism was, in essence, a repudiation of the Old Testament. Montanism, on the other hand, was of purely home growth. It was originally simply an "enthusiastic" movement, like Protestant revivals, particularly the American brands. It announced itself as an outpouring of the Spirit, the reign of the Paraclete promised by Jesus in the Gospel of St John. Montanus was a converted eunuch-priest of Cybele, who commenced as a prophet in the year 172, in a little township on the frontiers of Mysia and Phrygia. He enlisted the support of two females, Priscilla and Maximilla, who shewed themselves to be as glib and ardent as their master. Montanus was soon claiming to be the Holy Spirit in person, and that his revelation superseded all former revelations, including that of Christ and his apostles.

The heresy spread rapidly, not only in the east, but in the west as well. Its most illustrious convert was Tertullian himself. In retrospect, the importance of Montanism is twofold: first, it illustrates an aspect of Christianity which it is all too easy to overlook, namely, that from the very beginning, the gift of prophecy was an accepted manifestation of the Holy Spirit. It is constantly mentioned in the Acts and Epistles. It is recognized equally in the earliest Christian manuals.

Montanism could not have come into being were this not the case. To belittle the importance of prophecy as a vehicle of divine influence is to fall into an error analogous to that of Marcion. We may consider that prophecy is "not quite the thing" in our day and sophisticated generation; but it certainly was in the dawn of the Faith. We cannot simply overlook or omit the references to it in the New Testament just because we do not like it. In fact, it is one of the most misunderstood, and neglected, aspects of the Christian experience. Specially in these psychological days, it were better to study than to mock it. It is no good saying that it isn't done: it *was* done.

Not less important than the fact of Montanism was the Church's attitude to it; and that brings us back to the thesis stated at the outset of this chapter: that heresy benefits the Church, not the heretics.

The threefold threat of the Gnostics, the Marcionites and the Montanists produced a spirited and bracing reaction on the part of the Church: it also produced a remarkable man to give unity and effect to it, namely Irenaeus. The story of Irenaeus is in itself a commentary of the first value on the development to which the Church had attained little more than a century after its foundation. It shews how utterly false is the idea that Christians were a few communities here and there of slaves and other low persons, lurking in catacombs, unwanted and unwashed.

Irenaeus, as a boy, had known Polycarp, the saintly martyr-bishop of Smyrna. Writing to a friend, Florinus, about the year 190, he says: "I saw you when I was still a child, in lower Asia, with Polycarp; doing brilliantly in that royal hall, and trying to stand well with him. I remember those days better than more recent events, because what I learned when I was small has grown up with my soul and has become one with it, so that I can tell you just where the blessed Polycarp used to sit when speaking, how he came in and went out, how he lived, what he looked like, how he got on with people, how he used to tell the story of his relations with John and the other disciples who had seen the Lord, how he would recall their words, and the things he had heard them tell about the Lord, about his miracles, about his teaching; how Polycarp had received all this from witnesses who had with their own eyes seen the Word of life, and discoursed on it in perfect harmony with the Scriptures." All these discourses Irenaeus says he had by heart, so that he can bear witness that if Polycarp had heard anything like the Gnostic heresy into which Florinus had fallen, he would have cried out and shut his ears and said, as was his custom: "Good God! To what times have you preserved me that I should have to put up with this."

Polycarp suffered martyrdom in 155, so that if Irenaeus was born about 140, he would be a man of fifty when he wrote this famous letter, which is preserved for us by Eusebius (*Church History* V, xx). In it, we can trace the pure, unbroken tradition, which ran like an electric power-line from Jesus himself down to Irenaeus—and to hundreds of others. The validity of this tradition is of vital importance. True, the Scriptures were of prime value too, as we shall shortly see; but in the Levant, then as now, it was the oral transmission of ideas that was the more highly esteemed. In Judaism, as in Islam, the teachings of rabbis or prophets were to be memorized as well as read. To this day, it is by no means uncommon for a child to learn the whole of the Koran by heart, and to be able to recite it from memory. The same attitude was not unknown in the west, either. Seneca, a bookish character if ever there was one, said that he valued the living word more than books. As late as the days of Augustine and Ambrose, the sight of the former reading without moving his lips—that is, truly reading, not speaking it to himself—moved the latter to wonder, just as the same process still does in Levant primary schools. Ten years before Irenaeus was born, bishop Papias of Phrygia had confessed that he preferred "things spoken by the living, perishable voice" to the contents of books. No wonder that Irenaeus took the same view. All the more remarkable, then, is the value that he and the Church in general placed upon the Scriptures: this was the first, and priceless, gift which the reaction against the Gnostics and Marcion bestowed.

Irenaeus, the native of Asia Minor, was chosen to be bishop of Lyons after the persecution there in 177. During the next ten years he wrote his extremely successful treatise called "The exposure and refutation of the false *gnosis*", or more often, after the Latin version, simply "Against Heresies". Bearing in mind that Polycarp's episcopacy covered almost the whole of the period between the writing of the later books of the New Testament and their being accepted as canonical, and the vigour of the oral tradition mentioned above, we can see the irresistible force of Irenaeus' argument. It is that the teaching of the apostles had been handed on by their successors, whose names are known, to the churches of his own day, in particular that the Church in Rome was founded by Peter and by Paul in co-operation, and that from that day the names of the bishops are recorded, down to Eleutheros who was the present bishop. There had never been any break in the apostolic chain, and the four evangelists, Matthew, Mark, Luke and John, had given the true account of the life and teachings of Jesus. There is nothing Gnostic about them. Similarly with the other books of the New Testament. These are the authorities, and the only ones, for deciding what is apostolic and what is not. The future development of Christian ideas will be an unfolding, an "evolution" in the literal sense, of what the apostles taught, as preserved in their writings. Irenaeus is indeed a landmark in the history of the Church. With him, Catholic theology is established. How modern he sounds: his doctrine of perennial evolution might have come from the pen of Teilhard de Chardin. But then, Catholic theology is modern, because it takes no account of time.

As for the Scriptures themselves, it is clear from the foregoing that the canon was already established. In fact, the authenticity of the books of the New Testament as we possess them to-day is far superior to that of any classics. The first codices, written on the "leaf of Pergamum" that is "parchment", such as the *Sinaiticus* in the British Museum, date from the fourth century, so that there is a gap of only 300 years between the original and the earliest known copies. In the case of Aeschylus, Sophocles and Aristophanes, the gap is 1,400 years; 1,600 in the case of Euripides. Of portions of the New Testament, we have far earlier copies. For instance, the papyrus copy of St John's Gospel in the Bodmer Library at Geneva (see Plate 1 (*a*)) must have been written within half a century of the original.

In addition to the work of theological consolidation, and to the establishment of the canon, to which Irenaeus so splendidly contributed, we may note two other aspects of the contemporary Church which he exemplifies. The first is how catholic in the physical sense the Church had now become. Irenaeus is at one and the same time a son of Asia, a Roman and a bishop in Gaul, working, as he says, among Celts. He binds them all together in a really catholic charity. When there was a dispute between the Churches of Asia and that of Rome and the west about how to calculate the date of Easter, it was Irenaeus who was to intervene, in so pacific a manner that in the end the controversy solved itself.

Finally, it is already clear that the see of Rome had acquired a primacy. The confessors of Lyons sent their bishop on a mission to the bishop of Rome, to convey their disapproval of the heresy of Montanus. The bishop of Rome had in fact considerably earlier, in the days of Domitian, intervened to still controversies in the Church of Corinth. Ignatius of Antioch, who was martyred at Rome in 107, had written to his brother of Rome as leader of "the church which presides in the region of the Romans". After all, it was but natural that the Church which had been established not by one apostle only, but by two, the Church of the capital of the world, should enjoy in the spiritual realm a primacy analogous to that of the seat of the

Caesars in things temporal. It was felt and acknowledged before it was defined.

It will now be appropriate to examine the interplay between the two forces which was to take place in that same city, the juxtaposition of the dynamic soldier sun-worshipper, and the Church, no longer an imported eastern cult, but an international society, founded on a firm tradition, bound together by bonds which knew no barrier of race, conscious of unity under the guidance of its bishops of whom that of Rome was pre-eminent, and dedicated to a view of life and human destiny that could compromise with no other.

Chapter X

"IRON AND RUST"

WE must now take up the narrative of Septimius at the point where it was left at the end of Chapter VI. If the African saw himself as a second Hadrian, he lacked both Hadrian's fortune and his political suavity. It was all very well for him to be delighted by the omen, as he saw it, that when he first visited Rome he had come on a man "reading Hadrian's life", or that when he was in command in Spain he had a dream in which "first he was bidden to repair the temple of Augustus at Tarraco"—just like Hadrian—"and then from the top of a very high mountain he beheld Rome and all the world". Later on in the east he would deliberately do what Hadrian had done. But whereas Hadrian had succeeded to supreme authority without serious opposition and had then done all in his power to promote "peace, retrenchment and reform", Septimius was seriously challenged, and after overcoming his rivals, indulged in expansionist wars, more in keeping with the colonialism of the last century than the "partnership" policy of his own. The statement on page 52 above that Severus had defeated "Niger in the east, Albinus in the north" is a brief résumé of two civil wars, of a savagery and destructiveness such as Rome had not experienced since the last days of the Republic.

One quality which Septimius did possess in common with Hadrian was energy. Realizing that he could not possibly fight a war on two fronts, he anticipated, or rather as it turned out· postponed, the campaign in the north by offering his fellow-African Albinus the rank of Caesar, which Albinus was content to accept. This pleased the senate, and left Septimius free to march against Niger in Syria. Having ordered the IIIrd, Augusta, to move to the eastern region of "Africa", so as to forestall any attempt on Niger's part to interrupt the supply of Egyptian corn to Rome, he set out from the capital only five weeks after entering it by the Flaminian Way, the road that led to the north, in order to assure himself of the loyalty of the Danube troops, and then, moving south through what is now Bosnia and northern Greece, arrived at Perinthus, on the European shore of the Bosphorus, fifty miles west of Byzantium. This great and beautiful city declared for Niger, and his troops scored an initial victory over the Severan advance-guard. But the major part of his army, which had been despatched by sea, established itself at Cyzicus on the Asian side of the Sea of Marmara, thereby compelling Niger's general, Asellius Aemilianus, a former governor of Syria and now proconsul of Asia, to abandon Byzantium and retreat southwards. He was killed in action at Cyzicus shortly afterwards. Niger could count on no less than nine legions—three in Syria, two in Cappadocia, two in Palestine (of which one was soon to turn against him), one in Arabia and one in Egypt: in fact the whole of the east had rallied to him. He was no mere mushroom usurper: it would need a full-scale war to defeat him.

Severus was equal to the challenge. He himself could rely on the loyalty—though not on the effective presence—of the four Rhine legions and the twelve Danube legions. The three in Britain were commanded by Albinus. By the beginning of the year 194, Niger, who had established his capital at Antioch, realized that he could no longer hold Asia, in face of the now greatly strengthened Severan army. He therefore withdrew to Syria, hoping that Severus would be halted at the famous Cilician Gates (Gülek Boghaz). The position, strong by nature, had been further fortified by Niger; but a torrent of rain and melting snow carried away his works, whereupon the defenders retreated, and Severus' general, Candidus, stood victor on the Gulf of Issos. Egypt had already rallied to Severus. The end came soon. Amid dissension and wavering, such as the retreat of an army in that part of the world always stimulates, Niger, supported by an ardent cadet-corps from Antioch, decided to make a stand on the battlefield where Alexander had defeated Darius. As at the beginning of the campaign, Niger's troops scored an initial success, but once again, as at the Gates, nature intervened on the side of Severus. A violent thunderstorm, sweeping in from the west, seconded the assault of the Illyrian legionaries. Niger fled from the field, leaving 20,000 dead behind him. He made for Antioch, where he was forced to skulk in the suburbs until he could make off towards Parthia. He was overtaken, killed, and his head sent to Severus. The victorious emperor ordered it to be exhibited outside the walls of Byzantium, but to no effect: the town was to hold out for another two years.

Severus had shewn the greatest acumen and confidence throughout the campaign. Instead of taking the field himself, he had remained at Perinthus. He was thus able to keep touch with the west, and to direct affairs in Asia from a convenient base. He had no intention of allowing disaffection to make head in Europe while he was out of sight and out of mind in the wintry highlands of Asia Minor. At the same time, he had full trust in his generals and in his troops—he knew that they would not go over to Niger, or attempt a *coup d'état*. He understood, from the beginning of his career until, literally, his last hour, that his authority depended on the army, and on nothing else. It is true that Trajan had been a soldier-emperor, and so had Hadrian. It was also true that both of them had declared themselves the obedient servants of the senate, which they had then flouted. Severus had made just the same declarations, with just the same reservations. But he was the first emperor to admit openly and frankly that it was the army on which he relied solely and implicitly, that the army was in fact the source and guarantee of his sovereignty.

It is very hard for a Briton or an American, citizens of a group of states whose armies have proved themselves unconquerable in two wars, to understand the position of a "political army". Ever since the defeat of the regicides, England has been free from military dictatorship: the last attempt by an English administration to use the army as an instrument of domestic policy resulted in passive resistance, of the army, not the civilians. But other countries have not been, and are not, so happy. In France to this day, the army is a political factor that any would-be ruler must placate or control. In undivided Germany, in Fascist Italy, it was the same. In the new states of Asia and Africa, the pattern is monotonous: independence, the creation of an army as a symbol of independence, usurpation by the army, and the creation of a military despotism.

The great dilemma was stated by Abraham Lincoln in a famous phrase: "Must a government, of necessity, be too strong for the liberties of its own people, or too weak to maintain its own existence?" Severus was one of those who unhesitatingly chose the former alternative.

Such was the man who now entered Antioch as victor. Like Hadrian before him, Severus had taken a dislike to the Antiochenes, and with reason, because they had treated "the African" with contumely when he had been their governor under Marcus Aurelius. They now had cause to regret their haughty behaviour. Hadrian had considered dividing Syria into two, in order to reduce the power of its governor, and to humble the arrogance of these sneering pseudo-Hellenes. Severus now did so. *Coele-Syria*, or Hollow Syria, consisted of the northern part of the province, with Commagene added. Antioch was no longer to be the capital, that honour being transferred to Laodicea (Lataqia). Only two legions were now stationed in the truncated province. *Phoenician Syria*—the epithet is significant —comprised the south as far as the borders of Judaea, including the cities of Emesa, Damascus and Heliopolis (Ba'albek). Towns which had helped Niger, such as Berytus (Beirut) and Neapolis (Nablus), were deprived of their privileges and fined, to provide indemnities for their loyal rivals, Tyre and Samaria.

The "Eastern Question", as ever, awaited a solution. The Parthian king had assisted Niger, and so had several of the border princelings. But Severus shewed a statesmanlike caution in dealing with them: he had no wish to be embroiled in the east when he might have to defend his position in the west. Also, although the Parthian king was weak, his armed forces were being reorganized and re-equipped by refugees from Syria, Romans who had sided with Niger—an occurrence which has a strangely topical ring to our twentieth-century ears. He therefore contented himself with a show of force beyond the Euphrates, and the chastisement of the rebel chieftains. He was careful not to offend the Parthian king by assuming the title "Parthicus". The time for that would come. For as Severus had foreseen, Albinus had turned against him. Cheered by the news that Byzantium had fallen at last, Severus hastened to Europe. Before he left, knowing that it was members of the senate who had egged on Albinus, Severus announced that he was adopted into the Antonine family (see page 52) and had his army proclaim the deification of Commodus, his "brother" (see Plate 6).

It was again the army which proclaimed Severus' elder son, Caracalla, Caesar, the title formerly bestowed upon Albinus (see page 72). This action shewed a cold disdain for the senate, and at the same time outlawed Albinus.

Severus led his troops back to Europe along the route by which he had approached the east. After a flying visit to Rome, where the senate was dragooned into denouncing Albinus as a public enemy, Severus went north for what he knew was to be the decisive battle of his career. Hitherto, Dio tells us, he had never taken the field in person; he now realized that, at this supreme crisis, it must be himself and no other who directed the campaign. His instinct was right. At the battle of Lyons, on the 19th February, 197, Albinus was utterly defeated. He committed suicide. Severus sent his head to the senate as a present. The frightened fathers took good care to despatch a deputation to Severus to express their loyalty. Severus now divided Britain into two, just as he had divided Syria, and for the same reason. When, in June, he reached Rome, he executed twenty-nine senators who had supported Albinus, and confiscated their property. He needed the money: he gave a handsome bribe to the populace, and increased the soldiers' pay by a third. He allowed the legionaries to contract legal marriages while on active service (which they had formerly been forbidden to do), and extended to senior NCO's as well as to centurions the privilege of wearing the gold ring which had formerly been the insignia of the knights. The senate were shewn what their relative position now was, by being forced to confirm the army's proclamations in regard to Caracalla and Commodus (see page 75). He had already told them that he intended to model himself on the severity of Marius, Sulla and Augustus.

Never, in all Rome's long history, had so radical a change of régime been accomplished in so short a time. The process which had started with Sulla had, half a century later, evolved a form of government of which Augustus was the embodiment—rule by "the first citizen", supported by the senate and by obedient legions. The republican forms had been preserved; above all, it was a civil government. For two centuries it had lasted, down to the death of Marcus. Now, in less than two decades, that conception and practice had been replaced by a bold, brazen military dictatorship, and the dictator was a bold, brazen African.

Chapter XI

THE PROUD PAGAN

"TO be thus is nothing, but to be safely thus": Severus, by birth an Othello, by career a Macbeth, eclipsed the success of both, suffering the misfortunes of neither, and the reason was largely that his wife was neither a Desdemona nor a Lady Macbeth. The sagacious and domineering Julia, once her husband had established himself as master of Rome, was determined that Syria should be the scene of her own triumph: she was to be the prophetess honoured in her own country, Severus her capable consort. Thus it was that in August of 197 the emperor and empress with their two sons landed in Syria. Severus brought with him a detachment of European troops, to reinforce the armies of the east.

He also went one better than his model Hadrian: he had contrived to raise three new legions, the Ist, IInd and IIIrd, Parthian, presumably from Syrians and frontiersmen attracted by the increased pay and better conditions with which Severus had conciliated and caressed the army. One of these legions, the IInd, he had stationed at Albano, now the Pope's summer resort, just south of Rome, to make sure that the capital would remain "loyal", and to shew it and the world that in the African's estimation, Italy was just one more province, like the rest.

By this and other kindred measures Severus had completed a process begun by Hadrian, namely the assimilation of all the provinces of the empire. The modern analogue is the transformation of a British Empire directed from London into a Commonwealth of which the membership, and thus the initiative, becomes increasingly African and Asian. Severus and Julia now wished to demonstrate that it was from Africa and from Asia that the life and leadership of the Roman empire had sprung. "Phoenician" Syria—and Herodian, himself a Syrian Greek, says that the province included the "Phoenician nation"—still spoke and wrote the Phoenician language, just as Severus' own Africa did. Syria, therefore, was to be the scene of a magnificent durbar, of the revival of an ancient race. Severus would call the old world into existence, to redress the balance of the new. That was his policy, and brilliantly he carried it out. "The remote nations of the Levant," says Herodian, "so far disjoined by sea and land, scarce hear the name of Italy." He even talks of "Rome, which is not very far from Britain", so Syria-centred was he. But, as he makes Pompeianus say to Commodus, *"Ubi imperator, ibi Roma"*— where the emperor is, there is Rome. For almost the next five years, Rome was to be in Syria and Egypt. No emperor had ever given so haughty a proof of the primacy of the Levant, of the superiority of its twin capitals, Antioch—which was to be restored to its former pre-eminence in 201—and Alexandria, over Rome.

Septimius and Julia intended to make the region of her origin even more brilliant than it had been; but first, the clever African saw that, for western consumption, what was needed was a resounding military victory over a foreign enemy, because only thus could the corroding memories of two civil wars be allayed. What better than a successful invasion of the territories of the hereditary foe, Parthia? Would that not elevate him in popular esteem above Marcus Aurelius (see page 36), above Trajan, above Augustus himself? As soon as he took the field, the trimmers were his: the king of Armenia, excusing himself for having helped Niger under duress, sent hostages and money and concluded a treaty with the Romans. Abgar IX, king of Osroëne, which lay south of Armenia, and east of the Euphrates in what is now the extreme east of Turkey, in return for the flattering title *king of kings* bestowed on him by Septimius sent a corps of archers and his sons as hostages. Vologases IV of Parthia withdrew from Nisibis (now Nisibin, the frontier town on the Turkish side of the border with Iraq), which enabled Septimius to move south to Syria, to concentrate his forces, and to move into the heart of Parthia. Part of the army travelled by water, down the Euphrates, part overland. The invasion had become a triumphal progress. As in 166 (see page 36) Seleucia was taken, Babylon too. Finally, crossing the Tigris where Baghdad now stands, the Roman armies assaulted and seized the capital, Ctesiphon. Once again the town was sacked, the defenders massacred, and fifty thousand prisoners taken. *Parthicus Maximus!*—as such Septimius' soldiers acclaimed him. Yes, he could wear the title now, as of right. At the same time, the last link was forged in the family's dynastic chain: the army (who cared any longer about the senate—here in the east?) having decorated the father, now proclaimed Caracalla, aged eleven, joint Augustus with him, transferring the title Caesar to the younger brother, Geta.

Septimius had made good the boast which Dio records him as having uttered three years earlier: he had created a really strong bulwark to the Euphrates frontier of Syria, and he could now turn westward towards Syria and the arts of peace. What he did not realize was that by humbling the Parthians, he was preparing the way for the Persian Sassanids, who were eager to regain the power which the Arsacids had wielded for four and a half centuries. Throughout her history, Rome never did succeed in finding a radically stable solution to the problem of east–west relations. Co-existence, based on mutual distrust and fear, was the best that an Augustus or a Hadrian could achieve. Military intervention never brought any permanent amelioration in the Roman position, and was often the precursor of disaster. Trajan's conquests had melted away, Verus had brought back with him the fatal infection of the plague (see page 36). Rome was to rue the day, not so far distant, when, as the result of Severus' crushing Parthia, the renascent Persians would challenge the authority of Rome.

On his way back to Syria, Septimius tried once more to reduce the desert fortress of Hatra, the ruins of which still stand stark and calcined in the desert to the west of Mosul. It was a sort of junior Palmyra, and the sculptures from Hatra which now gaze at us in the Baghdad museum, in their hybrid garishness, their mixture of eastern and western styles, remind us of those from Palmyra. Trajan had besieged Hatra, and had failed to take it. Severus had been no more successful on his way to Ctesiphon. Nor would he succeed now. The defenders resorted to an interesting prototype of bacteriological warfare: they hurled down on the Roman assailants earthen vessels in which they had assembled various venomous winged and creeping creatures, which caused widespread distress. Hatra remained, for the third time, inviolate.

Back in the Levant, Septimius and his wife proceeded to elevate the already opulent provinces to an unprecedented zenith of prosperity and magnificence, of which the vestiges, even after the devastations of eighteen hundred years, the ravages of war, rapine and earthquake, still delight and thrill us. At the same time, the vindictive African continued, in Abel's words, "to gather grapes after the vintage", that is to say to pursue personal enmities, under the influence of his wife. Antioch had to wait for a year and a half before its ancient rights were restored, whereas Laodicea (Lataqia), dignified with the double title of colony and metropolis, was presented with a hippodrome, a hunting-theatre (the forerunner of our greyhound racing tracks), a public bath and an avenue with a grand colonnaded portico. Palmyra, too, became a colony with "Italian rights", and took the name Septimian. In the great temple of Bel (see Plate 25) a citizen placed a dedication to the emperor and his two sons. In the market was another, which mentioned the emperor, his wife and their elder son Antoninus, for so Caracalla was officially styled. The colony of Heliopolis, or Ba'albek, it too granted the Italian status, saw its famous sanctuary enlarged and enriched (see Plate 24). From this epoch representations of the great temple begin to appear on the city's coins. A statue of the ruler was set up in the shrine in answer to a request of the sun god, communicated by an oracle. Despite the labour lavished on this temple, so huge was it, so complex its adornment, that work on it was not discontinued until fifty years later, and even then, as we can see to-day, parts of it were left unfinished. Nevertheless, there it stood, in the hollow plain between the Lebanon and the Anti-Lebanon mountains, three thousand feet above the level of the sea, to which height had been hauled granite monoliths hewn in Egypt to match those carved in local quarries, its grand columns glistening against the snow-capped summits, and visible from the northern limits of the plain, from which run the springs of the river Orontes. Nature and art had collaborated to produce this marvel, the greatest, most august temple in the world, the abode of the sun god, the patron deity of the world's sovereign. What other religion could hope to rival such compelling glory?

Tyre, Ptolemais (Acre), Damascus, all received embellishment. Ulpian, the celebrated jurist who was a member of Septimius' privy council, and himself a Tyrian, lauds his master's generosity as follows: "It should be known that there are colonies which enjoy Italian Rights, such as the most splendid colony of the Tyrians, of which I am a native . . . of great antiquity, strongly fortified, very faithful to the alliance it has concluded with the Romans, on which, in fact, the deified Severus, our emperor, bestowed Italian Rights because of its outstanding loyalty to the Roman Republic and Empire." The passage is of particular interest, because it shews the juridical concept of the relation between Rome and the free cities in the Septimian epoch.

In Arabia, the provincial capital, Bostra, struck coins honouring the emperor, in Jerash three inscriptions recorded the pious veneration of its citizens. The roads were repaired, from Palmyra to Emesa, from Ba'albek to Aleppo, and the great Way of the Sea from Laodicea to Tyre and beyond. If we can credit Herodian, Septimius even despatched an expedition, perhaps a commercial mission, to the rich spice-bearing region of Arabia Felix (the Yemen and Aden).

In Palestine, the chief recipient of imperial favour was Sebaste, the ancient Samaria, where, on the débris of the city of Omri and Ahab, Herod the Great had erected a new town. Earthquakes and insurrections had done it much damage. Now, particularly as its neighbour and rival Neapolis (Nablus) had supported Niger, Sebaste was promoted to the rank of colony, and the ruins of temple, theatre, stadium and colonnaded streets to this day attest the imperial benevolence. In Jerusalem, or Aelia as it was now called, the upper aqueduct was repaired at Septimius' behest. Lydda, which had strong Jewish and Christian elements among its citizens, was re-dedicated to Zeus. The little village of Beit Jebrin, south-west of Hebron, was transformed into a colony, and erected into the metropolis of the whole of southern Palestine.

The architecture of this region and epoch, of which we possess such abundant remains, is valuable evidence of the region's vitality. There is nothing decadent about it. On the contrary, the Syrian architects always seemed to be able, as the great builders of the renaissance were later to prove themselves, to evolve new, arresting, virile versions of traditional styles. True, a certain lushness is apparent in some of the ornamentation, but that is more than offset by the general integrity of the design. The meretricious frippery that degrades much of the later work at Lepcis is absent in its Syrian counterpart.

Moreover it was in this region that, some time towards the end of the second century, an unknown genius discovered how to construct a dome on pendentives, that is, how to place a dome on a square building, in such a way that it shall be part of the supporting structure. The four earliest examples of this construction are at Petra, Sebaste, Jerash and near Amman—all in our area. This discovery was to prove one of the great liberating influences in architecture, which ultimately produced such soaring masterpieces at the dome of St Sophia.

Fourteen miles to the west of Rafa, the imperial suite crossed the frontier into Egypt, where, careful to follow the Hadrianic precedent, Septimius offered sacrifice to the shade of Pompey, at the monument which his model had raised. Two wings of cavalry, one from Gaul, the other Thracian, escorted the sovereign to Alexandria, to which city Septimius now granted the long-coveted restoration of the right to administer their own affairs. Like Hadrian, Septimius visited the principal monuments of the country, made a trip up the Nile (see p. 90), and took special care to investigate the religion of Sarapis, whom alone of alien gods Hadrian had honoured in a shrine which still exists in his villa at Tibur. Special orders were given that the fellahin should not be impoverished by the imperial progress: Septimius was determined to be not only all-powerful but popular as well.

So it came about that this man who had raised himself to an unprecedented height of authority and might, of secular power conjoined with religious veneration, became the first ruler of Rome personally to confront the Christians, in what had already become one of their chief strongholds.

Chapter XII

CHURCH AND STATE

BY the turn of the century, the Christian Faith had won adherents not only in almost every province of the empire, but also in every rank of society. The idea that Christianity was the religion of the poor and humble only is mistaken. The majority of its adherents were, it is true, of the poorer sort, for two reasons. The first is that in Roman society, founded as it was on a slave economy, there were far more poor than rich, so that any faith which made a universal appeal, as Christianity did, must of necessity attract more of the lower than of the upper ranks of society. The second reason is that in a society which was static in its outlook, as Roman society was, any innovation was regarded as subversive; in fact, the very phrase *novas res*, new things, was the accepted synonym for insurrection. Nevertheless, from the very outset, Christianity had attracted men and women in the upper ranges of the social scale. Joseph of Arimathea, Joanna, the wife of Herod's steward, Sergius Paulus, governor of Cyprus, Publius, the chief citizen of Malta—these were only the first of many. By the time of Septimius, not only were catholic belief and practice defined and established, but the Church, as such, was formed and braced for the inevitable struggle with the pagan state. The most crucial period in the whole life of the Church was to be the third century—as we now retrospectively call it: for the Romans, it was the period in which their eternal city was to celebrate its millennium, on the 21st April, 248—because only during this century were efforts made not merely to punish Christians, but to root out Christianity altogether. This onslaught was the culmination of a long process, obscure in its origins, its motives and its development, which it is now necessary to attempt to analyse.

Eusebius tells us that Ulpian (see page 80) drew up a list of all the imperial edicts relating to Christianity. This, not surprisingly, has not come down to us. We therefore have no connected story of the state's hostility to the new faith. There are, however, certain landmarks. First, there was the savage attack of Nero, who in the year 64 tried to divert the guilt of having burnt the city from himself to the Christians. That was a mere shift, not a settled policy. In the last decade of the century, Christians, among many others, fell as victims of the loutish

83

brutality of Domitian. Here again, there is no evidence of any thought-out and enduring legal procedure. Only in the year 112, or thereabouts, do we receive a direct ray of light, from the enquiry which the younger Pliny, then governor of Bithynia, addressed to Trajan, asking for guidance as to how he should treat the Christians. Trajan, like his predecessors, had no settled policy with regard to them. "Nothing", he says, "can be laid down as a general ruling, involving something like a set form of procedure. They are not to be sought out; but if they are accused and convicted, they must be punished." This principle was preserved by Trajan's successor, Hadrian, as we know from a letter of his to the governor of Asia.

Hitherto, it seems evident, authority was uncertain how to treat the new religion: perhaps it would die out, perhaps it was not so subversive after all. Yet every now and then, even in these early days, there were outbreaks which ended in martyrdom. These generally started not with the authorities, but with the populace. The rulers then intervened, and in order to restore order, and to appease the mob, punished the Christians. Such may have been the case with Ignatius, who was sent to Rome and there executed in Trajan's time, and certainly was the case with Polycarp, and others, who were martyred at Smyrna about the year 155, and a throng of Christians of both sexes who were done to death at Lyons in 177, in an orgy of the most disgusting cruelty. On the other hand, except for such outbursts, the Christians remained tolerated. They asked again and again that their legal position be defined, but always in vain. Nevertheless, whenever proceedings were taken against them, the aim of the magistrate was not so much to punish, as to persuade: apostasy, not martyrdom, was what Caesar desired.

What lay behind this curiously indefinite attitude of Rome towards the Christians? What was their crime, in the eyes of the law?

No one charge covers every instance. To discover the root of the matter we must go back to Tacitus. He had been governor of Asia, about the same time as Pliny was in the neighbouring province of Bithynia, and so he must have been quite familiar with Christians and Christianity. This is what he has to say about their origin: "Christus, from whom the name had its origin, suffered the extreme penalty during the reign of Tiberius at the hands of one of our procurators, Pontius Pilate, and a deadly superstition, thus checked for the moment, again broke out not only in Judaea, the first source of the evil, but also in the City, where all things hideous and shameful from every part of the world meet and become popular." Christ, the founder of the new faith, was a condemned criminal: he had been executed for a political offence. That was the basic fact, as seen by the world. It followed, in the general estimation, that those who not merely venerated, but actually worshipped a criminal must themselves be criminal. That the Christians were themselves aware of this is to be inferred from the fact that in the early centuries they almost never used the crucifix as a symbol or ornament. They preferred to represent Jesus as the Good Shepherd (see Plate 20), or as the Child with his Mother (see Plate 23). The representation of the Crucifixion in Plate 29 (a) is one of the earliest known. It dates from an era when crucifixion was no longer a common punishment, and the Christian could openly worship his Lord as he wished.

Next, there was the attitude of the Christians to the state. This was, in brief, that while they were ready and anxious to pray *for* Caesar, and, as their Master had taught them, to render unto him the things which were his, they refused to pray *to* him. This attitude simply confirmed the belief that they were a seditious and subversive organization. Thirdly, there were slanders which arose from the manner and liturgy of Christian worship. As we learn from Acts, it was the custom of the first Christians to assemble for worship in private houses. This continued to be their custom; and the earliest churches in Rome, e.g., St Martino ai Monti, St Pudenziana, or Ss Giovanni e Paolo, are actually built over the houses which they superseded. In these private dwellings baptized Christians would assemble before dawn, to celebrate the Eucharist, which was both a thanksgiving and a love-feast. It was known that the sacrament entailed the consuming of the "body and blood of the Son of Man", and that the Christians addressed each other as brothers and sisters. Malice was not slow to fabricate stories of cannibalism and incest. These were widely believed. Fronto himself, for instance, credited them; from which can be gathered the depth of prejudice with which Christians had to contend.

These three sources of hostility combined to make the mere *name* of Christian an offence, because it was well known that the Christians were extremely resolute. They could not be induced to compromise with their principles: their "obstinacy" had become proverbial: Marcus Aurelius cites it, not in condemnation of the Christians, but in parenthesis, as a stock example of stubbornness. The behaviour of the early martyrs wholly bore this out; and it was the admiration which it excited that contributed so notably to the spread of the Faith.

Finally, there was the general demeanour and behaviour of the Christians themselves. This was bound to set them apart from their pagan fellow-citizens. It is very hard for us who live in a society which if not Christian does at least, in its ordinary relationships, its moral sanctions, its ethical standards and its communal behaviour observe a decency which is founded on Christian concepts, it is hard for us to imagine what a pagan world was like. Bloodshed was the major sport and spectacle of rich and poor alike, and it was the blood not only of countless rare and beautiful beasts, but of men and women too. Obscenity, in literature and on the stage, was not merely tolerated but encouraged. In sexual relations, every form of lewdness and perversion was accepted as normal and natural. How could a people who regarded life as sacrosanct, purity as a virtue, and marriage as the sole and indissoluble union live otherwise than as strangers, as the "third race", alongside pagans and Jews?

If it was hard for the Society of Friends to avoid persecution in a Christian society, how infinitely harder must it have been for the first Christians (on whom the Friends modelled themselves) to have escaped it in a pagan one? And yet, like the Society of Friends, the Christians attracted admiration and respect by their standards of conduct, which made those who differed from them tolerate them, if not imitate them. To this tolerance the growing Church of the second century responded with a positive propaganda, the productions of the so-called apologists, for the Church was now strong enough to take the initiative, and to try to commend itself to the cultivated world. The first apologists, in the days of Hadrian, wrote in Greek, which indeed remained the language even of the bishops of Rome until the middle of the third century. The earliest apology which we possess is that of Aristides, an Athenian "philosopher", who addressed his work to Antoninus. His concern is simply to tell who the Christians are, what is their origin, who Jesus was, what his commandments are. Aristides' work was, as it was intended to be, a nice little Religious Tract. With his contemporary, Justin of Neapolis (Nablus) in Palestine, we begin to swim in far deeper waters. Here was a pilgrim who had visited many a shrine, and finally, converted to Christianity, had set up a school of Christian instruction in Rome, where, in the year 165, he died as a martyr. Justin, of whose works we still possess three, is the most important of the second-century propagandists: he set out to prove not only that the Christians were not atheists, but that their faith was founded in antiquity, and consonant with Greek philosophy. Justin evaluates the doctrine of the *Logos*, or Word, which shines from the splendid exordium of the Gospel of St John—a doctrine so fundamental, so omnipresent that it is recited every day at the conclusion of the mass.

Justin was followed by other writers, who sought to commend the new Faith, as a rational sequel to the antique philosophies. It is nevertheless to be doubted whether they made any deep impact on the general public, in a region which has always respected the spoken more than the written word. What moved Septimius to action against the Christians was not what he read—and he was a great reader— but what he heard and saw, there in Alexandria. For in that great city, the hearth of Hellenism, there flourished, at his coming, an open, established and confessed school of Christian doctrine.

Chapter XIII

"HAIL, O LIGHT"

THE origins of Egyptian Christianity are obscure. The earliest names that have come down to us are those of heretics. We do know that the Gospel of St John was current there in the second century (see Plate 1 (a)). Whether the other Gospels were also in circulation so early we cannot tell. There was a local work called *The Gospel according to the Egyptians*, which bore the taint of Gnosticism. Given the close bonds and easy communications, both by sea and by land between Palestine and Egypt, it is more than probable that Churches were established in Egypt in apostolic times, reinforced by refugees from the two Jewish wars of 66–73, and 132–5. Thus the legend that the Church of Alexandria was founded by St Mark—a legend unknown to Clement and Origen, the great Alexandrine churchmen—may rest on fact. What is certain is that the Church of Alexandria, in later centuries, maintained a particularly close relationship with the see of Rome; and it has been plausibly suggested that this originated in the gratitude of the Alexandrine Christians for Rome's help in purifying their Church of heresy.

By the end of the second century there was established in Alexandria what is known as the catechetical school, an oral university which was the Christian predecessor of the later Muslim Al-Azhar in Cairo. Ever since the second Ptolemy had founded his Museum, or "home of the Muses", and library in the third century BC, Alexandria had been a centre of diverse cultures. The city was touched not only by Hellenic and Roman influences, but by those of antique Egypt itself and even of the further orient. The milieu of a city in which cosmopolitan society and learning had existed for so long, where a shipmaster from Spain, a philosopher from Athens, a general from Italy might jostle a visitor from India or a Negro from the deep south was just that in which the new faith was most likely to find its first platform: where so many different schools of thought and doctrine already existed, one more would hardly be regarded as out of keeping, even if it could not share in the official, state-maintained academic life; just as in modern universities there exist religious colleges which are not members of the university. The school was, in fact, as we know from Eusebius, founded very early.

The first director to become famous was a certain Pantaenus, who is recorded to have gone on a missionary journey to "India"—a term which could mean any country from what is now Somaliland eastwards. As a former Stoic philosopher, he was held in high esteem. Of his works we possess nothing. His successor was Clement, who held his chair for approximately the last two decades of the second century. Clement came from Athens, where he had been born a pagan, and after his conversion undertook a long pilgrimage with the object of consulting the foremost Christian teachers of his day. One of them, from Asia Minor, he found in Greece, a Syrian and an Egyptian in Magna Graecia (that is the Greek cities of southern Italy and Sicily), a fourth in Assyria, a fifth—a Christian of Jewish origin—in Palestine. Finally, as he says, "having run down my quarry as it lay concealed in Egypt, I took my rest", that is, became the pupil of Pantaenus. Apart from its testimony to Clement's zeal, the catalogue of his spiritual mentors shews how widely the reputation of outstanding Christians could now spread, and how widely, too, they themselves were able to travel.

Clement's first aim was to maintain Catholic tradition; and it was with this end in view that he had visited so many instructors, for "these men", to quote his own words preserved for us by Eusebius, "maintained the true tradition of the blessed teaching straight from the holy apostles Peter and James, John and Paul, as son inheriting from father . . . and came under God even to our own time, to deposit those seeds of their ancestors the apostles".

Having established the Catholic purity of the faith he had received and taught, Clement set out to challenge pagan philosophy. It was commonly charged against the Christians (see page 83) that they were revolutionaries. Here is Clement's answer to the accusation, which occurs in his *Protrepticus*, or *Hortative* (X, 89):

"You say it is unreasonable to overthrow a way of life that has been handed down from our forefathers. In that case, why do we not go on using our first food, milk, to which, as you will admit, our nurses accustomed us from birth? Why do we add to or diminish our family property, instead of keeping it at the same value as when we received it? . . . So in life itself, shall we not abandon the old way, which is wicked, full of passion, and without God? And shall we not, even at the risk of displeasing our fathers, set our course towards the truth and look for him who is our real father, discarding custom like some deadly drug? There is no doubt that the noblest of all the tasks we have in hand is simply this: to prove to you that it was from madness, and from this thrice miserable *custom* that hatred of godliness sprang? . . . Away then, away with forgetfulness of the truth! Let us shake off the ignorance and darkness that spreads like a mist over our sight; and let us get a vision of the true God, first raising to him this voice of praise: 'Hail, O Light.' Upon us who lay buried in darkness and shut up in the 'shadow of death' a 'light shone forth' from heaven, purer than the sun and sweeter than the life of earth. That light is life eternal, and whatsoever things share in it, live. But night shrinks back from the light, and setting through fear, gives place to the day of the Lord . . . He it was who changed the setting into a rising, changed crucified death into life. He snatched man out of the jaws of destruction. He raised him to the sky, transplanting corruption to the soil of incorruption, and transforming earth to heaven.''

Here indeed was a new voice! No pagan had written with such a jubilance and vigour for many a long year. Clement claimed that Christianity was the only true basis for a science of world history: far from there being an antagonism between Greek philosophy and Christian doctrine, it was philosophy which had prepared the way for the Gospel, just as the Hebrew scriptures had: "Philosophy then before the advent of the Lord," says Clement in his *Stromateis*, or *Miscellanies*, 1, 5, 28, "was necessary to bring them to righteousness, but now it is profitable to bring them to piety, because it is a sort of training for those who are gaining the fruit of faith for themselves by means of demonstration; for 'your foot will not stumble', He says, if you refer good things to providence, whether the good things be Greek or Christian. God is the cause of *all* good things—of some primarily, such as the old and new covenants, and of others consequentially, such as philosophy. It may be that it *was* given primarily to the Greeks in the days before the Lord called the Greeks, also; because philosophy educated the Greek world as the Law did the Hebrews—'to bring them to Christ'. So philosophy is a preparation, making the way ready for the man who is being made perfect by Christ."

This fusion of philosophy and faith produced the *true* 'man of knowledge' or 'Gnostic', in Clement's view. Thus it was that he was able to appeal to Christians, philosophers and Gnostics alike. In the late Professor Burkitt's words (CAH, xii, 480): "The real value of Clement's writing . . . consists in the picture that he unconsciously draws of a paganism attracted by the Christian system and willing to accept it if it can be shewn to be not inconsistent with a cultivated and enlightened view of the universe, and on the other hand of a Christianity willing to express its beliefs in a way consistent with the best pagan culture."

Clearly, such a system must hold a threat for a man like Septimius who wished all men to see in *himself*, not in faith or philosophy, their guide and goal. Nor was it only in the Greek-speaking east that the old "custom" was now being vigorously attacked. From the Latin west the assault was duplicated, not in Greek, but in Latin, not from Italy, but from Africa, from Carthage itself! Quintus Septimius Florens Tertullianus—Tertullian to us—was born in Carthage about 160. Like Clement, he was born a heathen and was converted in adult life. He was well versed in Greek and Latin, in rhetoric, philosophy and law. His was a bold, fiery spirit, full of contradictions. An African, he was to become, after Irenaeus, the founder of western, European, Catholic theology. He was an ardent and eloquent defender of the Catholic Church against heretics, Jews and pagans. He then became a heretic himself, a Montanist (see page 67), and thereafter displayed the same vigour in attacking the Catholic Church as he had formerly shewn in its defence. At his best, Tertullian is splendidly stimulating. In outlook he cannot be said to resemble Clement; and yet that very fact is a tribute to the universality of the new light, for the worlds of both are illuminated by the same radiant warmth, a warmth which pagan literature now wholly lacked.

Tertullian's best-known work is his *Apology*, because it has the most general appeal to a modern reader, to whom all heresies (except his own) seem unimportant. Here is the passage, in Chapter XVII, which contains the famous phrase *testimonium animae naturaliter Christianae*: "Would you have us prove him to you from his own works, in all their plenitude, all their character, those works that contain us, sustain us, delight us—yes, even terrify us. Would you have us prove him to you from the witness of the human soul itself? Yes: the soul, be it cabined and cribbed by the body, confined by evil nature, robbed of its strength by lusts and desires, enslaved to false gods—none the less, when it recovers its sense, as after a debauch, or sleep or some illness, when it regains its proper health, the soul names *God*, and for this reason and no other, that, if language is properly used, He is the one true God. 'Good God!' men say, 'Great God!' 'God grant!' That he is also *Judge*, is shewn by such phrases as: 'God sees'; 'I leave it to God'; 'God will repay me' *Oh the witness of the soul by nature Christian!* Then, as it says in these words, it turns its gaze not to the Capitol, but to heaven. For it knows the abode of the living God: from him and from heaven it came." (It may be noted that Tertullian here, although he writes in Latin, is thinking as a Semite: phrases such as he cites are constantly on the lips of modern Arabs, and the penultimate one, "I leave it to God" may be seen written in Arabic on scores of lorries and buses throughout the Levant.)

How far he was from the Greek approach of Clement may be gathered from the following passage, taken from *About the prescription of Heretics*, vii:

"Philosophy is the material of the world's wisdom, the rash interpreter of the nature and dispensation of God. Indeed, heresies are themselves instigated by philosophy. From this source came the 'aeons' and I know not what infinite 'forms', and the 'trinity of man' in the system of Valentinus: he was a Platonist. From the same source came Marcion's better god with his tranquillity—he started as a Stoic." It is the same, he goes on, with Epicureans as with the followers of Zeno or Heraclitus: they all foster heresy. "The same subject-matter is discussed over and over again by heretics and philosophers; the same arguments are reconsidered. Whence comes evil, and why? Whence comes man, and how? Besides the question which Valentinus has recently put forward—'Whence comes God?' No doubt from *Desire* and—abortion" [that is, Hachamoth, the monstrous creature to which Wisdom gave birth, as the result of her illicit desire for the Abyss, in the Valentinian scheme of things] . . .

"What indeed has Athens to do with Jerusalem? What has the Academy to do with the Church? What have heretics to do with Christians? Our instruction comes from the Porch of Solomon" [as opposed to the Porch, the *Stoa*, at Athens where Zeno, the founder of the *Stoic* philosophy taught] "who had himself taught that the Lord should be sought in simplicity of heart. Away with all attempts to produce a Stoic, Platonic and dialectic Christianity! We want no curious disputation, once we have possessed Jesus Christ, no inquisiton after receiving the gospel. When we believe we desire no further belief. For the first article of our faith is this: that there is nothing beyond this that we need believe."

This Semitic revulsion from Hellenism, this burning, almost desert fundamentalism is curiously prophetic of that very Semitic creed of Islam which over four centuries later was to win the whole of north Africa, and to hold it until this day: it is an astonishing psychological presage. At the same time, it shews how widely, in the context of the age in which Clement and Tertullian lived, the Faith could be interpreted, and what fervour it inspired in each of its different interpretations.

Tertullian wrote so much, and in so vigorous and challenging a style, that it would be easy to compose a Christian anthology, and a most readable one too, wholly from his works. But we must press on, content with one last citation, which is not only typical of the man; but, to those familiar with the Coronation Service, shews, in its final sentence, the model on which one of the most beautiful prayers in that service (the *Benediction*) is based.

Tertullian is answering the charge that Christians are "disloyal". In those days, as in our own, the word was often misused. Tertullian was at pains to shew that it was not the Christians who had assassinated emperors, for instance: in this passage, again from the *Apology* (c, 30), he puts the positive case: "We, on behalf of the emperors, invoke the eternal God, the true God, the living God, whom the emperors themselves prefer to have propitious to them beyond all other gods. They know who has given them the empire; they know as men who has given them life; they feel that he is God alone, in whose power and no other's they are, second to whom they stand, after whom they come first, before all gods, and above all gods. Why not? seeing that they are above all men, and men, at any rate, live and so are better than dead things . . . Looking up to heaven the Christians—with hands outspread, because innocent, with head bare because we do not blush, yes and without anyone to dictate the form of words, for we pray from the heart—we are ever making intercession for all the emperors. We pray for them a long life, a secure rule, a safe home, brave armies, a faithful senate, an honest people, a quiet world—and everything for which a man and a Caesar can pray."

Such a new power over the minds of men, such a potent influence on their minds and actions, was bound to affront the lord and master of the sublunar world. The magic-ridden African, who had demanded of Dio that he compose him a dream-book, the classical dilettante who prided himself on his knowledge of Greek and Latin authors, the warrior who had triumphed in the west and the east over Roman and Parthian alike, such a man would never tolerate a race of men who laughed magic to scorn, who held that ancient philosophy was, at best, but the preparation for their own faith, and who, in general, though not wholly, held it inconsonant with their profession to serve in the wars. Septimius was bound to chastize the Christians. But how was it to be done?

The emperor, once more copying Hadrian, made a trip up the Nile. He visited Memphis, he visited Thebes, and there, like his predecessor, he visited the famous statue of "Memnon" (Amenophis, III) and heard it "sing" at dawn. He then had the neck and head restored, with the result that from that day to this, the statue has sung no more. Did the superstitious emperor see in this an omen of the end of a dispensation?

Just when he made up his mind, we do not know: Clement had

quitted Alexandria soon after the emperor's arrival, and had taken refuge in Cappadocia with an old pupil, Alexander, now a bishop and destined one day to rule the Church of Jerusalem; from which it is clear that the Alexandrian Christians had a good idea of what was coming to them. The actual edict, or rescript as it more probably was, appears to have been issued after Septimius' return to Rome, in the spring of 202. Clearly, the emperor had long pondered the matter, before deciding on what precise form his anti-Christian policy should take. As finally promulgated, it surprises us by its sense of compromise, rather than by its ferocity. Septimius did not attempt, as later emperors did, to extirpate the Faith altogether: he simply tried to "contain" it, as we should say nowadays. He merely forbade Christian proselytism, making those who made converts and the converts themselves equally guilty. This was ingenious, because although it permitted those who were already Christians to remain Christian, it contrived to hit with particular force the propagandists of Alexandria, and that, as Eusebius tells us (VI, i), is exactly what it did: even the anchorites of the Thebaïs were rounded up and brought to Alexandria for slaughter. In fact, although Eusebius places it in the year 202, the persecution in Alexandria seems to have been a pilot project, because the authorities agree that Septimius was in Egypt when it broke out.

Nevertheless the Church as such continued to exist. What had led Septimius to adopt this compromise? There appear to be two main reasons. The first is indicated in the words of the *Augustan History* announcing the change of policy from that which had been formerly in force: "The emperor forbade conversions to the Jewish religion under threat of serious penalties, and he took the same decision with regard to the Christians." In fact Jewish proselytism had been forbidden ever since the days of Antoninus Pius, who was moreover regarded as a benefactor by the Jews because he had modified the harsh edict of Hadrian which had forbidden circumcision of anyone, whether Jew or Gentile: Antoninus had permitted it for Jews. Septimius now makes a similar decree. In fact the Jews had flourished since the days of Antoninus. Their existence was officially recognized, they were allowed to aspire to civil honours, they had at their head a patriarch who, says Tertullian, differed but little from a king. The office was held from the days of Marcus Aurelius right down to those of Caracalla by Rabbi Judh I. This great man was given the privilege of travelling in the most splendid carriage, the *carruca*, of which there seems to be a representation in one of the sculptures of the synagogue at Capernaum. The age of Septimius and his son was to

94

see the construction of a series of magnificent synagogues throughout Galilee, which could only have been erected with full official approval.

If, therefore, this was the result of the edict concerning the Jews, it seems at least possible that Septimius had designed a similar status for the Christians, not realizing that the Christians were far more ardent in their proselytism than the Jews. Why differentiate between these two sections of the community who were, after all, akin in their beliefs?

The second reason was personal. In his earlier days Septimius had been not unfavourable to the Christians. He gave his son Caracalla a Christian nurse, as we learn from Tertullian (*Ad Scapulam*), just as he allowed him a Jewish playmate. He was said to have been cured of some disease by a Christian doctor. Moreover the Christians of Palestine had shewn no enthusiasm for the cause of Niger. When Byzantium fell in 196, one of Niger's officers had cried out, "Now, Christians, you can rejoice!" Then, too, there was his wife's influence. As already noted, her family had been allied, two centuries earlier, with the royal house of Judaea. She herself was surrounded with philosophers of the stamp of Diogenes Laertius and his friend Galen, the great doctor. Galen criticized the attitude of both Jews and Christians towards empirical knowledge, and their reliance on faith as the one guide; but it could not be said that he, any more than the naturalists Aelian and Oppian, were inhumane. On the contrary, Galen in another context commends the Christians for their constancy and continence—the first great pagan to do so. Even the lawyers, like Ulpian and Papinian, the former of whom was certainly opposed to Christianity, were nevertheless the advocates of justice: is it not to Ulpian that we owe the great maxim that "by the law of nature all men are born free"?

Taken all in all, therefore, it seems probable that Septimius really did believe that his new policy would "stabilize" a difficult situation. It nevertheless marks a decisive stage in the development of relations between Church and State. First and foremost, it is a positive policy: it replaces the Trajanic tolerance with an injunction that demands positive action on the part of Caesar's subordinates. In fact, although those subordinates, egged on by the mob, were to take savage measures against individual Christians, or whole communities, the policy was to prove a failure, as must any which enriched the Church with deaths so splendid as those of Felicity and Perpetua at Carthage. Such was the resilience of the Church, so vigorous its generative force, that it must inevitably invoke upon itself still sterner sanctions. As inevitably, it would render them ineffectual.

Chapter XIV

FATHER AND SONS

BEFORE leaving Alexandria, Septimius visited the tomb of Alexander the Great, its founder. Augustus had done the same, touching the face, and, it was said, breaking a bit off the nose. Septimius—and this pre-Christian veneration of relics is not without interest—entered the monument, took away, as was his custom, any liturgical books which he thought might contain arcane lore, and then had the tomb sealed up, that he might be the last ever to view the features of so great a man. On Caracalla, now in his sixteenth year, the incident, as we shall see, appears to have made a deep impression. The winter was spent at Antioch, now restored to favour, and it was here that on the first day of the year 202 Septimius assumed his third consulship, with Caracalla as his colleague. From Antioch the imperial party journeyed towards Rome by way of Thrace, Moesia and Pannonia. That northern frontier—it was essential to ensure that it was faithfully and efficiently held. There was, too, another object in the emperor's visits to the military posts. The permission he had granted to the soldiers to marry (see page 76) had meant that cantonments had been transformed into garrison towns, and he wanted to inspect the new married quarters. He was apparently pleased by what he saw, and did his best to encourage the new deal. At Viminacium, at the confluence of the Morava and the Danube east of Belgrade, he and Caracalla are recorded to have reconstructed the *canabae* or faubourg of the VIIth, Claudian. Carnuntum, twenty-five miles east of Vienna, at Hainburg on the Danube, and Aquincum, the modern Buda-Pesth, both important military stations, were promoted from the rank of *municipia* to that of colonies.

Septimius reached Rome in time to celebrate, from the 2nd to the 8th June, 202, his *decennalia*, or tenth anniversary of his reign. It was almost five years since the emperor had seen his capital, to which, indeed, he had made but three short visits, in 193, 196 and 197, amounting to less than a twelvemonth in all. The proceedings were impressive, though not as splendid as those which had marked the emperor's first entry into Rome ten years before, which Dio says were the most magnificent he ever saw. On this later occasion, the emperor was unable to stand in a chariot, owing to gout, and so there

Constantine, the first Christian emperor, born, probably at Nish, about 280, hailed as Augustus at York in 306, sole emperor 324–337. This colossal "Byzantine" head, impersonal and hieratic, the right hand raised as if to warn or bless, was found in the basilica of Constantine in Rome (Plate 9) and is now in the Palazzo dei Conservatori on the Capitol there.

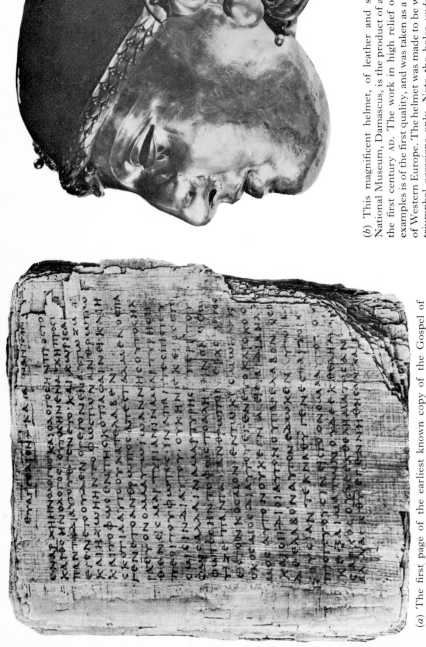

(b) This magnificent helmet, of leather and silver, now in the National Museum, Damascus, is the product of an Emesan artist of the first century AD. The work in high relief on this and similar examples is of the first quality, and was taken as a model by artificers of Western Europe. The helmet was made to be worn on formal and triumphal occasions only. Note the holes *under* the eye-slits, to enable the wearer to see where he was going as he marched with head erect in the proud procession (page 50).

(a) The first page of the earliest known copy of the Gospel of St John. It is almost complete. This copy is also the earliest known papyrus *book* as distinct from roll. It may be dated, by the script, as a product of the late second century.

(b) The "Thundering Legion" (page 40), as represented on the column of Marcus Aurelius in the Piazza Colonna, Rome. The incident is portrayed in the middle band, where the rain-god is shown with showers dripping from his outstretched arms.

(a) The Temple of Artemis, Jerash, dedicated in the year AD 150.

Plate 2

"Iron and Rust." The emperor Commodus, son of Marcus Aurelius, dressed as Hercules, from a bust in the Palazzo dei Conservatori, Rome. By this epoch, in Roman portrait busts the iris and the pupil of the eye are worked and the face polished, to contrast more vividly with the hair, which is emphasized by undercutting and drilling. Commodus resembles his father as a travesty resembles its original

(page 42)

Plate 2

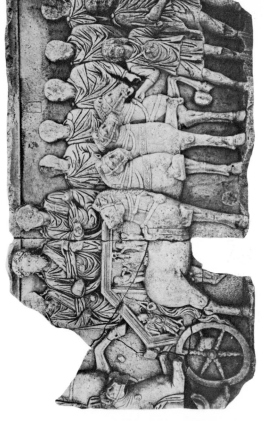

(b) Septimius and his sons Caracalla and Geta in a triumphal chariot, from the Arch of Septimius at Lepcis. Note the "frontality" of the figures, which reflects Syrian or Mesopotamian influence (cf. Plate 7).

LEPCIS MAGNA

(a) The Severan Nymphaeum. The columns and entablature are purely decorative, *appliqués*, like those at the back of a Roman stage. The lower columns are of *cipollino*, the upper ones of red granite. The Septizonium in Rome, designed to recall Lepcis, was constructed on a similar plan (page 98).

Plate 4

(a) Septimius Severus, from the bronze statue in the Cyprus Museum, Nicosia. The statue, which is a little over life-size, was found in fragments at Kytherea in Cyprus in 1928. It is possible that the head of Septimius has been added to an older torso.

(b) Julia Domna, wife of Septimius Severus, from a head in the Ny Carlsberg Glyptotek, Copenhagen. Note the firm mouth and chin.

IMP · CAES · DIVI ·
[A]NTONINI · PII · GERMANICI
SARMATICI · FILIVS · DIVI ·
[C]OMMODI · FRATER ·
DIVI · ANTONINI · PII · NEPOS · DIVI · HADRIANI
PRONEPOS · DIVI · TRAIANI · PARTHICI I ·
ABNEPOS · DIVI · NERVAE · ADNEPOS ·
[·] SEPTIMIVS · SEVERVS ·
PIVS · PERTINAX · AVG ·
[A]RABICVS · ADIABENICVS · P · MAX ·
[T]R · POT · IIII · IMP · VIII · COS II · P · P ·
[C]OLVMNAM · VII · TEMPESTATE ·
CONFRACTAM · RESTITVIT ·

MAIAS · PONTIFICAT

Retrospective adoption (page 52). This inscription of the year 196 from Ostia, now in
the Lateran Museum, gives the clearest possible exposition of Septimius' (purely
fictitious) claim to be an "Antonine". It records his restoration of a pillar of a public
building and reads:

The emperor Caesar son of Marcus Antoninus Pius Germanicus Sarmaticus
brother of the deified Commodus grandson of the deified Antoninus Pius great-
grandson of the deified Hadrian great-great-grandson of the deified Trajan
Parthicus great-great-great-grandson of the deified Nerva Lucius Septimius
Severus Pius Pertinax Augustus Arabicus Adiabenicus Pontifex Maximus
holder of his IVth Tribunician Power hailed as Imperator for the VIIIth time
Consul for the IInd time Father of his country restored the seventh column
which had been shattered by a storm.

Plate 6

Septimius and Julia Domna sacrificing, from the "arch of the Moneychangers", Rome. The heads of both are veiled, as Roman ritual practice required. Note, as in Plate 4 (*b*), the frontality of the figures and the oriental exuberance of the decoration of the pilasters. Similar motifs may be seen at Lepcis. This monument is visible evidence of the eastern influence that now invaded Rome, a reaction from Rome's influence on Syria and Parthia (cf. Schlumberger, *Syria* xxxvii, pp. 265 *et seq.*).

Plate 7

The Arch of Septimius Severus in the Forum, Rome. The arch was originally surmounted by a bronze six-horsed chariot carrying the emperor and his sons. The sculptures on this elevation, facing the Capitol, represent on the lower right-hand side the siege of Hatra (page 79) and on the left-hand the crossings of the Tigris and Euphrates (page 78).

Plate 8

The Temple of Vesta in the Forum which Julia Domna restored (page 98). Immediately behind and to the right is the House of the Vestals. On the horizon, athwart the Sacred Way, is the Arch of Titus. On the left, behind the campanile of S. Francesca Romana, is a vestige of Hadrian's Temple of Venus and Rome, with the Colosseum at the very back. On the extreme left, behind the standing columns, is the Temple of the deified Romulus, son of Maxentius, and a fragment of the Basilica of Constantine.

Plate 9

Croy Hill, in Scotland, from the air. At the base of the hill may be seen a portion of the Antonine Wall, running from Forth to Clyde (page 30.) In the National Museum of Antiquities in Edinburgh there is a distance-slab from this wall, worked by a member of the IInd, Augusta, which shows on the right the Roman *suovetaurilia*, sacrifice of ox, sheep and pig, and on the left a Roman horseman despatching a couple of natives. The inscription reads: "In honour of the emperor Caesar Titus Aelius Hadrianus Antoninus Augustus Pius Father of his country the IInd Augustan Legion completed 4652 paces."

Plate 10

Caracalla, from a head in the National Museum, Naples. Note the treatment of the eyes and the contrast between flesh and hair already evident in the head of Commodus (Plate 3). This head shows Caracalla as he liked to appear to his contemporaries (page 103).

Plate 11

The Baths of Caracalla, Rome, one of the most stupendous
ruins of all antiquity. They represent the functional
"engineering" architecture of Rome at its boldest and best.
This aspect of the structure is easier to appreciate now than
when the walls were covered with marble and the ceilings
with stucco ornament. It was here, in 1819, that Shelley
wrote the second and third acts of *Prometheus Unbound*,
"upon the mountainous ruins . . . among the flowery glades,
and thickets of odiferous blossoming trees, which are ex-
tending in ever-winding labyrinths upon its immense platforms and dizzy arches suspended in the air". The glades
and thickets are gone now, but the platforms and arches
remain. The Baths were begun by Septimius Severus in 206,
inaugurated by Caracalla in 217, finished by Elagabalus and
Alexander and restored by Aurelian.

Plate 12

Roman sport. From a mosaic floor from Abu Qumeira, Libya, now in the Tripoli Museum. A prisoner bound to a stake is being pushed in a cart towards a waiting panther, the animal being egged on by the *bestiarius*, goad in one hand, whip in the other. These wild animals were specially trained to attack human beings. Tertullian refers to this savagery in his *De Spectaculis* xxiii, *ad fin.*: "I say nothing of the man who pushes another in front of himself to the lion—in case he is not quite murderer enough when he cuts his throat afterwards." Other scenes in the same mosaic show man fighting man, to the accompaniment of organ, horn and tuba, with a gaudy bier waiting for the loser (page 49).

Plate 13

Julia Mammea, mother of Severus Alexander. Compare this face with that of her aunt Julia Domna (Plate 5 (*b*)) and her son (Plate 15). This head is now in the *Terme* National Museum in Rome.

Plate 14

Severus Alexander, from a statue in the National Museum, Naples. He has the face of a thinker rather than of a man of action. It is not hard to picture him under the influence of his dominating mother.

Plate 15

(a) Elagabalus, from a head in the Capitoline Museum, Rome. Note the change in the treatment of the hair in this and the preceding plate, compared with Plates 3 and 11. This head, with its staring eyes and loose mouth, conveys very well the mentally deranged and morally unrestrained character of the Syrian boy-emperor.

(b) The Black Stone being conveyed to Rome, as shown on a coin in the Bibliothèque Nationale. The inscription reads SANCT DEO SOLI—"to the holy god the sun" and, below, ELAGABAL.

Plate 16

(b) Philip the Arab, from a coin in the British Museum, issued in 248, the year of Rome's millennium (page 133). Philip is wearing the *corona radiata*, the radiate crown, the attribute of deity. The inscription reads IMP PHILIPPUS AUG. The reverse bears a representation of the Arabian oryx, a beautiful animal which is now almost extinct. The inscription reads SAECULARES AUGG in commemoration of the millennium and below is the figure VI, indicating that it is Philip's sixth issue.

(a) This fine mosaic from Philippopolis (page 132) is now in the National Museum, Damascus. The figures of Greek mythology which it represents would not be intelligible to the Arabs of the Hauran without the Greek "captions", giving the names of the Winds, Agriculture, Triptolemus, Prometheus, etc. Even the *putti* representing Dew (top middle) have their names attached to them.

Plate 17

(*a*) Valerian a captive kneeling at the feet of Shapur, from the rock-cut monument at Naqsh-e-Rustam, near Persepolis. The standing figure in Roman garb is Mariada (page 144).

Plate 18

b) Decius. This eloquent head is now in the Lenbachhaus at Munich. The process noted in Plate 16 (*a*) has been carried a stage further, and the hair is now represented by chisel strokes. Like other emperors of the third century Decius looks tired and perplexed, as well he might (cf. Plate 27).

(*a*) Mithras: Rome. Mithraeum of the second century AD below the Christian church of San Clemente, which supplanted it. On the altar Mithras is represented slaying the bull.

(*b*) Mithras: London. This relief, found at Walbrook in 1889, is made of sandstone, and shows Mithras slaying the bull, accompanied by the usual attendants with torches, also a dog, snake, scorpion and bird. Signs of the zodiac surround the central figure. In the corners, *top r.h.*, moon-chariot drawn by bulls, *l.h.*, sun-chariot drawn by horses, *bottom r.h.*, Boreas, *l.h.*, Zephyrus. Both these examples show Mithras in his customary Persian garb; but a statue has recently come to light at Ostia representing Mithras slaying the bull dressed in a Greek *chlamys*—so acclimatized in the west had this eastern deity become.

Plate 19

(a)

(b)

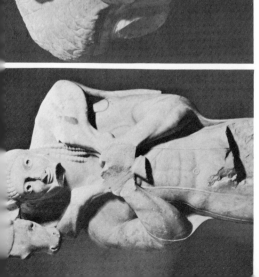

(c)

Plate 20. Christian symbols: The Good Shepherd. This most popular of Christian symbols was, like others, adopted from current secular imagery. It has a long history, being modelled on aspects of the god Hermes, whose office it was to accompany the souls of the departed. This plate shows (*a*) Hermes Moschophoros, or calf-bearer, archaic, sixth century BC, in the Acropolis Museum, Athens; (*b*) Hermes Criophoros, or lamb-bearer, fifth century BC, in the Barraco Museum, Rome; (*c*) the Good Shepherd, about half life-size, third century AD, in the Lateran Museum, Rome. Its size suggests that it was originally made for a private shrine.

The Catacombs were decorated with simple frescoes, representing such subjects as the Eucharist, praying figures, Old Testament prototypes of Christ, and Christ himself, sometimes under the guise of deities such as Orpheus or the Sun, or, as here, as the Good Shepherd. This picture is in the catacomb of Priscilla on the Salarian Way, the oldest in Rome. The fresco is of the third century.

Plate 21

A favourite subject for early Christian sculpture was Jonah and the Whale—a prototype of Christ's death and resurrection (Matt. xii, 40). A subject like this (from a sarcophagus in the Lateran Museum), even where the execution is rough and unskilled, infused a vigour and novelty into representative art which it had lacked for centuries.

Plate 22

The Magi were naturally a popular theme in Eastern Christendom. This charming "primitive" comes from Syria, and is now in the National Museum, Damascus. The three Magi are dressed as Persians. In accordance with a convention of eastern art, the Madonna is represented as larger than the other figures, because she is more important

Ba'albek. An aerial view of the majestic ruins, showing the *temenos*, the great temple of the Sun and the lesser so-called "temple of Bacchus" (page 80). This and the following plate are from photographs kindly supplied by the Institut Archéologique Français of Beirut.

Plate 24

Palmyra. An aerial view, showing the temple of Bel, after clearance, with the triumphal arch and colonnaded streets. At the top left hand may be seen some of the "tower tombs" (see Plate 26).

Plate 25

(a) Funeral relief from Palmyra. Tomb-reliefs in the Palmyrene style are found as far afield as South Shields, which has produced two, one for a resident Palmyrene, one for a Spanish soldier.

Plate 26

(b) Interior of a tomb, reconstructed in the National Museum, Damascus. Note the Persian head-dresses of the two principal figures on the central couch.

(a) Diocletian. This sad, puzzled face in the Ny Carlsberg Glyptotek may well be that of Diocletian. It still holds something of the old Roman *gravitas*.

(b) Gallienus. This head in the Ny Carlsberg Glyptotek marks a turning-point in the history of sculpture. For the very last time an attempt is made to revive classical dignity and realism. The face is, nevertheless, marked by the *angst* of the age.

(c) Aurelian. This coin shows the emperor wearing the "radiate crown" of his patron god, the victorious Sun (see Plate 17 (b)). The reverse, with the inscription ADVENTUS AUG, celebrates his arrival in Rome.

(d) Zenobia, from a coin in the Bibliothèque Nationale. She has the aspect and air of a twentieth-century sovereign.

Plate 27

(*a*) Split. A reconstruction of Diocletian's Fortress-palace (page 170).

(*b*) Split. A portion of Diocletian's palace as it is to-day. Note the arches springing directly from the columns. This un-Greek innovation may be seen at Pompeii and Lepcis, but here brought to a maturity which was powerfully to influence Byzantine, Muslim and Renaissance architects.

Plate 28

(b) The earliest Christian coin, showing Constantine on the obverse, and on the reverse the *labarum* and the imperial family.

(c) Diocletian. The obverse well illustrates his character as planner and man of action. The reverse shows the four tetrarchs in front of a fortified camp, with the inscription VICTORIA SARMATICA.

(d) A coin of Carausius (page 172), founder of the first British empire. This coin is unique, in that it is the only Roman coin to embody a quotation from Virgil, EXPECTATE VENI[S] (*Aenid* ii, 282) "Longed for thou comest", with which words Britannia is represented on the reverse welcoming her "liberator".

(a) One of the earliest known representations of the Crucifixion, from the fourth century. Christ is represented clothed, and fastened by the wrists, not the hands, to the upper side of the crossbeam, and at ground level, not raised aloft. At his side are two

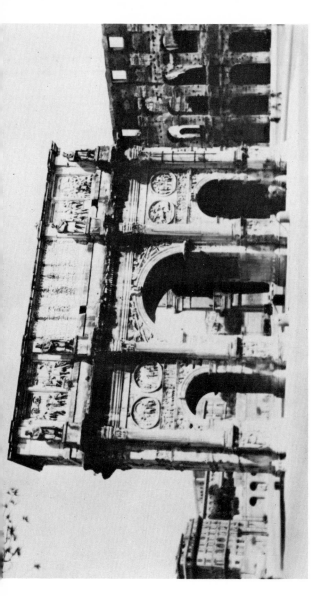

The Arch of Constantine, erected in Rome near the Colosseum, as a war memorial, in 315. The architectural structure, in contrast to the Arch of Septimius Severus (Plate 8), is inspired by a strong classical sentiment. Part of the decoration is taken from earlier work. The contemporary panels exhibit no Christian symbols nor any reference to Constantine's visions (page 175). On the other hand the "prompting of the deity" is acknowledged—a fair compromise, because although the emperor was a Christian, even if an unbaptized one, the Roman Senate and People were still predominantly pagan. The inscription reads:

To the emperor Caesar Flavius Constantine Maximus Pius Felix Augustus the Roman Senate and People dedicated this arch decorated with his victories because by the prompting of the deity by the greatness of his mind he with his army at one moment by a just victory avenged the state both on the tyrant and all his party.

To the liberator of the city to the establisher of peace.

The battle of the Milvian Bridge is represented in the panel over the right-hand archway.

Plate 30

was no formal triumph. But neither the populace nor the praetorian guard had any cause to complain: each citizen who was entitled to free grain, and each member of the guard, received ten gold pieces, one for each year of the reign.

As a permanent record of the event, a splendid building programme was inaugurated. The fire of 192 (see page 45) had ravaged both the Forum and Palatine: only now, eleven years later, in a Rome victorious and at peace, could the task of restoration be undertaken. But before the old was repaired, there was one new, personal, addition to be made to the Roman scene: a triumphal arch (see Plate 8). It stands there still, at the north-west end of the Forum, or rather in the north-west corner of it; for the arch itself, magnificent as it is, is nevertheless dwarfed by its nearness to the Capitol, which overtops it. It is, too, almost jostled by the curia, or senate house, on the north-east, and by the temples of Concord, Saturn and Vespasian between it and the Capitol. Even the rostra seem to confine the newcomer on the west side. Why then did this proud man choose such a site, instead of placing his memorial on a ridge such as that which supports the arch of Titus at the other end of the Forum, or out in the open, as Constantine was later to do? (see Plate 30). The Forum, it is true, was by now fairly cluttered up with memorials great and small; but was it necessary to have the arch in the Forum? Yes, it was: for in the very next year, that is, in 204, Septimius had decided to celebrate the Secular Games. These solemn exercises had been founded in 509 BC, and under the early Republic had been held at intervals averaging about a century, hence their name. Augustus had revived them in 17 BC, and had commissioned Horace to write his stately *Carmen Saeculare* for the occasion. Claudius, Domitian and above all Antoninus Pius had revived them. The new Antoninus must do the same; and it should be through his own arch, the record of his own victories, that the sacred band of lads and virgins, chanting their hallowed hymns, should pass on their way to the Capitol. So there the arch had to be set. That it should be within fifty paces of the meeting place of the senate, athwart the way between it and the acropolis of the city, may well have given an ironical pleasure to the man who had so conspicuously humbled the hostility of the conscript fathers.

The arch which, even if it were constructed in a hurry, has weathered eighteen centuries, stands as an eloquent exposition of the man who ordained it, of his character and his achievements. It is a family, a dynastic memorial, recording the triumphs of the father and his two sons (though the name of Geta was later replaced by other words), who "restored the commonwealth and promoted the rule of the Roman people by their outstanding merit both at home and abroad". Septimius himself, so run the graven titles, is hailed as *Pontifex Maximus*, *Father of his Country*, four times *Imperator*, holder of the tribune's authority, *Parthicus Arabicus*, *Parthicus Adiabenicus*. The sculpture of the arch illustrates and corroborates these ascriptions. The lower panels are representations, in the classical manner, of Romans leading Parthian captives. The upper sections, on the other hand, picture events in the campaigns in the more popular cursive, or "strip", technique used on the columns of Trajan and Marcus Aurelius. Here sculpture is imitating painting, the scenes being taken no doubt from the paintings which, Herodian tells us, were paraded at the *decennalia*. There is also here, as in the contemporary arch of the Moneychangers (see Plate 7) both in the arrangement of the figures and the decoration, a Parthian influence—a *quid pro quo* for Rome's impact on Parthia.

Septimius restored the portico of Octavia, near the theatre of Marcellus, and repaired the Pantheon. Julia his wife, tactfully if inappropriately, rebuilt the temple of Vesta, a pretty little feminine rotunda in the middle of the Forum, and the house of the vestals which adjoins it. It seems rather large for the six ladies who inhabited it; but we must remember that it was also the repository of wills and testaments, the Somerset House of Rome. Julia put the restored temple on her coins (see Plate 9).

Septimius' greatest works were on the Palatine, and in the region to the south of it. Facing the Appian Way, Septimius built what was called the Septizonium, or Septizodium. This was apparently a three-tiered portico, like a nymphaeum, and probably modelled on the nymphaeum of Lepcis, because the object of the portico was to remind wayfarers from Africa (who would enter the city on this side) of the glories of their native land, now installed here in Rome—a sure psychological touch. We have early engravings of the structure, and it is represented in one of Botticelli's frescoes in the Sistine Chapel; but unfortunately the last traces of it were demolished by Pope Sixtus V in 1588–9.

On the Palatine above, Septimius erected a series of buildings, supported on brick substructures, which for audacity and grace are not to be surpassed. These new buildings included a bath, for which water was conveyed through a branch of the Aqua Claudia, spanning the valley between the Palatine and the Caelian hill at an altitude which recalls the aqueduct of Segovia.

Finally, to the south arose the great Antoninian baths, a vast structure of which the ruins remain one of the most impressive relics in the whole range of Roman antiquity (see Plate 12). These were started by Septimius and finished by Caracalla, by whose name they are popularly known. It was from the ruins of these baths that many of the finest pieces of statuary in the Farnese collection, including the famous bull, now in the Naples Museum, were recovered. It has well been styled (CAH XII, 552) "one of the mightiest ruins in the world".

To commemorate this renovation of the city, Septimius had a map of it engraved on marble, 18 metres wide and 20 high, the scale being 1 : 250. At various dates since 1562 fragments of it have come to light. They are now preserved in the Capitol Museum and wear a curiously precise and modern aspect.

The ultimate development of the imperial city was to be achieved in the latter years of the century, at the hands of Diocletian, Maxentius and Constantine. Nevertheless, to stand on the Palatine to-day, and to contemplate the work of Septimius, on the hill itself, in the Forum to the north, and in the great baths to the south, is to realize what imagination, what energy the African had brought to Rome.

For the author of this majestic achievement the world still held its problems—and its humiliations: he had passed his zenith.

As part of the *decennalia* celebrations, Septimius had arranged that his son Caracalla should marry not one of the daughters of the Roman aristocracy, but Plautilla, the daughter of the praetorian prefect, Plautianus. This proud and evil man was, like Septimius, an African. Over the emperor he exercised an arrogant ascendancy, amounting almost to blackmail, which may have originated, as Herodian suggests, in an indiscreet boyhood association. Plautianus became so insolent that, for instance, when one day at Tyana he lay sick, and the emperor called to enquire, Plautianus' bodyguard would not allow Septimius to enter with his suite. On another occasion, a court usher refused to call a case which Septimius wanted to judge, saying: "I dare not do so without the orders of Plautianus." This man had been praetorian prefect since 197 or earlier, and for most of the time sole prefect, because he very soon liquidated his colleague: his aim was to be, as Dio says, not merely sole prefect, but permanent prefect. During the absence of an emperor from Rome, the praetorian prefect was now to all intents and purposes emperor. Plautianus behaved as though he actually were, recklessly abusing his authority. He insulted the empress, to such a degree that she took refuge in her philosophical study-circle. No favourite since Sejanus in the reign of Tiberius had held such power. At one period Septimius was piqued because Plautianus' statues began to outnumber his own, and the prefect even presumed to have his own likeness placed among the imperial portraits. This antagonized even the doting emperor: Plautianus was in disgrace. But not for long; and woe betide those who had dared to assume that he was done for! Plautianus soon had them put to death, even so eminent a man as a governor of Sardinia.

Dio gives a long catalogue of his crimes. "He wanted everything," he says, "asked everything of everybody and took everything. He left no province and no city unplundered, but snatched and gathered in everything from all sides; and everybody sent a good deal more to him than to Severus. Finally he sent centurions and stole horses with tiger-like stripes, sacred to the sun, from the Islands of the Red Sea [Zebras from Somalia] . . . At home he castrated a hundred citizens of noble birth—though none of us knew of it until after he was dead . . . Nor was it boys and youths alone that he castrated, but grown men as well, some of whom had wives. His purpose was that Plautilla, whom Antoninus Caracalla afterwards married, should have only eunuchs as her attendants." It was this pampered Plautilla that brought about Plautianus' downfall.

The year 202 marks the apogee of his power. It was in that year that his daughter became the wife of Caracalla, and thus he himself the father-in-law of a future emperor. The match disgusted Caracalla, because, despite the prefect's drastic precautions, Plautilla, besides being low-born, was vicious and dissolute. To make the enmity between Caracalla and his father-in-law irremediable, in the following year Plautianus became consul, and with Caracalla's own brother Geta as his colleague. This was too much. For one thing it was still regarded as improper that the same man should be both prefect and senator, though there had been previous cases, and the dual honour was later legalized by Severus Alexander; for another, although Septimius had bestowed the consular insignia on Plautianus, he had never held the office, and so should now have assumed his first consulship, instead of which he flaunted his second. With his brother, whom he already disliked, gone over, as it were, to the enemy, Caracalla felt isolated. He determined to be rid of this incubus, who now presumed to pry into all his son-in-law's affairs, even the most private. Both Caracalla and his brother were, it is true, given to lechery with both boys and girls, but Plautianus was even more notorious for his debauches with both sexes.

During the year 203, Septimius was absent in Africa, inspecting military posts, arranging for Numidia to be separated from Africa and to become a separate province on the model adopted for Syria and Britain (see pages 74 and 75), revisiting his native land, crushing raiders from the south and reorganizing the frontier defences, a process which was to be continued by Caracalla and completed by Alexander. By the spring of 204 he had returned for the celebration of the Secular Games. Early in 205 Caracalla decided to strike. He suborned a centurion, called Saturninus, to warn Septimius that he and nine other centurions had been drawn into a plot against the emperor's life by Plautianus. Septimius sent for Plautianus, who fearing nothing repaired to the palace, into which he alone was admitted. Septimius taxed him with conspiracy, but very mildly, only asking him: "What made you do this, why did you wish to kill us?" Plautianus, taken aback, started to make his defence. Caracalla, fearing that once again he would succeed in winning over his father, rushed up, seized the prefect's sword, and struck him with his fist. Septimius tried to intervene, but Caracalla ordered one of the attendants to kill Plautianus then and there.

The next day, the 23rd January, Septimius made a speech to the senate, in which he merely blamed himself for being over-indulgent towards the dead man. Caracalla would have liked to murder his wife and brother-in-law, but the emperor saved them, temporarily, by banishing them to the Lipari Islands. Many others, too, were banished, and some executed. So vast were Plautianus' riches, that a special commissioner was appointed to administer them.

The story of Plautianus has been told at some length, first, because it is as vivid a miniature as we have of the prevailing moral and political standards of the day, so like, in some respects, those of a later age, in which one man could commit outrage after outrage, and the "respectable" sections of the community say, as Dio said, "though none of us knew it until after he was dead"; secondly, because the emotional havoc which these incidents worked on the nature of Caracalla were to have disastrous consequences.

After the downfall of Plautianus, Severus felt bewildered and wounded. He really had been fond of the man. He had even written in a letter once "I hope I may die before him". Now he was alone. He retired to Campania with his sons, hoping that country life would distract them from the snares of the city. But trouble pursued him. First there was an alarming outbreak of brigandage. A certain Bulla Felix terrorized Italy for two whole years, at the head of a gang recruited from disbanded legionaries, the jetsam of the victorious wars, and the victims of Septimius' proscriptions and confiscations. Bulla shewed the greatest audacity, often impersonating imperial officers and hoodwinking the simple soldiers despatched to catch him. In the end he was betrayed by a woman, captured and thrown to the beasts, and his gang dissolved. It appears from Tertullian (*Apology* II) that the aftermath of the wars had produced similar unrest in other provinces as well as Italy.

Another more personal humiliation befell the emperor. His sister decided to pay him a visit accompanied by her son. The poor woman, who had lived all her life in Lepcis, could hardly speak Latin. The emperor, we are told, was constantly blushing for her. It was indeed humbling for the lord of the Roman world to be thus reminded of his un-Roman origin. He loaded her with presents, decorated her son with the "broad stripe", the mark of senatorial rank, and packed them off back home. The boy, we are told, blankly, "died a short time afterwards". We are left wondering why.

In the end, the aging emperor decided that the only way to restore his own peace of mind and the harmony of his family was to undertake yet another military campaign. He was now sixty, and suffering so severely from gout that he could hardly walk. Nevertheless he set out for Britain, "although he knew he would never come back". As usual, the natives were shewing signs of insubordination: only half the island, says Dio, was in Roman hands. The Britains were hardy, brave and predatory. Most of the autumn and winter of the year 208 was spent in preparations, such as repairing roads and bridges. The campaign, of which we possess no connected account, appears to have been a success, despite the skill of the Britons in ambushing and skirmishing. Dio tells us that Septimius reached the extremity of the island, where he verified Ptolemy's calculation of the solar parallax; but just how far north the "extremity" really was we cannot tell. Throughout the campaign, the behaviour of Caracalla became more and more intemperate, passionate and menacing: on at least two occasions he attempted to murder his father, who shewed a fatal forbearance towards his son. Finally, Septimius died at York, on the 4th February, 211, "not without help, they say, from Antoninus [Caracalla]". On his death-bed he is reported to have said to his sons: "Agree: enrich the soldiers: despise all the rest."

So died Septimius Severus, in the sixty-fifth year of his age. He had done well by Rome, this African. He had established a military dictatorship as the basis of power; but that was merely to acknowledge a *fait accompli* which he must either control or be ruined by. He had restored the frontiers of Rome, he had augmented her glory, he left the city's granaries full, the provinces tranquil and well governed. If only he had not also left Caracalla!

Chapter XV

CARACALLA

CARACALLA'S first care, after the death of his father, was to kill his brother. For his part in the British campaign, Geta had been raised to the rank of Augustus: he was co-equal with Caracalla and, like him and their father, had assumed the honorific of *Britannicus*. Caracalla had no intention of sharing his authority; his "Alexander complex" had now taken complete hold of his neurotic nature. "Alexander and his achievements were ever on his lips." The power which he had enjoyed since a boyhood corrupted by his father's indulgence had demolished the last shreds of his self-control: the personal humiliations described in the last chapter had sharpened his innate savagery. He was now, as his portraits suggest (see Plate 11), perfectly schooled for evil-doing.

But he could not kill Geta in Britain, much as he would have liked to: the legions were too fond of the boy, both because he was modest and because he bore a personal likeness to his father. It would be easier in Rome, whither Caracalla was anxious to return from this cold and uncouth island. He came to terms with the Britons, evacuated the territory his father had won, "and abandoned the forts". Late in the year he and Geta began their homeward journey, bearing with them the ashes of their father in a golden urn, to be placed in the mausoleum of the Antonines, which Hadrian had built by the Tiber. It survives to this day, as Castel Sant' Angelo.

Knowing the soldiers' love for Geta, Caracalla "went to the praetorian camp, and complained there to the soldiers that his brother was forming a conspiracy against him". But Geta was guarded day and night by soldiers and athletes. Caracalla therefore induced his mother to summon both him and Geta to the palace, where the three of them could meet in private. Caracalla's assassins were in waiting. They rushed upon Geta, who clung to his mother, and was stabbed to death in her very lap. The crime aroused the resentment of the IInd, Parthian, stationed at Albano (see page 77): they refused the now sole emperor admittance to their camp, until he had repurchased their allegiance with an enormous bribe. He overawed the senate by stationing armed men in the chamber. Soon, he had kindled a holocaust of proscriptions, in which anyone who had incurred his displeasure or that of his creatures was put to death, from Papinian, the great jurist who had become praetorian prefect, to a retired champion charioteer who had supported the rival faction in the hippodrome, Caracalla himself being a Blue. In compassing the destruction of his victims he displayed a disgusting niceness. He chid the man who had killed Papinian with an axe: "You should have used a sword", he said. To Laetus, probably Papinian's colleague, he shewed the attention of sending him the necessary poison himself. Men were seized while at dinner, even in the public baths. Dio says that no less than twenty thousand people were despatched in all. Caracalla ordered that Geta's name be deleted from inscriptions throughout the empire; and surviving memorials not only in Rome (see page 97) but in places as far apart as Jerash in Jordan and Hexham in Northumberland bear witness to the efficacy of a Roman emperor's writ.

Like his father, Caracalla relied solely and openly on the army as the basis of his power. Septimius had increased the legionaries' pay from 350 denarii a year at which Domitian had fixed it—it had been 225 in Augustus' day—to 750. Caracalla now augmented it by fifty per cent. He used to say that he alone ought to have money, so that he could give it to the soldiers. This reckless expenditure, coupled with his many other extravagances, soon turned the surplus which Severus had left into a deficit. Like his father, he debased the coinage, reducing the size of the gold piece, and putting into circulation a new coin called an "Antoninian", which rated as a double denarius, although it was actually worth only one and a half. Cities no less than individuals were constantly called upon to supply "coronation money", an "indulgence" which had originally been levied at the accession of a new emperor, though many had remitted it in whole or in part, and was now extorted to celebrate any "victory" the emperor might care to name. Regular taxation was increased, too. The rates on the manumission of slaves, and death duties, were raised from five to ten per cent, the exemption formerly granted to near relatives being abolished.

Since their introduction by Augustus, death duties, like many other taxes, had been levied only on Roman citizens. Caracalla, in the year 212, extended Roman citizenship to all free inhabitants of the empire. The *Constitutio Antoniniana*, as it is called, sounds as though it were a great liberal gesture (even though it provided for a small class of exceptions), but in fact, as Dio tells us, "his real purpose was to increase his revenues by this means, inasmuch as aliens did not have to pay most of the taxes". The practical consequences were small: the edict merely ratified what was almost a *fait accompli*. It underlined the diminished status of Italy: it gave an un-Roman emperor an opportunity of enhancing his political stature in the name of Rome.

The new Alexander must prove himself in the field, in which, to do him justice, Caracalla had been at home since childhood. The Alemanni, a confederation of German tribes from the region of the Elbe, whose name survives in many languages as a generic term for German, were now threatening the frontier. Caracalla conducted a successful campaign against them, assumed the title *Germanicus Maximus*, and consolidated the frontier. It was from this campaign that he came back wearing the *caracalla*, the Celtic tunic which he lengthened into a sort of cassock, and by which he has ever since been known. Owing to his adoption of it, it plays henceforth a prominent part in the history of Roman dress.

Caracalla was ailing, both in body and mind. His debauches had enfeebled him, and he was pursued by visions of his murdered brother. Neither the Celtic god Grannus, nor Aesculapius nor Sarapis sent him any help, despite his unremitting devotion to them, and his many gifts. "While claiming to be the most pious of mankind, he indulged to an extravagant degree in bloodshed, putting to death four of the Vestal Virgins, one of whom he had himself outraged—when he had still power to do so, for later he became entirely impotent."

As is often the case with the mentally unstable, Caracalla sought relief in physical movement. It was his ancestral Levant, the country in which he had spent so much of his boyhood, that now summoned the restless wreck. Passing through Thrace, and finding himself near the borders of Macedonia, "he was Alexander": he trained a phalanx, in which he enrolled sixteen thousand Macedonians and armed them like Alexander's spearmen. He used various cups and weapons which he believed to have belonged to his hero. He even took a troop of elephants with him on his travels. That his admiration of Alexander might not be without its opportunity for doing harm, he persecuted the Aristotelian school of philosophers, on the ground that Aristotle had had a hand in Alexander's death—a silly fiction known to, but rejected by, both Arrian and Plutarch. He ordered the books of the Aristotelians to be burnt, and abolished their privileges, including their collegiate mess in Alexandria.

The winter of 214–15 was spent at Nicomedia; then in the spring the court moved to Antioch. Here Julia Domna was on her own ground: she felt it possible and indeed prudent to emerge from her philosophical seclusion to take over the control of affairs; for Caracalla was now quite unfitted to direct them. He despatched an expedition into Armenia under his former dancing-master, Theocritus, who quite understandably led it to disaster. Caracalla made his way to Alexandria. The citizens already had their grievances against him. He had, as already mentioned, humiliated their Aristotelians; his creature, Theocritus, in a fit of pique, had ordered the execution of Flavius Titianus, the imperial procurator. Nor could the murderer of Geta be other than loathed in a city where the lad had been known and liked. *Geticus Maximus*, the Alexandrians called him in mockery, Geta meaning Goth, as well as being a proper name. Caracalla now determined to get even with them. The leading citizens met him in the suburbs. He smiled and smiled, invited them to dinner and killed the lot. He then proclaimed a curfew, posted troops in the streets and —the first essential for controlling a town in the Levant—on the flat roofs as well. This done, he ordered a general massacre and pillage, and the expulsion of all foreigners except the merchants, who were reserved for plunder. Caracalla had his headquarters in the temple of Sarapis, from which he directed the proceedings. He informed the senate that he was performing "rites of purification". These included the dedication to Sarapis of the very sword with which he had killed his brother. All public entertainments were banned, Alexandria was partitioned by means of a wall, and troops were posted to prevent any intercourse between the two zones.

Confident that he had now nothing to fear from any possible insurrection in Egypt, Caracalla returned to Antioch to plan yet another eastern campaign. As a preliminary he gave orders for the repair and realignment of the great coast road where it crosses the Dog River just north of Beirut—as an inscription records, one of many that decorate the rock wall, ranging in date from Rameses II in the thirteenth century before Christ to the Australian army in the twentieth after. Caracalla here styles himself *Parthicus Maximus, Britannicus Maximus, Germanicus Maximus*, and says that the work was carried out by "his own" IIIrd, Gallic, whose name was later deleted (p. 116).

During his warlike preparations, the emperor and his mother (no doubt on the initiative of the latter) found time to promote works of peace, and those most likely to flatter and conciliate the inhabitants of the country—their country, too. At Ba'albek, the great temples were at last finished: the dedication of the Propylaea is in the names of Caracalla and Julia Augusta. Another long inscription records that one of the reconnaissance-corps of the IIIrd, Gallic, had presented two gilded bronze capitals in honour of the great gods of Heliopolis and for the safety of the emperor and Julia Augusta, *mother of the camp*. Caracalla bestowed on Ba'albek the *Italian privileges* and founded games there. These were becoming, in imitation of Grecian models, increasingly popular throughout the empire, even in quite small towns, as the innumerable vestiges of hippodromes and theatres shew. A champion of Caracalla's day, from Laodicea, records that he was victorious in boxing and running contests in no less than twenty-seven towns, including his birthplace, where he carried off the prize in the games newly instituted by Caracalla.

The winter of 215–16 was again spent at Antioch. In the spring, the emperor sent the kings of Osroëne and Armenia an invitation to pay him a visit, and, when they arrived, made them prisoner. The king of Parthia, Artabanus V, was as impotent as his displaced brother Vologaesus V, or their father Vologases IV (see page 78), had been to resist the Romans; but when Caracalla asked him for the hand of his daughter, he felt bound to decline because he knew it was simply a ruse for annexing his kingdom. The new Alexander hoped that by marrying a Parthian wife he would unite Romans and Parthians in a single empire. In the summer of 216 he marched through Mesopotamia, crossed the Tigris and reached the eastern borders of Adiabene, roughly the area of the modern Kirkuk oilfield. He never saw an enemy, and the only effect his demonstration, and the excesses that accompanied it, had on the Parthians was to provoke them to resistance. Caracalla retired to Edessa for the winter, to prepare for a new campaign. But he no longer commanded the loyalty of his troops.

In the spring of 217, on his birthday, the 6th of April, he decided to visit the shrine of the moon goddess at Carrhae. He was accompanied by the successor of Papinian as praetorian prefect, Macrinus, who had been with him throughout the eastern journey. An African seer had recently foretold that both Macrinus and his son were to be emperors, and this had been noised abroad. The seer had been sent for at Rome, where he had repeated the prophecy to Macrinus' deputy. This officer had at once written to warn Caracalla; but the letter, like all official correspondence, was diverted to Julia Domna at Antioch. Caracalla therefore never received the warning, though but a few days before an Egyptian had told him to his face that he had not long to live, for which the man was executed. Macrinus, on the other hand, did receive a letter from a friend in Rome, from which he realized that he must act quickly. The journey to Carrhae offered an opportunity. Caracalla dismounted to relieve himself. His equerry, while helping him to remount, stabbed him with a dagger. Everyone knew who had instigated the murder. As it happened, Macrinus was himself fulfilling the dying prophecy of Papinian, that "whoever succeeded him would be an absolute fool if he did not take vengeance for this savage attack on the prefecture". So died one of the worst rulers Rome ever knew.

It might naturally be supposed that under the tyranny of "the Ausonian Beast" as he was, and enjoyed being, called, the Christians would have fared ill. In fact, they did not. Caracalla did not repeal his father's edict, but he did nothing to enforce it. There were isolated acts of persecution, such as those of Scapula, proconsul of Africa at the beginning of the reign. To him Tertullian addressed a scalding letter, which seems to have abashed Scapula, because the persecution died down, and the Church of Africa had peace until the middle of the century. There were, too, proceedings against the heretics of Osroëne, who were grouped around Bar Daisan, a famous astronomer and astrologer who became a Christian at the age of twenty-six, in 180. He invented a cosmic system which is chiefly of importance to-day as being that on which Mani later built his own cosmogony. It was not the heresy of Bar Daisan's followers which irked the state: it was that they had been associated with the local dynasty of the Abgars, converts who had been deposed by Rome. These were purely local affairs: there is no sign of any general onslaught against Christians. What was the reason for this indulgence? To say that Caracalla and Elagabalus after him left the Christians alone out of indifference and inertia is to say too little. The real reason lies deeper.

With the accession to power of Septimius, a Semite became master of Rome. This alone had a profound effect on the psychology of both western and eastern Semites: they felt that they were no longer ruled, but rulers. This feeling of superiority was greatly enhanced when the emperor married Julia Domna. It reached its apogee when Julia's own son, and Julia herself, shared the dominion of the Roman world. Anyone familiar with the Levant knows that this regional, racial loyalty is one of the strongest forces, political, social and religious, throughout the whole region, particularly when it can display itself in rivalry with, or superiority to, the west. Thus it comes about that in times of political tension between "east" and "west", "eastern" religious communities, such as the indigenous Churches of the Levant, will meet with a tolerance which their "western" fellow-Christians may be denied, not on religious grounds at all, but on racial and political ones. The minorities thus protected shew their gratitude by the solidarity with which they accept and promote the policy of the dominant majority.

The same lines of force, and fission, operated in the second century: they are absolutely basic to the spiritual make-up of the Semites. That the inhabitants of Syria were proud of their Syrian empress and emperor there is abundant evidence. The coinage exalts Julia, *mother of the camp, mother of the fatherland*. Among the cities which honoured her, or her memory, with a special issue were Tyre, Tripoli, Byblos, Ptolemaïs (Acre), Bostra, Rabbath-moba (near Kerak), Petra, Diospolis (Lydda), Aelia (Jerusalem), Gaza and Neapolis (Nablus). The inscriptions are, if anything, more eloquent. At Zebireh, a village in the "lava-district" of Trachonitis, two tribes, who were employed as shepherds by the inhabitants of a neighbouring town, erected a shrine to Fortune for the long life of Antoninus Caracalla. 'Atil, in the Hauran, can shew three or four dedications to the same emperor, of which one is the gift of a soldier of the IIIrd, Cyrenaican-Antonine, who sets up an altar by order of his father Sabinus; and another tells of the construction of a door for a temple to Theandrios, a god specially venerated at Bostra. (On this, as elsewhere, Geta's name has been defaced.) At Dera'a, a veteran of the Ist, Parthian, sets up a column, and the fellahin of the inhabitants dedicate a statue of Victory, both for the health and success of Caracalla. Soldiers, veterans, shepherds, peasants—dedications by such as these shew how popular Caracalla was with the Semitic masses, and also how prosperous the region had become.

That Caracalla and Julia should have reciprocated this proud gratitude by indulgence to their fellow-countrymen is not to be wondered at, nor that they would view at least without disfavour cults which had sprung not from the west, but from that very land itself. So far as the Jews were concerned, we have already seen (see page 94) how they flourished at this period. In any case, the prohibitions by successive emperors of circumcision, even of non-Jews, must have remained a dead letter in a region where the rite had been practised since time immemorial by all and sundry. To this day it is observed by Jews, Muslims and Copts alike. The ban, if strictly enforced, would certainly have penalized Julia's own family. If the edict against Judaizing remained in abeyance, it is not to be wondered at that its corollary, against Christianizing, was equally disregarded, given the similarity, in pagan eyes, of the new and the old, and, above all, its Palestinian origin.

An "accidentally preserved notice of a flood at Edessa in AD 201 mentions the 'temple of the Christians' as an important building" (CAH XII, 496), from which the status of the Church may be inferred. Even in Rome there was a change. The faithful still met for worship in private houses (see page 85); those houses of which the relics, in such striking contrast to the splendid basilicas which now surmount them, are one of the most poignant and arresting testimonies to the triumph of the Church. But gradually the houses came to belong not to individuals, but to the Church itself.

It is the same with the cemeteries, the famous catacombs. The word catacomb is an adaptation of the Greek *kata kymben*, meaning "near the dell", that is, the area near the ancient church of St Sebastian on the Appian Way, the only "region" of its kind to be known and venerated in the Middle Ages. Gradually the term became generic. The catacombs were not, as is sometimes suggested, "secret meeting-places" of the oppressed Christians. To start with, anything less secret than a catacomb it would be difficult to imagine. As the law required, these burial-places were outside the walls, in most cases a mile or so outside. Who would walk a mile in open country, in full view of any watcher on the wall, past the guards at the gate, if he desired to remain unseen? Those who were so rash as to do so fell an easy prey to the waiting police. Records of several such arrests have come down to us, including that of a bishop of Rome himself (p. 145). Secondly, as anyone who has been in a catacomb knows, the space is so restricted as to induce claustrophobia. Only rarely, here and there, has a tunnel been enlarged into a mortuary chapel such as that in which Bishop Xystus met his end. The real value of the catacombs to-day is that they shew the extent to which the Christian Church had expanded by the third century—those miles, literally, of galleries must have been the repositories of scores of thousands of corpses. They were in use from the second century until 412, when Alaric ravaged the countryside around the city and security vanished. So important and honourable, indeed, was the office of administrator of cemeteries that in the year 217 one of them, Callistus, became pope. This in itself shews that the cemeteries were now the property of the community, no longer of individuals. In fact, Roman law would protect the dead, even when it proscribed the living. Funeral guilds were not only tolerated but encouraged, and from the first the Christians had no doubt profited by this policy. It may be asked why they buried their dead at all, in an age when cremation was the prevailing fashion. The answer is, first, that inhumation was the custom of the Jews, whom in this as in other matters the first Christians followed; secondly that their Lord had been buried in a tomb; and thirdly that burial was considered to be more appropriate to a community which held to a literal interpretation of the doctrine of the Resurrection of the Dead.

These cemeteries, like their modern successors, became places of resort. The tombs of relatives, of martyrs, were visited and venerated. So gradually evolved the decoration of the walls which preserves for us some of the earliest known examples of Christian art. These are of more than sentimental interest. They shew the themes that were held to be most eloquent of the Faith. The Good Shepherd is there again (see Plate 21), even Christ represented under the guise of Orpheus or the radiant Sun, the "orant", or praying figure, the Eucharist, associated with the Feeding of the Five Thousand, and Old Testament figures such as the Three Children.

In Rome, no less than in the east, the dawn of the third century witnessed a Church which, if not openly recognized, was nevertheless firmly rooted in the hearts and lives of its members. It was confident of itself, and was learning to express itself and its beliefs not only for the edification and comfort of the faithful, but also for the enlightenment and persuasion of those without the fold.

Chapter XVI

SYRIAN SUNSET

COMPARED with those who came before and after him, Macrinus was but "a transient and embarrassed phantom", his reign but an interlude in the dominance of the Syrians. Septimius and Caracalla had together reigned for twenty-four years; Elagabalus and Alexander would add another seventeen to the tale of the dynasty. The activities of the two earlier sovereigns had been largely martial: those of the two later were to be predominantly civil, indeed spiritual, and in their different sphere as remarkable as those of their predecessors. The brief usurpation of Macrinus, seen in retrospect, bridges the interval between the end of the old régime and the beginning of the new.

Macrinus was, like Septimius, an African, from Caesarea, now Cherchel, in Mauretania. He was a competent lawyer, had been superintendent of the post-service on the Flaminian Way, the Great North Road of Rome, treasury council, one of the commissioners in charge of Plautianus' confiscated wealth, and finally, like Plautianus himself, praetorian prefect. He was a knight—the first ever to become emperor—but was granted the consular insignia. He wholly lacked the ambition, tenacity and initiative of Septimius: the senate accepted him out of relief at being rid of Caracalla, and ratified his nomination to the willing army of his own ten-year-old son as Caesar. Macrinus might have taken warning, though, from the soldiers' insistence on giving him the additional name of Severus and his son that of Caracalla: they still hankered for the old dynasty. Moreover such was now its hold upon the eastern armies that they desired its presence in fact, not in name only.

Julia Domna, too proud after her years of imperial glory to accept the station of a private citizen, starved herself to death at Antioch. She was later deified. But if the great Julia was dead, there was no lack of ladies to carry on her tradition. And here Macrinus made an irreparable blunder. Instead of relegating Julia's sister and her two nieces to separate domiciles in the west, he sent them all three, with their children, back to Emesa, the very hearth and home of their influence and prestige. Moesa (see Table II), Julia's younger sister, was a woman of the same stamp—determined, dominating and devoted.

She had married Julius Avitus, a Roman of proconsular rank, who had successively administered Asia, Mesopotamia and Cyprus. Her early married life had taken her from one government house to another, and it was only in 193, the year of Septimius' accession, that she was able to join her sister in Rome, and settle down to enjoy the splendid and lucrative leisure of the court. Already, or shortly afterwards, a widow, she could now give her time and talents wholeheartedly to her own enrichment and the advancement of her daughters. Of these the elder, Suheima—or Soaemias in western form—was married to a Syrian from Apamea, above the Orontes, thirty miles north-west of Hama. His name was Sextus Verus Marcellus, and he was an imperial procurator who had become a senator before his early death. His only surviving son was Avitus Bassianus, later Elagabalus. Moesa's younger daughter, Mammaea, married Gessius Marcianus, from Arqa, an important cult-centre of Astarte, fifteen miles north-east of Tripoli. All we know of Gessius is that he held more than one post of imperial procurator. He was of lower rank than Mammaea, but Severus and Caracalla jointly granted her the privilege of retaining her senatorial status. The only son of this union was Alexander, who was born at Arqa, and was only nine when he was sent back there, so that he always retained a Syrian cast of speech and manner of which he was very conscious. Alexander's father too died young.

The three widows, with the two children, were now once more in Emesa. Their situation engaged the sympathy of their fellow-countrymen, their place of exile provided them with the best possible base for exploiting that sympathy and the pride and loyalty which the presence of these royal ladies, so recently the stars of Rome itself, excited and diffused.

As a first step towards the restoration of the family's dynastic fortunes, Avitus Bassianus became high priest of the mountain god, that is Ela-Gabal, who was venerated at Emesa in the form of a large conical black stone, which was said to have fallen from heaven. Macrinus, although he had been praetorian prefect, was no soldier: like Papinian before him and Ulpian after him he had been appointed for his legal not his military talent. In Dacia, he forestalled a war by returning hostages which Caracalla had taken; he cut short the Armenian war by nominating as king one of the sons of the very monarch whom Caracalla had imprisoned (see page 107). In Mesopotamia, he was defeated by the Parthians, but purchased peace at the cost of an egregious bribe. The armies had no more lust for battle than Macrinus; but they resented these humiliating transactions and the implied slight on the memory of Caracalla, whom the armies compelled Macrinus, his murderer, to deify! Back in Antioch for the winter of 217–18 Macrinus issued several salutary ordinances. He halved, to five per cent, the rates on death duties and manumissions which Caracalla (see page 104) had raised to ten per cent. But he was savage in his military punishments, reduced the privileges which the army had enjoyed under Caracalla, and announced that new recruits were to be paid on the Septimian scale, a measure that not unnaturally excited the suspicions of the legionaries. Finally, instead of dispersing the army, which had been on active and inglorious service for four years, to their winter quarters, he kept them concentrated in Syria. "It needed", says Abel (II, 166), "all Macrinus' mediocrity not to understand that the discontent of soldiers mobilized with no object at a point in Syria was bound to be disastrous for his cause." It was.

The IIIrd, Gallic, "Antoninus' (Caracalla's) Own", were encamped near Emesa. The soldiers, coming into the town to attend the ceremonies in the temple, were carried away by the youthful pontiff. Looking like Bacchus, he was arrayed in a long purple robe bordered with gold, and wore a crown encrusted with precious stones, which glittered and flashed in the sunlight, as he danced to the melody of a flute, attended by a train of lads and girls of the country. That hardened Roman soldiers should be captivated by such an exhibition may strike us as strange, until we recollect the conquests made in our own age and society by gaudy adolescents, who by antics more tasteless than those of Elagabalus reduce to hysteria admirers whose mental standard is about that of the Roman peasant. Moesa, at any rate, very sensibly took the demonstrations at their face value: she let it be known that Elagabalus was really the son of Caracalla, for both her daughters, she said, had formed part of that prince's *seraglio*. To give an edge to the effect which this disclosure produced in the camps near Emesa, the astute grandmother put it about that she had at her disposal an enormous sum in gold, amassed partly from her perquisites and pickings while at court, and partly from the oblations of princes and satraps to the sanctuary of the family god.

To the soldiers, a new accession seemed to offer a gilt-edged security. Having thus cogged the dice, Moesa resolved to risk all on a single throw. She made her way by night to the neighbouring camp of the IIIrd, Gallic, taking with her a wagon full of gold and her precious grandchildren. The gates were opened to her, and the soldiers acclaimed with fervour those whom they regarded as the natural heirs of their own Augusta, Julia Domna, and her son. The next morning, the 16th April, the whole army saluted Elagabalus as emperor under the name of Antoninus. The legionaries then called in their wives and children from the neighbouring villages in which they were billeted, and laid in stores for a long siege.

Macrinus sent against the rebels a detachment which included Moorish soldiers, under the command of Ulpius Julian, a praetorian prefect. Macrinus temporized, breaking off the engagement in the hope that the besieged IIIrd would surrender. They merely paraded on the walls the new Antoninus, together with the sacks of gold with which they had already been refreshed. It was an irresistible lure. Macrinus' troops killed their officers and went over to Elagabalus. Julian's head was sent to Macrinus, carefully wrapped up, and sealed with Julian's seal, as though it were that of Elagabalus. The shocked and nauseated Mauretanian made one more effort: he marched south from Antioch to meet the insurgents on the border of Syria and Phoenicia. Spurred by the tears and objurgations of Moesa and Suheima, the rebels at length bore down the praetorians. Macrinus decided to retire to Rome, but was captured and executed, as was his son also. On the 9th June, Elagabalus entered Antioch. Once again the army had triumphed; once again the Syrians had asserted themselves. Where now were the *senatus populusque romanus*, the senate and people of Rome?

The imperial party wintered at Nicomedia in Bithynia, where the emperor-priest, who was only fourteen, insisted on celebrating the bizarre rites of his religion. Moesa, who knew Rome, was disturbed by this; but her remonstrances only resulted in the headstrong boy killing Gannys, one of his most trustworthy advisers, who had been largely responsible for his elevation. It was a bad beginning. He then wrote to the senate, calling himself son of Antoninus and grandson of Severus, with the titles *Pius Felix Invictus Augustus*, which henceforth became the official style of the emperors. Moesa and Suheima were each made Augusta.

Thus in the summer of the year 219 Rome beheld the arrival of this exotic boy-emperor, habited in garments of silk embroidered with purple and gold, wearing bracelets, a collar of gold, and a crown in the shape of a tiara, embellished with pearls and gems. He was accompanied by the black aerolith. Once again Moesa begged him to wear woollen clothes, in the Roman style, and not to affront the citizens of the capital. Once again, he paid no attention to her.

The name of Elagabalus has for centuries been a synonym for every sort of neurotic lechery. It is irrelevant, as it would be unprofitable, to turn yet again the pages of that well-thumbed catalogue. The sight of a lad from the Levant, bedizened like some Indian queen, making his sinuous and silken progress through the courts of the Palatine, attended by a giggling gang of epicene orientals, did, no doubt, excite the disgust of the Romans, habituated though they now were to every eccentricity of natural or unnatural vice. But it was not the personal excesses of the boy that caused the sharpest repercussions, specially as his grandmother took over the direction of affairs. She was introduced into the senate and sat with the consuls. She fulfilled all the functions of a senator, the first and last woman ever to do so. A number of hungry Syrians had arrived with the imperial family, and they were now satisfied with jobs and sinecures. On the Quirinal, the emperor instituted a female senate, where his mother, not so adept at public administration as Moesa, regulated such vital matters as female fashion, rank, the transport permissible for different social classes, the right to wear trinkets of bone, ivory or silver, gold embroidered slippers, and precious stones.

The general administrative machine was robust enough not to break down under the vagaries of the supreme ruler. There was, it is true, some disaffection in the army. Elagabalus was disgusted to learn that his own IIIrd, which had been the first to acclaim him, had sought to advance a rival. He disbanded them with ignominy, and ordered the deletion of their name from inscriptions (see page 106). It was Elagabalus' religious policy that aroused the keenest opposition, for here was no question of personal behaviour, but of public and official conduct. Roman religion, as will already have appeared, was by the end of the second century as easy-going as it was eclectic. Elagabalus decided to put an end to such tolerance, or, as it seemed to him, indifference, and to rally mankind, and the Roman state, to the worship of one supreme god. This in itself was a remarkable conception for a fifteen-year-old boy to entertain. The measures he took to enforce it hastened his overthrow.

Sun-worship was no new cult in Rome. Augustus himself in 23 BC had brought from Heliopolis an obelisk of Rameses II, so old that Moses himself might have gazed upon it, and had set it up as an offering to the sun in the Circus Maximus, where Tertullian saw it two centuries later. For the Christian zealot (*De Spectaculis* VIII) it was an outstanding symbol of idolatry. This obelisk, together with the original dedication, but now surmounted by a cross, is still to be seen in the centre of the Piazza del Popolo in Rome. The obelisk of Monte Citorio bears an identical inscription. Augustus placed it on the Campus Martius, where, as we know from Pliny, it formed the gnomon of a gigantic sundial. The worship of the sun, therefore, was established and respectable—in its Roman form. But that it should be enforced by an eccentric boy, a Syrian, a circumcised Augustus who abstained from pork, as the one supreme cult, of which he was the supreme hierophant, and to which all other forms of worship must give place—that was to prove too much for Rome. Elagabalus was formally recognized as priest by the senate, included his priesthood among his official titles and recorded it on his coins. The black cone was installed in a shrine next to the emperor's own home on the Palatine. Among the ceremonies of the god, many of which aroused dark suspicions on the part of the citizens, the most splendid was the celebration of Midsummer, when the sacred emblem was conveyed in a procession, led by the emperor himself, to a temple on the outskirts of the city. Senators and knights were held to be honoured by participation in these proceedings. A spouse was found for the god, first Minerva, and then, more congenially, the Punic Tanit. The union was celebrated at a public festival. To supply an earthly version of these heavenly nuptials, Elagabalus divorced his first wife to marry one of the Vestal Virgins, excusing the sacrilege on the ground that the marriage was a religious act. The coinage ratified it. (It did the same, out of flattery, for all his four, or perhaps five wives. In the end he went back to his Vestal; although that did not prevent his continued indulgence in extra-marital excesses in a depraved spirit of give and take.)

Moesa looked ahead, and saw the inevitable catastrophe that awaited her unbalanced grandson. She therefore arranged that he should adopt his first cousin, Alexander, the son of Mammaea and Gessius Marcianus. It was her last political coup, and it was a brilliant one. Alexander was only four years younger than Elagabalus, but the rules were waived, and on the 10th July, 221, Alexander was proclaimed Caesar.

Elagabalus' plan for enforcing uniformity had been ruined by his vanity and egotism: it was not the sun, but Elagabalus himself, not a universal, but a particular, Syrian deity that men were called upon to worship. They turned away in disgust.

Alexander's popularity made Elagabalus regret his advancement of him. He twice tried to have his cousin assassinated. This goaded the praetorians to action, probably with the connivance of Moesa. On the 11th March, 222, both Elagabalus and his mother were killed in the palace, and their corpses dishonoured.

The nineteen-year-old Elagabalus was succeeded by his thirteen-year-old cousin. Alexander was a character of a very different stamp.

Moesa, her work accomplished, died the year after his accession; but Mammaea was as determined as her mother to direct and safeguard the policy and interests of her son. She was hailed as "mother of Augustus and the camps". She was not allowed to sit in the senate, but sixteen of their number were chosen to form a council of regency.

That Alexander was a biddable lad and that his tolerant and gentle character was improved by a careful and liberal education there is no doubt. It is also clear that he was of a reflective rather than an active disposition (see Plate XVII). Unfortunately, our knowledge of his reign is drawn almost entirely from the *Augustan History*. For some reason Lampridius, the author of Alexander's *Life*, which is dedicated to Constantine, chose this emperor to represent the "model ruler". He receives more space than any other emperor or usurper in the whole collection. In contrast with Elagabalus, who was all black, Alexander is painted as all white. Some of the incidents in the *Life* are demonstrably false, which tends to undermine our faith in the work as a whole. Herodian treats of Alexander, but his account is almost wholly concerned with the Persian war. Dio, after recording Alexander's accession, says "for subsequent events I have not found it possible to give an accurate account, for the reason that I was seldom in Rome". He was serving abroad as a provincial governor most of the time. He returned to Rome in 229 to hold his second consulship as Alexander's colleague, but from fear of the soldiery, whom as governor of Pannonia he had dared to restrain, he preferred to live at Capua, retiring soon after to his native Bithynia, where he completed his work. We are therefore more than ever dependent on the *Augustan History*.

That the general prestige of the senate was respected, if not restored, seems to be clear; but there are no grounds for believing that the rule of the senate was substituted for that of the army. In fact the evidence points in the opposite direction. Dio, in an earlier book of history (LII), inserts a debate between Augustus' two ministers Agrippa and Maecenas, in the presence of the princeps, as to whether the republic should be re-established or a monarchy put in its place. This, in accordance with the accepted literary practice of the age, is a "set piece", and reflects Dio's own views. Agrippa defends the republic, with arguments drawn from the armoury of rhetoric and theory. Maecenas, on the other hand, advocates a monarchy, and a monarchy such as was in fact the régime in the period we are now considering. The senate is recognized as being what in another context Dio calls "the ornament of the state", but it is the ruler who directs affairs. The knights are to have a larger share in administration, Italy is to be treated as a province—both features of the Roman polity at the beginning of the third century. Dio, as a senator, was always sensitive to the status which his rank bestowed. It is significant that he makes Agrippa, the more capable and practical of the two ministers, speak for the senate: it no doubt expresses what Dio would have liked to see. But from Maecenas it is that we learn what he actually saw, even if he did not approve it. Against the evidence of this eye-witness, who took part in the affairs he chronicles, that of the *Life*, which has been described as a historical novel, cannot prevail.

It is in the spiritual sphere that the reign of Alexander is of particular interest. Internally, tranquillity was preserved, after a domestic disturbance caused by Alexander's marriage. Mammaea had chosen as his bride a lady of senatorial rank called Orbiana. She was declared Augusta and her father Caesar. Exasperated by Mammaea's domination of her son, he fled to the praetorians. Orbiana was banished, her father executed, at the instance of the vengeful and all-powerful Mammaea. Ulpian, the great jurist, was a praetorian prefect. He tried to bring the soldiers to reason, but met his death at their hands.

For the Christian Church the reign of Alexander was a time of rest and consolidation. Elagabalus had been personally vicious, and in addition had tried to relegate both Judaism and Christianity to the position of being two among many other cults subordinate to his own personal religion, a position which both Jews and Christians would rather die than accept. Alexander was the very opposite in respect both of his own morals and his conception of religion. He was simple in his dress, temperate and chaste. He did all in his power to purge Roman society. He forbade the use of the baths by both sexes at the same time. Others before him had imposed a similar ban, but it had been disregarded. He banished eunuchs from the court, degrading them to the position of slaves of his wife and friends. Women of ill-repute he rounded up and consigned to the public stews. The taxes levied on pimps and prostitutes of both sexes were now paid into a special fund, which was used to repair ancient monuments, such as the theatre of Marcellus, the Colosseum, the Circus Maximus and the stadium in the Campus Martius (now the Piazza Navona). It is to this unusual source of revenue that we owe in part the preservation to our own day of the two former buildings. Catamites were deported. Alexander wanted to abolish male prostitution altogether, but he was dissuaded from doing so on the ground that "such a prohibition would merely convert an evil recognized by the state into a vice practised in private"—an argument which has been advanced in a similar context in more recent ages. It remained for another Syrian, Philip the Arab, to disestablish this perversion.

So good, so austere a man, of such humane and gentle tendencies might well be expected to shew tolerance to the Christians. In fact he went further: he took an active interest in their doctrine. The Faith might disconcert those who were convinced that it was only the "old religion" that could hold the state together, even if, unlike the Christians, not a single one of them was prepared to suffer for their beliefs. The Syrian court had long been illuminated by a more glowing spirit. Julia Domna herself had bade the sophist Philostratus compose a life of Apollonius of Tyana, a philosopher and thaumaturge, gifted with second sight, who had lived in the days of Domitian. We still possess the work, and very interesting it is, not so much for what it tells us, but because later in the century it was actually used as a sort of counterblast to the Gospel story of the life of Christ. The life of Apollonius reads more like that of Sinbad the Sailor: that it should ever have been relied on to counter Christianity is a telling indication of the poverty and paucity of the resources on which a fading paganism was forced to rely. Mammaea had carried on the philosophic, eclectic tradition of her aunt. While the court was at Antioch, Mammaea, "a religious woman if ever there was one", says Eusebius, sent a military escort to bring to her side the great Origen himself.

Origen towers above his age. He was born in Egypt of Christian parents about 185. He was the pupil of Pantaenus and Clement. When his father suffered martyrdom in 202, Origen was only restrained from sharing his fate by his mother. At the age of eighteen he became the unofficial head of the Catechetical School. In the year 215 after Caracalla's massacre (see page 106) he was forced to quit Alexandria, and took refuge in Palestine, with the bishops of Caesarea and Aelia (Jerusalem). Origen later returned to Alexandria, and embarked on a brilliant career as head of the School, a post he was to adorn for fifteen years. He was soon internationally famous, his advice and presence sought by prelates and laymen far and wide. Ammonius Saccas, the philosopher who at this period was educating the young Plotinus in Neo-Platonism, counted Origen as his friend.

In the year 230 a breach occurred with Demetrius, the bishop of Alexandria. Origen, on his way to Greece, was ordained priest by his friends the bishops of Caesarea and Aelia. Demetrius protested, on the ground that it was improper to ordain eunuchs (Origen, in an access of asceticism, had castrated himself), though he may well have been actuated, as Eusebius implies and Jerome declares, by jealousy.

Origen, his journey completed, tried to resume his chair, but the rift had gone too deep, and he spent the last twenty years of his life at Caesarea. He was arrested and tortured in the persecution of 250 (see page 140) and died three years later.

Origen's work was as important as it was profuse. The greater part of it is concerned with the Bible. He constructed a Sixfold Version of the Old Testament, or *Hexapla* as it was known in Greek. This consisted of the Hebrew Old Testament, the same transliterated into Greek characters, the Septuagint (the Greek version made in the days of the Ptolemies and the official Greek version of the Jews), alongside three other versions by individuals. One of these "was found at Jericho in a jar" in the days of Caracalla—the forerunner of the now famous "Dead Sea Scrolls". This vast work, six times the size of the Old Testament, has perished, except for a few fragments. Origen himself emended the Septuagint text, using an asterisk * for the passages which he added from the other versions, and an obelus † for passages found in the Septuagint but not in the Hebrew, thus introducing the familiar signs of modern textual criticism.

It was not only his treatment of the text that was modern: his interpretation of it was equally so. Like most of his contemporaries, he had adopted the Jewish method of allegorizing the Scriptures, but with the difference that Origen adopted it to give him freedom of thought: he held that the literal meaning of the book was secondary to its spiritual meaning. "What man of sense", he writes, "will suppose that the first and second and third day, and the evening and the morning existed without sun and moon and stars? Or that God walked in the garden in the evening and that Adam hid himself under a tree? Or that the Devil took Jesus into a high mountain from which he could see the kingdom of the Persians and Scythians and Indians?" Such passages are valuable only for their higher meaning. Origen was equally frank about discrepancies between the Synoptic Gospels: they, he held, are merely media through which the divine Gospel is expressed, the Fourth Gospel a symbolic exposition. By these methods, Origen saved the Old Testament for the Church, and helped both the Old and the New to commend themselves to the educated pagan.

It was to this end that his great apologetic work, *Against Celsus*, is directed. Celsus lived in the age of Marcus Aurelius. He wrote a book called *The True Word*. This we do not possess, but Origen's refutation is so closely argued that we can almost reconstruct the text of the earlier work. Evidently it had enjoyed a certain vogue, so that seventy years later, when his friend Ambrosius shewed him a copy,

Origen thought it his duty to answer it. Celsus puts forward all the familiar arguments—that Jesus was an impostor who relied on wonder-working, that Christianity appeals not to the intellect, but to a blind faith. He knows the Scriptures. He ends with the usual appeal to the Christians to support the empire under which they, no less than their pagan fellow-citizens, live and prosper.

Origen's refutation, written on the eve of the Decian persecution, is in eight books, all of which have come down to us. Although throughout he writes as a devout and fearless Christian (as he was so soon to prove himself to be) Origen shews that he is learned in all the wisdom of the Greeks. He can meet Celsus halfway when it comes to a philosophical approach to the Faith. On the other hand, Origen sees no reconciliation between Church and pagan state—he is more deeply antagonistic to pagan culture than his predecessor Clement. Christians, he says, should be excused military service; nor are they bound to pray for all emperors automatically, but only for the good ones, and only for the soldiers when they are engaged in a just war. Clearly, the Church had still far to go, before it could come to terms, its own terms, with the state.

Meanwhile, the state was tolerating its existence. Alexander placed in his private chapel statues of the best emperors, and also of Apollonius of Tyana, Orpheus, Abraham and Christ. He would have liked to build a temple to Christ, and to have the senate admit him among the recognized gods of the state. He had the Golden Rule, which he had heard on the lips of Jews and Christians, engraved on his palace and on public buildings, and had a herald recite it at the punishment of malefactors. Alexander went further: he established direct relations between himself and leading Christians. Julius Africanus, a Christian historian, was invited to Rome, and founded a library there. The empress-mother's patronage of Origen has already been mentioned. St Hippolytus of Rome, whose almost contemporary statue, with a table for finding the date of Easter engraven on his chair, presides over the Christian Museum of St John Lateran, dedicated a treatise on the Resurrection to her. The emperor, when he decided that the choice of magistrates should receive popular approval, quoted the Christian use in like case; when he was called upon to arbitrate between the Church of Rome and the city guild of tavern-keepers on the possession of a disputed building he gave the following sentence: "Better that God be worshipped in any manner whatsoever in this place, than that it should be handed to the tavern-keepers as a gift."

To end this sketch—for it is nothing more—of the interplay of society and the Church at this period, mention may be made of the most attractive and luminous of the Latin apologies, the *Octavius* of Minucius Felix, "the pearl of apologetic literature" as Renan called it. The setting is as charming and natural as anything in Latin literature. It is the long vacation, the Roman law-courts are closed. Minucius and his friends Octavius, a Christian, and Caecilus, a pagan, have gone down to Ostia, as Romans do to-day, to bathe and stroll on the seashore. There are the boats hauled up on their baulks, there is the breakwater, and there are the young, playing ducks and drakes. As they walk along in the wash of the waves, Caecilus blows a kiss to an image of Sarapis; and that starts the disputation. It is conducted on forensic lines. Caecilus produces all the standard arguments against Christianity. Octavius in reply patiently answers the well-worn slanders, but in language so gentle, so persuasive, so stylish, that the reader feels that he is confident not only of his own salvation, but in the ultimate and inevitable salvation of all men through the God of the Christians. "Do you suppose we conceal our object of worship because we have no shrines and altars? What image can I make of God when, rightly considered, man himself is an image of God? What temple can I build for him, when the whole universe, fashioned by his handiwork, cannot contain him? . . . Is not the mind a better place of dedication, our inmost heart of consecration?" For English readers this beautiful little work has a particularly endearing appeal, because among the arguments adduced for the operation of Divine Providence is the Gulf Stream: "It is not for the whole only that God takes thought, but likewise for the parts. Britain, for instance, lacks sunshine, but gets warmth from the surrounding sea."

Taken all in all, the reign of Alexander seems to be the threshold of a door through which the Christian Faith might emerge into acceptance. The Faith was tolerated, yes. But toleration implies compromise. Christianity could not compromise. No great cause has ever been vindicated by compromise. So it came about that, at a point in time when it seemed that the struggle was over, it was in fact only about to begin. In the next half century, the Church was to face the most terrible travail it had ever undergone or was ever to undergo, nothing less than a savage and determined effort to wipe it wholly out.

Chapter XVII

THE LONG NIGHT

IT is to the life of Severus Alexander that, as already noted (page 15), the *Augustan History* devotes its longest essay. At first reading this may seem puzzling: would not some of his predecessors, Hadrian, for instance, or Septimius, or even a successor such as Aurelian, have been worthier of this pre-eminence? The reason is that, seen from the age of Constantine (to whom the *Life* is dedicated), Alexander's reign represented the last epoch of true Roman greatness, which Constantine's own era had not yet, in the estimation of mankind, either equalled or surpassed. The half-century which separated the two régimes was to be the darkest and most disastrous that Rome had yet known; and across this sea of troubles the reign of Alexander shone like a beacon.

It was his mother who brought about his end. The masterful Mammaea, determined as she was to promote her son's and her own fortunes, ended by ruining them both. Alexander might well have quoted the bitter quip made by his model, Alexander the Great, that he had had to pay a heavy rent for the months he had spent in his mother's womb. When Alexander had succeeded to the purple he was only thirteen, and there was some reason for his clever mother to reckon that he needed her guidance. Thirteen years later, she was still his mentor. The soldiers, in particular, resented this: in the closet, a woman might plot and plan for all they cared, but not in the field: it was an insult to their superior sex. Besides, it was Mammaea's meanness that had led Alexander to cut down on Elagabalus' lavish wooing of the troops' attachment. So it came about that one day when the army was encamped near Mainz, the rumour went round that Mammaea was trying to dissuade her son from continuing the campaign, and urging him to go back to the east, where she could queen it once again on her own ground. A conspiracy was quickly rigged, and mother and son stabbed to death. He was only twenty-six. As a philosopher and reformer, he had been noteworthy; not so as a man of action. In the year 232 he had tried conclusions with Ardashir, only to be ignominiously repulsed by the rejuvenated Persian army. While he was negotiating with Ardashir, news came of a fresh threat on the northern frontier. Ever since the days of Augustus, the spectre of a war on two fronts had haunted Roman policy. Augustus had averted it by negotiation with the Parthians: Germany was the scene of the one military disaster of his reign. Trajan had fought aggressive and victorious wars both in the north and in the east; but his successor, Hadrian, had no sooner assumed the *imperium* than he abandoned all Trajan's eastern acquisitions—or such of them as remained. He knew that the Euphrates was the natural limit of the west. Those who came after him were less far-sighted, and Mesopotamian "adventures", very much in the manner of the gunboat-happy imperialists of the nineteenth century, had become commonplace. The new Persia was not the old Parthia, and henceforward the resurgence of this power in the east, combined with the restlessness of the tribal waves in the north, was to prove the greatest single factor in the decline of Rome. The crisis occurred in 260, when the lord of the Roman world became a Persian captive (see Chapter XX). Alexander escaped that ignominy; but it was because his north-European troops thought that their homes were threatened that he was compelled to break off the eastern campaign, and because those same troops thought that he was negotiating at Britzenheim near Mainz what would later come to be known as a "Munich", that he was killed. It was indeed, as Dio had foreseen, an age of "iron and rust":

"The last of these Syrian emperors could not fulfil his rôle," in the words of Ensslin (CAH XII, p. 72), "since he was neither a Severus nor an Alexander."

His supplanter was a Thracian *condottiere*. A tough and gigantic peasant, he had risen from the ranks under Septimius, who in his last days had been attracted by this champion wrestler, with his dark eyes and dazzling complexion. "He could obtain from the emperor whatever he wanted"—and he knew what he wanted. He refused Elagabalus' lewd proposals and during that reign he had to remain content with a military tribuneship. But Alexander had given him command of a legion, had made him a knight, and during the Persian campaign, had appointed him governor of Mesopotamia. The troops loved him, called him Hercules, Achilles, Ajax, and so he was entrusted with the training of the recruits, whose preference for their flashy commander its object did nothing to abate. Maximinus is the prototype of the soldier "liberators" who have swarmed over Asia, Africa and parts of America in our own day. Almost his first act after murdering his benefactor was to double the pay of the soldiers whose seditious loyalty had elevated him. His opponents, real or imagined, he slaughtered. He crossed the Rhine near Mainz, and succeeded in defeating the Germans, thanks chiefly to his contingents of eastern archers and African pikemen.

At long last the Romans had realized that the legion was not the answer to every military problem. Armies are notoriously conservative. Napoleon insisted on maintaining the outdated column formation, despite the demonstration by the British that the line, which they had been constrained to adopt in the wooded terrain of North America, was, particularly when armed with the new rifle, a far more effective array. So earlier, the Greeks had relied on the Macedonian phalanx, until the Romans routed it at Cynoscephalae in 197 BC. The Romans in their turn, despite the valour of the Persian light and heavy mounted archers—the ancient analogue of the airplane and tank respectively—clung for centuries to their own renowned legion, as the basic unit of the army. Only now, in the third century, were they willing to admit that the horse and the bow could prevail over the infantryman and the sword. And even now, it was from their eastern "allies" that the new arm was principally recruited.

Maximinus needed money, and it was his avarice that destroyed this greedy dolt, after but three years and three months of power. His procurator, or financial agent, in Africa had shewn such brutal rapacity that a number of those whom he had despoiled and ruined mobilized their tenants and set on and killed the obnoxious official near Thysdrus, the modern Al Djem in Tunis. They went further: they acclaimed the proconsul Gordian as emperor, despite his eighty years, and Gordian associated his son with himself as co-emperor. The senate, who had been compelled by *force majeure* to stomach the Thracian, now saw an opportunity of reasserting their traditional prerogative. They confirmed the appointment of the Gordians. But those who thought that the grand days of government by "The Senate and People of Rome" were about to return were disappointed: civil disorder was all that the senate's gesture produced. Gordian's agents succeeded in killing Vitalianus, the commander of the guard. Egypt, Syria and the armies in Gaul supported the new government; but Capellianus, the governor of Numidia, remained loyal to Maximinus and moved east to crush the revolt. The younger Gordian was killed, and his poor old father hanged himself after a reign of just three weeks. But the senate did not give in. An action committee of twenty members was set up. The Gordians were deified, as Alexander had now been, and two new Augusti were appointed: Pupienus, to take command of the armies, and Balbinus to assume charge of the administration. Anti-Thracian riots broke out in Rome, the city prefect was murdered, and the followers of Maximinus were hunted down and butchered. It was now the middle of April, 238. News of the African revolt had reached Maximinus at Sirmium. After two days' deliberation he distributed a handsome "refresher" to his troops, which now included a contingent of Germans, mostly cavalry from beyond the Rhine, and moved south. His path to Rome was barred by the fortress of Aquileia. As the siege dragged on, Maximinus, humiliated and desperate, raged against his officers, and even executed several of his generals. This was too much for the men of the IInd, Parthian, whose wives and families were at Albano, and so in the power of the senatorial forces. They assassinated Maximinus while he was taking his siesta, and with him his son, and sent their heads to Rome.

The populace was in a frenzy of relief and delight at the news, and Pupienus and Balbinus made a state entry into the capital. With them, it seemed, constitutional government had returned. Alas for any such hope: the praetorians had decided otherwise. Strife broke out once more, during which a large section of the city was burnt. The two senatorial emperors met their deaths after a reign of ninety-nine days. The praetorians nominated as emperor Gordian III (as he is known) a nephew of the second, a lad of thirteen years. Tired of strife, senate, army and people welcomed the well-bred and charming boy as the gage of peace and reconciliation.

During this period of universal tumult it was not to be expected that the Christian Church would have escaped unmolested. Maximinus, so Herodian tells us (VII, 1), "dismissed all the officers who had been in Alexander's service so long, and put several of them to death whose crime was to have regretted so good a master and to have allowed their tears too free a course". Eusebius completes the picture (EH VI, xxviii). Maximinus, he says, "through ill-will towards the house of Alexander, since it consisted for the most part of believers, raised a persecution, ordering the leaders of the Church alone to be put to death, as being responsible for the teaching of the Gospel". This passage is of interest for two reasons. First, it shews that the Christians had already established their reputation for honesty and reliability, and had thus become predominant in the civil service, exactly as in later days the Christian Copts and Armenians were to do in the Ottoman empire. Secondly, it is apparent that even so limited an intelligence as Maximinus' could grasp the power which the Church now derived from its organization under a regular hierarchy, a campaign against which seemed the most effective means of countering that power. Pontian, the bishop of Rome, was deported to

Sardinia, together with Hippolytus, a learned schismatic. The climate soon killed them both. Origen, who tells us that Christian buildings were burned, was compelled to take refuge in Cappadocia. The priest of Caesarea in Palestine and Origen's patron Ambrosius were arrested. But the persecution was not maintained, and on the death of Maximinus it ceased altogether. With the exception of the three years of Maximinus' rule, the Church enjoyed tranquillity from the year 222, when Alexander started to reign, until the year 250, when the Decian persecution began.

Chapter XVIII

MILLENNIUM

WELCOME as Gordian was, his appointment as Augustus at the age of thirteen made a mockery of any theory that Rome was to be restored to a constitutional régime headed by "the best citizen". Far from it: the bloody tale of war without and plots within was not yet told, nor would it be for another forty years. There is no direct correlation between the peace of the Church and that of the state, a fact which in itself refutes those who held that the Christians were the source of every secular disaster. The sad truth is that, whether the Christians were persecuted or tolerated, the disintegration of the state proceeded apace.

Gordian was fortunate in having, from the year 241, a loyal and capable guardian in his praetorian prefect, Timesitheus, whose daughter Gordian was to marry. The senate continued to exercise more than a merely nominal control over the policy of the new reign, since both the proconsul of Africa, later city prefect, and the governor of Lower Moesia had been members of the Committee of Twenty which had organized the successful resistance to Maximinus (see page 126). Guided by such tutors, the young prince shewed himself the friend of liberal justice. Informers were once again proscribed. A decree of September, 238, enjoins provincial governors to see that nothing should be done "which is not in accordance with the spirit of the age", a rather pathetic formula which, when first used by Trajan (in his famous rescript to Pliny on how to deal with the Christians) was not inappropriate, but a century later sounds sad and hollow. In provincial administration, the encroachments of the military and of the treasury officials—always the twin bugbears of colonial governments—were restrained. The law was not to be stretched in favour of civil servants; nor was the favour of the treasury to be obtained by ceding to it a part of the property involved in a dispute. Imperial officials were not to act as money-lenders, either openly or covertly. Municipal administration was reviewed. Alexander had forbidden treasury officers in the provinces to inflict punishments—that was the business of the courts. Gordian placed a similar prohibition on municipal supervisors. On the other hand, councils were allowed to dismiss the schoolmasters they had appointed if they turned out to be incompetent.

These measures, if they shew that the old Roman sense of justice and decency was by no means dead, shew also how lax, in these last troublous years, Roman standards, specially in the provinces, had become. In these reforms we may see the influence of Timesitheus, who knew the provinces from long experience. He had served in Spain with the auxiliaries, he had been finance officer in Belgium and Arabia, where he had twice been deputy-governor. In Rome he had been head of the death-duties office. In Syria and Palestine he had again been special financial commissioner, to collect the taxes which had been levied for Alexander's Persian war. He had gone back to Belgium as deputy administrator of Crown property, and was at the same time vice-governor of Lower Germany. Then he was special commissioner in Bithynia, Pontus and Paphlagonia, next deputy governor in Asia, and finally governor of Southern Gaul and Aquitania. This *curriculum vitae*, which is preserved for us in an inscription from Lyons, is of the greatest interest, as shewing how various could be the activities of a Roman civil servant in the third century, and also as a tribute to the character of Timesitheus, who had succeeded in pursuing his beneficent and versatile career despite the frequent changes of emperor. Once again, we can admire the toughness of the Roman fabric. The machine was still in good working order: it was the motive power that was failing. Timesitheus also reorganized the army's commissariat. He ensured that every frontier town of importance contained a year's supply of food for an army and fodder for its horses, and smaller towns for shorter periods according to their size. Timesitheus also checked the abuse whereby the names of young boys and old men were inscribed on regimental establishments, so that their families might draw pay for their fictitious services. This form of misappropriation had been prohibited by Hadrian: as abuses are apt to do, it had evidently crept back.

In other respects, the army was fairly treated. Like the populace, it was given liberal presents; but the IIIrd, Augusta, for its complicity in the overthrow of the first two Gordians, was disbanded, and its officers and men distributed among other formations. Timesitheus (he had once been in charge of the imperial stage) also enlarged the barracks of the Marines who were employed at the Colosseum. They did not, like Her Majesty's Guards at Covent Garden, provide "supers" for the performances: their duty was to rig and dismantle the enormous awnings that sheltered the spectators. These were stretched from poles at the very summit of the vast arena, and only men thoroughly versed in sailcraft would have been able to manipulate them.

"The spirit of the age" was not to leave Timesitheus and his affable son-in-law leisure for the arts of peace: on the contrary, it was to engage them in wars, and then destroy them both. In 240 a rebellion in Carthage had to be crushed. Meanwhile, danger threatened both the northern and eastern frontiers. The Goths and their neighbours, the Carpi of Dacia, were on the warpath. The Goths had been bribed to withdraw, whereupon the Carpi remained quiescent for three years. In the east, Ardashir had occupied Nisibis and Carrhae while Maximinus was emperor. His son, Shapur I, who succeeded him in 241, was even more formidable. He crossed the Euphrates and menaced the city of Antioch. Gordian and Timesitheus set out for the east, chastising the Carpi, who had made a thrust into Thrace, on the way. They roundly defeated Shapur. In a swift campaign they retook Carrhae, and at Ras-al-'ain, on the upper Khabur, won a decisive victory which restored to Rome the possession of Mesopotamia, with Sinjar, Nisibis and Edessa. The last-named became a Roman colony, the remainder of Osroëne, in which it was situated, becoming once more a vassal state under Abgar X. (Osroëne was of great importance to Rome, just as Nepal was one day to become to England, for it was from this principality that many of their best archers were recruited.)

A further advance to Ctesiphon was being planned, when Timesitheus died, struck down by the dysentery which is a scourge of that region. He was succeeded as prefect by M. Julius Philippus, the son of an Arab sheikh in the Hauran (see Plate 17 (b)). Philip was forty-five, and had no intention of accepting a position of subordination to a lad of less than twenty. He fomented disaffection in the army by deliberately upsetting his predecessor's "Q" organization. Gordian tried to compound for the position of co-emperor, then when that was denied him by the haughty Arab, for that of Caesar, or even prefect—finally he begged for his life; but even that was refused him. Philip had him murdered by the soldiers. As late as the Persian campaign of the emperor Julian, Gordian's cenotaph stood near Zaitha, between Circesium and Doura-Europos, "At once", in Ensslin's words, "the record of successes gained under his name and a memorial which showed what forces were in fact at that time determining the empire's fate."

Philip lost no time in seeking the recognition of the senate, to whom he reported that Gordian had died, like Timesitheus, of natural causes. This version of events won general credence, both because the country was notoriously unhealthy and because Philip always paid the greatest respect to the memory of Gordian even when in the company of the very men who at his behest had committed the murder. The body was sent to Rome, where at Philip's bidding the senate duly elevated Gordian to the ranks of the deified.

The new emperor was anxious to reach Rome himself as soon as possible. He made peace with Shapur, and withdrew Gordian's army to Syria. By the terms of the accord Rome sacrificed all real control over Greater Armenia, but retained Mesopotamia, which Philip entrusted to his brother as governor. The rest of the family, as tribal custom demanded, were suitably provided for. His brother-in-law became governor of Moesia and Macedonia. His wife, Otacilia, was raised to the rank of Augusta. His son, aged seven, was proclaimed Caesar. Clearly, Philip intended to found a dynasty. To this end, even his father was posthumously deified, and was thus honoured on the coins of Philippopolis. This splendid city arose on the site of Philip's native village, Shuhba, which stands just where the "lava-country" of Trachonitis joins the grainlands of the Hauran, forty-five miles south-east of Damascus and sixty east of the Sea of Galilee. Remains of the city which have been brought to light in recent years shew that it was built on a rectangular plan, divided into four quarters by two intersecting main arteries, like a Roman camp. The town is an artificial creation, the product of a single mind. Part of the *enceinte* seems never to have been occupied. The remainder was furnished with all the amenities of a Graeco-Roman town—of which in this region Philippopolis is the latest example—temples, baths, theatre, administrative buildings, even a monument to Philip's deified father. The houses of the rich were embellished with magnificent mosaics, the finest of which, now in the Damascus Museum, is shewn on Plate 17 (*a*). For the whole region of Syria and Phoenicia, the good old days of Severus seemed to have returned— on all sides cities were honoured, including Ba'albek, where the little round temple had just been finished. Nablus was made a colony with the title Julia Sergia; Bostra became a "metropolis". Ptolemaïs, Caesarea and Rafa all struck coins in honour of the new ruler and his family. The new emperor's line was not destined to endure. Nevertheless, Philip the Arab is of more than passing interest in the sombre pageant of decline and fall for three reasons. First, he was the first Arab to attain to imperial dominion. Herod the Great was of Arab stock on both sides, but he ruled not Rome, only Judaea, by the grace of Rome. Septimius was a Semite, but, though by his marriage with Julia Domna he founded a Syrian dynasty, he himself was sprung from Africa. Philip was an Arab of Arabia, the lord of Rome and its empire, the true prototype of a long and illustrious line of caliphs and kings which has maintained its lustre down to our own day. That in itself is no small claim upon the regard of mankind.

Secondly, it was this son of a sheikh from the Hauran who was to preside, as Rome's master, over the celebration of Rome's millennium.

Thirdly, in the estimation of many, Philip was Rome's first Christian emperor.

By July, 244, Philip was in Rome. From the beginning his relations with the senate were cordial. The citizens were conciliated with no less than four donatives. In a contemporary encomium which has come down to us Philip is lauded as the ideal embodiment of the just ruler, the stoic paragon, the grand contrast to his sorry predecessors, the master, not the servant of the soldiers, etc., etc. Ambitious Philip may have been, but he was a conscientious ruler. He declared an amnesty for those who had been exiled, or condemned to *résidence forcée*. Like Gordian, he did his best to check the arrogance of treasury officials. Like Gordian, too, he kept an eye on municipal councils. His courageous decision to erase one of the darkest stains on Roman social life has already been noted (see page 120).

The year 246 found the emperor in Dacia—by now the war on two fronts had become part of the Roman way of life. At last that harassed province, so rich in precious metals, was given the right of coinage. Philip subdued the Germans, and exploiting the victory had his son declared Augustus, and his wife Otacilia honoured as "mother of Augustus, and of the camp, and of the senate, and of the fatherland". His son was also designated *Pontifex Maximus*, yet another step towards diarchy.

There now dawned the year 248, during which, according to the established reckoning, Rome would celebrate the millennium of its foundation. On the 21st April, which then as now was accounted the official birthday of the eternal city, the emperor was in the field, and so the solemn exercises were postponed until its close. The two Augusti, as the consuls for the year, attended the traditional religious ceremonies, presided over the lavish games in the Circus Maximus and the Flavian amphitheatre, during which were slaughtered thousands of men and animals which Gordian had assembled to adorn his Persian triumph.

Arab princes were later to lord it in Spain, in India, in Africa and in China; but never can there have been a stranger conjunction than this tribesman from the Hauran, who as a lad had gazed out over the silent·and deserted horizons of the east, enthroned now as emperor in the metropolis of the west, amid the trumpets and tumult of an alien capital which he had made his own, celebrating the pride of a people whose master he had now become.

This was to be Rome's last jubilee: the circumstances in which it was held led the fifth-century writer Orosius to believe that Philip had celebrated it in honour of Christ and his Church. Whether Philip was a Christian by conviction, or even by convenience, it is hard to say. Our written sources, scanty at the best of times, are for this period tantalizingly meagre. Herodian's history ends with the year 238, and in the *Augustan History* there is a gap from the year 244 and the end of Gordian, until the year 259 or 260, when we "come to", as it were, in the middle of a sentence about the last days of the luckless Valerian.

We have on the other hand this passage in Eusebius (CH VI, xxxiv):

"When after six whole years Gordian brought his government of the Romans to an end, Philip along with his son Philip succeeded to the principate. It is recorded that he, being a Christian, wished on the day of the last paschal vigil to share along with the multitude the prayers at the church, but was not permitted to enter by him who was then presiding, until he confessed and numbered himself among those who were reckoned to be in sin and were occupying the place of penitence; for that otherwise, had he not done so, he would never have been received by the president on account of the many charges concerning him. And it is said that he obeyed readily, displaying by his actions how genuine and pious was his disposition towards the fear of God."

Have we here an example of romantic hind-sight, such as that which made Antoninus, in Jewish eyes, an adherent of the Jewish faith? (see page 29). Or are we to see in the incident a precursor of Canossa, or of the remorse of our own Henry V at his father's usurpation? Eusebius does not mention his source, and he was a meticulous historian. On the other hand, why include the story if he did not credit it? St John Chrysostom, citing the tradition of Antioch, says that it was there that the incident took place, and that the bishop was St Babylas, who, as we know from Eusebius, was bishop at the time. St Jerome, in his *Famous Men* (LIV) calls Philip "the first of the Roman emperors to be a Christian". That Philip was well disposed towards the Christians there is no doubt: he and his wife corresponded with Origen, and he allowed Fabian, the bishop of Rome, to bring back to the capital the bones of Pontian, who had died in Sardinia (see page 128). But does this make Philip more of a Christian than Alexander? Of modern scholars, Duchesne and Abel regard him as having been Christian, Ensslin does not. The best summing-up is that of Zeiller, who says (page 121):

"It may be asked whether Philip himself was not a Christian. The way in which he rose to power, by killing his predecessor, would not favour the hypothesis, but Eusebius reports without guaranteeing it a tradition according to which the bishop of Antioch imposed penitence on the emperor before allowing him to enter his church on Easter day; St John Chrysostom has even stated that the bishop was St Babylas. It seems that such an occurrence must have made enough stir for a more definite memory of it to have been preserved. Eusebius knew of letters from Origen to the emperor and his wife Otacilia Severa which should, one would think, throw light on the problem; his diffident account of them can only enlist reserve. On the other hand, the correspondence with Origen is at least an indication of Christian sentiments, or sentiments orientated towards Christianity, on the part of the imperial couple. But it may well be that it was these very dispositions that later made them to be regarded as Christians. Let us add that bishop Dionysius of Alexandria makes allusion to the Christianity of Philip, which his birth in the Hauran, a country which in the third century was the home of many of the faithful, does not render unlikely.

"But if Philip really had adhered to the faith of Christ and merited the title given him by St Jerome of the first Christian emperor, it must be agreed that this adhesion had remained secret and had had no repercussion on his public life. Philip even presided at the secular games, as a prince who preserved for the ancient religion of Rome the respect of his predecessors. All in all, there is perhaps no ground for thinking that he professed towards Christianity more than a sympathy analogous to that of Alexander Severus."

From which it is clear that if the toleration of Christianity was now practical politics, its establishment was still a long way off.

Chapter XIX

FIRE AND STEEL

PHILIP'S downfall was as meteoric as his rise. Its fundamental cause was economic. Throughout the century, the value of money had been steadily falling. Inflation, and debasement of the coinage, the *sequelae* of civil strife, had brought increasing ruin upon the citizens of the provinces, just at a time when the defence budget grew ever larger. Taxation was increased, but taxes became progressively harder to collect, as is evident from the harshness of the treasury officials which both Gordian and Philip had tried to moderate, and the selection of such a man as Timesitheus to be special financial commissioner, charged with the collection of arrears (see pages 129–32).

Revolts broke out both against Philip's brother in the east, and against his brother-in-law in the west. In the border territory between Syria and Cappadocia there were tax-riots, which resulted in a certain Jotapianus (a scion of Julia Domna's Emesa dynasty) being acclaimed as emperor. In Syria yet another usurper appeared. Neither was to survive for very long; but the civil disturbances only made a bad economic situation a good deal worse. In the west, it was the army of the Danube which started the revolt, to be immediately seconded by the ever-alert and greedy Goths. Other tribes, including, ominously, the Vandals, followed their example.

In face of this redoubled opposition to his throne and family—and for an Arab it would be the insult to his personal honour, his *sherf*, that wounded most fatally—Philip offered to abdicate.

From this course he was dissuaded by the calm assurance of Decius, a capable general, and the only member of the senate to counsel resolution: the usurpers, he rightly foretold, would soon be brought to book. Philip accepted his advice, but on condition that Decius himself took the field in the north. Decius, who foresaw the fatal consequences of success, reluctantly agreed. His reluctance was justified: the victorious and grateful army hailed him as their ruler. Philip was forced to take arms against him, and so fell a victim, near Verona, to the very same circumstances as had led Gordian to succumb to him. On hearing of his death, the praetorians made away with his son.

Abel's description of the situation that now confronted Church and state cannot be bettered (II, 203):

"The prospect of a future trial of strength between Roman might and the teaching of the Gospel was, no doubt, quite foreign to the intelligence of a noble Illyrian, married to the descendant of a rich Etrurian family, Messius Quintus Decius, whom in September 249 his flatterers saluted as a new Trajan. The energy, the harshness even, depicted on the disdainful features of this old aristocrat accord well enough with those of a leader whose aim it would be to bring back the state to the times, manners and institutions of ancient Rome, the majesty of the senate, the exercise of the Censor's office and the worship of the divinities favoured by the old Roman fatherland, into which the recent celebration of the Millennium had infused new life. To neglect the cult of these born protectors of Rome's good fortune was to provoke their ire, and to draw down upon the empire the scourge of the elements and the inroads of the Barbarians. Was it not an abomination that the patrimony of Roman greatness should be entrusted to a secret contemner of the official religion, such as Philip the Arab, and to his Christian archers from Osröene? In the eyes of Eusebius, St Jerome, Rufinus and Orosius the persecution unleashed against the Christians by Decius was a reaction against the policy of Philip, a revenge taken by the pagan party against the reign of a prince who had favoured the disciples of the Gospel. In the modern view it is less the effect of personal animosity than the act of a will coldly dedicated to exorcizing the ruin of the state by re-establishing it on the foundation of the ancient religion of Rome, which was held to be the essential bond of the empire's unity. As sovereign pontiff, Caesar was to institute a solemn Act of Supplication, in which every subject of the empire without exception was to take part, by virtue of the solidarity which their common interest imposed upon them. Anyone who dared to neglect this religious duty would betray himself as the enemy both of the gods and of the state." (For Decius, see Plate 18 (b).)

The persecution which ensued was therefore in origin political, not religious. As in some future ages, it was not the faith, but the non-conformity, of the victims which irked the state. There were, it is true, sporadic unofficial anti-Christian outbreaks, such as that which had occured in the beginning of this same year 249 in Alexandria. An Egyptian mob has always been one of the most excitable and destructive to be found anywhere. On this occasion it was aroused by a crazy seer, a familiar enough type, "prophet and creator of evils for the city", as bishop Dionysius called him, who "was beforehand in stirring up and inciting the masses of the heathen against us", until the whole city was in an uproar. Of the Christians, an old man was blinded with pointed reeds, flogged and stoned to death. A woman was dragged over the stone-paved streets, beaten all the while, and likewise stoned. An old spinster, after all her teeth and her jaw had been smashed, was burned to death. Another Christian, his bones having been broken, was flung headlong from the upper storey of his own house. Houses were looted, and furniture smashed, until the city looked as though it had been sacked by savages. The rioters then started fighting each other, and the police had to intervene.

Within a year Decius had issued his edict. Of this, understandably, no copy has come down to us; but we know its import. Every man, woman and child in the empire was to sacrifice "for the safety of the emperor". As to which god the sacrifice should be offered to—that was a question of minor importance, as it had for so long been. Decius' innovation consisted in requiring that a strict register be kept of all those who had sacrificed, every one of whom must obtain a certificate of sacrifice. The rite was enjoined, in fact, rather as in some countries "loyalty tests" are to-day, and with the same ultimate object in view—the safeguarding of society, for it was in that light that Decius and his advisers regarded their action. A *pro forma* of this certificate, or *libellus*, was circulated to provincial governments, as we know from those which have been recovered, inscribed on papyrus, from the sands of Egypt. These are dated between the 12th June and the 15th July, 250. It is clear, then, that the persecution proceeded in three stages: first, at the end of 249, measures were taken, following the precedent of Maximinus (see page 127) against the Church's leaders. Fabian, bishop of Rome, was seized, thrown into prison and executed on the 20th January, 250. In March the inquisition becomes more intense, and by June it is working like a machine. Here are the texts of two of the actual *libelli*, issued in Egypt, which make clear exactly what was required of every citizen, how the prescribed duty was performed, and how the requisite certificate was issued:

"[*1st Hand*]. To the commission chosen to superintend the sacrifices at the village of Alexander's Isle. From Aurelius Diogenes, aged 72 years, with a scar on the right eyebrow. I have always sacrificed to the gods, and now in your presence and in accordance with the edict I have made sacrifice, and poured a libation, and partaken of the sacred victims. I request you to certify this below. Farewell. I, Aurelius Diogenes, have presented this petition.

"[*2nd Hand*]. I, Aurelius Syrus, saw you and your son sacrificing.

"[*3rd Hand*]. (A name, fragmentary.)

138

"[*1st Hand*]. The year of the Emperor Caesar Gaius Messius Quintus Trajanus Decius Pius Felix Augustus, Epeiph 2 (26th June, 250)."

The second *libellus* is of particular interest because it shews that pagans *who could be under no suspicion of being Christians* must nevertheless secure their certificates:

"To the commission chosen to superintend the sacrifices. From Aurelia Ammonous, daughter of Mystus, of the Moeris quarter, priestess of the god Petsouchos, the great, the mighty, the immortal, and priestess of the gods in the Moeris quarter. I have sacrificed to the gods all my life, and now again in accordance with the decree and in your presence, I have made sacrifice, and poured a libation and partaken of the sacred victims. I request you to certify this below."

Sometimes a man presented the petition for himself and his family, sometimes on behalf of someone who was illiterate.

Refusal to sacrifice amounted to a refusal to obey an order of the emperor, and as such was accounted treason, for which the punishment was death. The object of the state was not to eradicate the Christians, but to reform them. As St Cyprian the great bishop of Carthage puts it (Ep. 35) the rulers wanted to make not martyrs, but apostates. In the event they made both. Many Christians fell away. Eusebius compares the effect of the edict to "that which was predicted by our Lord, wellnigh the most terrible of all, so as, if possible, to cause to stumble even the elect"—a reference to Matthew xxiv, 24. "Everyone", he says, "was terrified; and of the more prominent people, many came forward at once through fear, others in public positions were compelled to do so by their business, and others were dragged by those near to them. When their names were called, up they went to the defiled and unholy sacrifices, pale and trembling, some of them, as if they were not sacrificing, but being sacrificed as victims to the idols. The large crowd jeered at them: it was obvious that they were cowards by nature, whether it was a question of dying or of sacrificing. Others ran eagerly towards the altars, affirming by their forwardness that they had never been Christians, even formerly. Of the rest, some followed suit, others ran away and were caught. Of these, some went as far as being shackled and thrown into prison, and then, after being shut up for some time, foreswore themselves before being brought into court. Others who had remained firm under torture for a time, finally gave in."

Thousands, on the other hand, did not. Not only do Christians like Dionysius, Cyprian and Eusebius bear witness to the steadfastness of the martyrs, and *confessors*, as those were called who though imprisoned and valiant unto death were not executed, but even such a sworn foe of the Faith as Porphyry, a well-informed contemporary. He records that thousands of Christians were put to death in this and subsequent persecutions. The rigour with which the edict was enforced, as in the case of later edicts imposing a "final sollution", varied from province to province. So did the methods of execution, for those who were faithful to the end. Some were despatched with a stroke of the sword; but others were burned at the stake, or flung into quicklime, or roasted on red-hot chairs. Others again were torn to pieces by wild animals. Thousands were sent to the living death of the mines, where in darkness and pain, riveted day and night to a fellow-prisoner, or penned in revolting promiscuity, they rotted away as swiftly as they might. Those who escaped the death penalty were subjected to the rack and the branding-iron. Imprisonment killed Babylas of Antioch and Alexander of Jerusalem, the founder of the great library which was to be of such service to Eusebius. Origen was so outstanding and important a victim that he was reserved for special treatment. Eusebius, who had read the letters Origen wrote in his last years, says that they gave a true and accurate picture of what he suffered. He was loaded with chains and shut up in a dungeon. The judge was determined not to make a martyr of so eminent a man, but to subject him to the torture of the stocks, to threaten him with the red-hot iron, in order to wear him down—in vain. Had not Origen himself written, in his *Against Celsus* (VIII, 44): "The judges are distressed by those who endure the outrages and tortures but exult whenever a Christian is overcome." It was Origen who overcame. The persecution had put an end to the misunderstanding between the bishops of Alexandria and Jerusalem (see page 120) over Origen's ordination, and Dionysius of Alexandria, who had just completed the panegyric of Alexander of Jerusalem, wrote him a comforting letter on martyrdom. The death of Decius set Origen free, nor was he molested when the persecution was renewed. He withdrew to Tyre to edit his letters, at long last suffered his sermons to be taken down in shorthand, and died there in peace, aged sixty-nine, in 253.

The persecution had failed. The death of Decius, while fighting in the Dobrudja in June, 251, brought chaos to the state and peace to the Church. The emperor had moved north in yet another attempt to check the audacious and ravaging Goths. When, with his elder son, he died on the battlefield, the troops hailed as his successor Trebonianus Gallus, governor of Lower Moesia, associating with him Decius' younger son, who was shortly afterwards carried off by the plague, whereupon Gallus put his own son in the dead boy's place.

He could not however prevail over the Goths. They had made appalling inroads, and had devastated Thrace. All that Gallus could do was to promise them an annual bribe to respect the frontier, and then perforce allow them to retire with their vast booty and a host of captives, which included many Christians. The Goths, knowing that these were persecuted by the Romans, treated them well, thus paving the way for their own eventual conversion.

To add to the general tribulation, plague had broken out again, and was to rage for fifteen years. The devotion of the Christians in tending its victims, comforting the dying and securing honourable burial for the dead, without any care for their own safety, made a deep impression on the pagan mind, notwithstanding which Gallus, as if to allay the depopulation caused by the plague, ordered new massacres of the impious Christians. Gallus had reigned for hardly two years, when he and his son were killed at Terni, just north of Rome, by Aemilian, who having succeeded him as governor of Lower Moesia had in his turn been proclaimed as emperor by the army in the spring of 253. After three or four months he, too, was dead. Valerian, having been adopted as emperor by the army in Rhaetia, became sole ruler in August, the senate in the following month associating with him his son Gallienus as Augustus. (See Plate 27 (b).)

The staying of the persecution had left the Church with a distressing and delicate problem—how to treat those who had sacrificed and now wished to be received back as Christians, the *lapsi*, or fallen, as they were called. Some were for harsh measures—permanent exclusion—others for gentleness. The division which this question provoked was understandably deep: those who had risked death in its most horrible forms, or whose relatives had suffered it, might not always find it easy to forgive or forget the lapse of weaker souls. On the other hand, it had become the custom for genuine confessors, who for all their steadfastness had escaped death, to intercede for the feeble.

Both St Cyprian of Carthage and bishop Cornelius of Rome called councils in 251 to deal with the matter. On the initiative of St Cyprian, a middle course was adopted. He knew well enough what apostasy meant. In Carthage, his own see, there had been mass defections. "They did not even wait to be arrested", he says in his work on *The Fallen*, "before they went up, or to be questioned before they made their denial . . . They ran to the market-place of their own accord . . . How many the magistrates had to put off until the next day, because it was near night?" But Cyprian was a true saint. He himself had retired from Carthage during the persecution, for which he had naturally been criticized. In a letter to the Roman Church he defended his action, which was dictated, he says, not by fear but by prudence, lest his presence in the city might be a further provocation to violence. That he, too, could be valiant to the death he was later to prove. He now called a synod of his bishops, which with Cyprian as president, ruled that all penitent *lapsi* were, without distinction, to be admitted to penance, nor in the hour of death "should the mercy of the Lord be denied to them that implore the Divine grace". Cyprian sent a full report of the proceedings and findings to the Church in Rome, which adopted the same rule. It did not please everybody, in particular a rigorist Roman priest called Novatian, who in any case was opposed to bishop Cornelius, to whose see he felt he should himself have been elected. The Council of Rome at length expelled Novatian, whereupon he founded a church of his own. He too was to die a martyr's death; his sect was still in existence at the beginning of the fourth century.

Chapter XX

NADIR

AFTER the confused and dolorous events related in the last chapter, it might well seem that Rome was doomed, that the empire would disintegrate, its fairest provinces raped and ruined by foes from without, its authority the prize of rival upstarts, its army a selfish rabble, its spirit rent and frustrated by dissension within. And yet, so hardy was its substance, so formidable the mere fact of a millennium of existence, that not only would Rome continue to exist, and a greater part of its empire as well, for ages to come, but before it recovered its balance, it was able to sustain shocks even more damaging, humiliation more shameful, than any it had yet undergone.

If, during the reign of Decius and his supplanters, the northern frontier had been reduced to a mere name, the east had remained in a state of uneasy tranquillity. Occupied as Decius was with the Goths, he could not campaign in the east as well. He was reduced to a strange expedient. The Arabs who roamed the desert between the province of Arabia and the Euphrates, the ancestors of the modern Shammar and Huweitat, were always ready to make a profitable raid into the fertile crescent, if the desert patrol relaxed its vigilance. Decius hit upon the idea of diverting to practical use some of the wild beasts which were destined for the amphitheatre. He had numbers of lions and lionesses brought from Africa, and turned loose to live and breed in the Syrian desert. The Arabs depended on their flocks for their livelihood, and thus were compelled to keep their distance from the hungry lions, whose progeny was still plentiful in the fourth century.

More direct measures were now required: it was the embattled Persians, not marauding Bedu, who had once again to be confronted. Gallienus was sent to command on the Rhine-Danube front, and there won some success, to judge by a coin struck at the beginning of the reign which is dedicated to Victorious Jupiter, and bears the words *Gallienus with his army*. This had not prevented the Goths, in 253, from raiding Asia Minor by sea, ravaging Ephesus, "the first and greatest metropolis of Asia", as its citizens called it, and destroying the great temple of Artemis (Acts xix). Not for three centuries, not since Pompey the Great had suppressed the last of the pirates, had anyone dared to challenge Rome's control of the "Roman Lake". The following year, another band of Goths, operating farther west, had once again over-run Thrace as far as the shores of the Aegean. In 256 a regular Gothic armada swept down through the Bosporus and occupied Chalcedon (whose craven garrison had fled), Nicomedia and other rich cities. Valerian could do nothing to check these devastations; but that did not prevent his describing the disaster on a coin struck at Antioch in 257 as *Victoria Germanica*, the counterpart of another which proclaimed an equally fictitious *Victoria Parthica*.

The true picture in the east was far different. In 253, while Gallus and Volusian were still alive, Shapur had invaded Armenia and Mesopotamia and had then seized Antioch, wrecking its proud buildings and massacring or leading captive its inhabitants. Had they not been encumbered with their vast booty, the Persians could have made themselves masters of the whole of Asia Minor. In this crisis, the lord of Emesa, conscious of his imperial connexions, declared himself independent (he had already flouted Philip's authority). He succeeded in checking the Persian hosts. It was essential that Valerian should regain Antioch. By the year 255 he appears to have established his headquarters at Samosata on the Euphrates, after vainly trying to dislodge the Goths from Bithynia. Valerian was no general; but he dared not rely on those who were, for as recent history had repeatedly shewn, that would be to invite his own eclipse. Paralysed by this dilemma, the unfortunate emperor drifted to his inexorable doom. Hormuzd, son of Shapur, captured the frontier-fortress of Doura-Europos, in 255 to judge by the coins found beneath the ruins of the citadel. A passing Roman success in 257 was followed by catastrophe. The Syrians had never liked the Romans (they never would), so that it was easy for a rich citizen of Antioch called Mariada to hand over the city to Shapur. Once again the city was burned and looted, but this time the inhabitants, who supported Mariada, were spared. Valerian, who had on another of his coins pathetically styled himself *Restitutor Orientis*, could fight no more. His army was afflicted by the plague, it had lost all spirit. Valerian decided to offer Shapur a large indemnity as the price of peace. Shapur refused his initial overtures, but then said he would like to meet his rival. Valerian walked into the trap, and thus the emperor of Rome became a Persian captive, together with many of his men. The exultant Shapur led his prisoners back to his capital. No less than five rock-hewn sculptures were to commemorate their humiliation. The chief scene shews Valerian, on his knees before the mounted king, amid a crowd of Persian warriors and Roman slaves, as they had now become, to be used, as the Romans used their own slaves, on the construction of public works (see Plate 18(a)). As a slave, too, Valerian was to die, and his skin, stuffed and tinted by the artistic Persians, was for long to adorn one of their temples.

Such was the end of this unhappy man. In the eyes of Christians of later generations it was regarded as a divine punishment, for Valerian had resumed the persecution in a more violent form. During the first three years of his reign the Christians had been unmolested; his own secretariat was largely staffed by them. But in the year 257, bludgeoned by disaster, he found himself in need of two things—money and a scapegoat. His evil genius, the secretary of the treasury, Macrianus, suggested that in the Christians he could find both. (There is a depressing analogy between the treatment of the Christians in the third century and that of Jews and Huguenots in later ages.) The ageing emperor—he was in his seventh decade—gave way, and issued the fatal edicts. Once again it was the Christian *society*, not the Christian *faith*, which was proscribed as illicit; the persecution was, as usual, based on political and economic, not on religious or theological, grounds. The bishops were ordered to sacrifice to the gods of Rome; public worship was forbidden, the cemeteries placed out of bounds on pain of death. It was in one of the cemeteries of Rome, one of the catacombs, that bishop Xystus was surprised with his clergy and beheaded there and then, on his own episcopal chair. In Spain, Fructuosus, bishop of Tarragona, was haled before the governor, where the following interchange took place: "You are a bishop?" "I am." "You mean you were", and off he was sent to the stake. It is surprising that in Africa, where the pliant authorities once again allowed the mob to sate its appetite for the most revolting cruelty, Dionysius and Cyprian were at first visited with exile only. Their respite was short; for a year later came a second edict, ordering the immediate execution of the clergy. Christians in high places were punished with both death and confiscation; those in the imperial household were deported, reduced to the status of slaves, or sent in chain-gangs to the mines, their goods being forfeit.

Dionysius and Cyprian were recalled, the former to Alexandria, the latter to Carthage. Dionysius had much to suffer, but he escaped execution—he held his see until the year 265.

Cyprian was altogether bigger game. He was famous, both as a bishop and as a writer, far beyond the bounds of his diocese. Having been born a pagan, he had been trained in rhetoric, and had studied Cicero to good effect. In Rand's words (CAH XII, 601), "Ciceronian art and Christian straightforwardness have become one in his clear and simple style." His Christian models were Minucius Felix and Tertullian, especially the latter: "Hand me the master", he would say daily to his servant. Cyprian's leadership in matters of Church discipline and policy has already been mentioned. He was also a pillar of catholicism. Just how he understood the primacy of Rome is still debated, but that he deferred to Rome as a matter of courtesy is beyond question. The Church must be one, as taught by both Peter and Paul. Before the Council of Carthage in 251 (see page 141) he had read his discourse *On the Unity of the Catholic Church*. "The spouse of Christ cannot become an adulteress", he says. "She is undefiled and chaste, owning but one home, and guarding with virtuous modesty the sanctity of one chamber . . . He can no longer have God for a Father who has not the Church for a mother."

To put this confident and commanding voice to silence would indeed be a triumph for secular authority.

So beloved and famous was Cyprian that a deacon, Pontius, wrote a *Life* of him immediately after his death. We also have the *Acta*, or minutes, of his two trials, which it had long been the custom (so admirable was the Church's organization) to compile and circulate among the faithful. Both trials took place at Carthage, and both before the proconsul. At his first interrogation, in 257, when adjured by Paternus, in accordance with the imperial mandate, "to return to Roman rites", Cyprian gave the by then standard answer: "I am a Christian and a bishop. I know no other gods but the one true God, who made heaven and earth, the sea and all that is in it. This God we Christians serve, to him we pray day and night, for ourselves, for all mankind, for the health of the emperors themselves."

"Do you persist in this purpose?"

"That good purpose which knows God cannot be changed."

"Then you must obey the mandate of the emperors [Valerian and Gallienus] and go into exile at Curubis" [about forty miles away on the Gulf of Hamamet].

"I go."

Before dismissing Cyprian, the proconsul tried to induce him to divulge the names of his priests against whom also he had orders to proceed. The brave bishop retorted that informers were forbidden "by the excellent and beneficial provision of the law". Priests would be at their posts in the towns; Christian discipline forbade anyone to offer himself for punishment; it was for the proconsul to carry out his instructions.

On the 14th September of the following year, 258, Cyprian, having been recalled from exile, appeared before the new proconsul, Galerius. Galerius was an ailing man—he died soon afterwards—and held his court in a country villa. Cyprian had been escorted thither in a chariot, with every mark of respect, by two staff officers, with one of whom he lodged "in Saturn Street, between the temples of Venus and Safety", a strange setting for the last days of a Christian saint. A great throng came to salute him, whereupon Cyprian bade them send the girls home, for their own protection: he knew what a Carthage crowd was like.

The trial was brief. When told that "the most sacred emperors have commanded you to conform to Roman rites", Cyprian answered:

"I refuse."

"Take heed for yourself."

"Do as you are bid: in so clear a case I may not take heed."

Galerius, after consulting his assessors, haltingly (whether from his infirmity or from embarrassment we do not know) pronounced the following sentence:

"You have long lived an irreligious life, and have drawn together a number of men bound by an unlawful association, and professed yourself an open enemy to the gods and to the religion of Rome; and the pious, most sacred and august emperors, Valerian and Gallienus, and the most noble Caesar Valerian [the emperor's younger son] have endeavoured in vain to bring you back to conformity with their religious observances: whereas therefore you have been apprehended as principal and standard-bearer in these infamous crimes you shall be made an example to those whom you have wickedly associated with you: the authority of the law shall be ratified in your blood. It is the sentence of this court (reading from his tablet) that Thascius Cyprianus be executed with the sword."

"Thanks be to God", said Cyprian.

The "case for the Crown" in this and similar trials could not have been more precisely stated.

So Cyprian was led away to martyrdom. He was accompanied by a vast crowd which the authorities dared not attempt to disperse. Arrived at the place of execution, Cyprian divested himself of his mantle, handed his dalmatic to the waiting deacons, then knelt in prayer. When the executioner arrived, he ordered that he be given twenty-five gold pieces for his trouble. He then bound his own eyes, and offered his hands to be tied by a priest and sub-deacon. The executioner struck.

Cyprian's body was laid out there for all to see; and when night fell it was escorted back to Carthage in a solemn pomp with torches and hymns, to be laid in a sepulchre near the Baths overlooking that lovely bay where he is still venerated.

Cyprian had won.

Chapter XXI

TOWARDS THE DAWN

NEVER again would both Church and State, at one and the same time, suffer such tribulation. Gallienus, as soon as he found himself, by his father's captivity, sole emperor, at once took steps to reverse Valerian's disastrous policy. It is true that, as we have seen, Gallienus' name had appeared in the "persecuting edicts"; but without openly opposing his father, he could hardly have had it omitted, any more than his young brother could. Once disembarrassed of Valerian (for it was in such a light, much to the priggish horror of his detractors, that he viewed his father's captivity), Gallienus set himself to do all in his power to arrest the disintegration of the empire. With so many foes without, so many upstarts within, it would be sheer folly, if nothing more, to continue the persecution of a community which had proved itself capable, loyal and above all steadfast to the point of death. He therefore issued an edict, of which the text is lost, and clarified it by a rescript to Dionysius and other bishops. This is preserved for us by Eusebius, and says that the emperor has ordered that "the benefit of his bounty should be published throughout the world, to the intent that they [i.e., the pagans] should depart from the places of worship, and therefore you also may use the ordinance contained in my rescript, so that none may molest you. And this thing which it is within your power to accomplish has already long since been conceded by me; and therefore Aurelius Quirinius, who is in charge of the Exchequer, will observe the ordinance given by me" (CH VII, xiii).

Here at last is an emperor of Rome guaranteeing the peace of the Church, "already long since conceded" by Gallienus, in will, if not in fact; and to make quite sure that there was to be no equivocation or evasion on the part of the treasury, the chief finance officer is told in terms to see that restitution is made. For, as we learn from Eusebius' next paragraph, other bishops were empowered to recover the sites of their cemeteries. This rescript *does not* proclaim the recognition of the Christian faith as such; but it does allow the Christians to possess corporate property, both churches and cemeteries.

Gallienus could hardly have done less, and survived. The year 260 was one of unparalleled disaster. Apart from the catastrophe in the east, where the Christians were so numerous that it was particularly desirable to conciliate them, there was a revolt in Numidia, two pretenders appeared in quick succession in the Danube lands, and the evil Macrianus had turned against Gallienus, proclaimed his sons emperors, and won over a large part of the orient. Yet a fourth rebel, an officer called Postumus, appeared in the north and succeeded in capturing Cologne, and with it Gallienus' son, whom he killed. Meanwhile Macrianus was moving west with an army of thirty thousand men. This invasion was halted in Pannonia by Gallienus' general Aureolus (he, too, would later turn against his master); the army surrendered and Macrianus and his son were put to death. Yet another insurgent arose in Achaea, but was disposed of by Macrianus on the way to meet his own end. Gallienus' troubles were by no means over: in 262 the prefect of Egypt, Aemilian, who had sided with Macrianus, attempted to dictate to Rome by withholding the corn convoy. He was suppressed and replaced by Theodotus who succeeded also in crushing a revolt led by a Moorish officer.

At the end of his nine years of reign, that is in the autumn of the year 262, the distracted emperor felt that, although much remained to be done, he could at least emphasize his survival by celebrating his *decennalia*, as none of his predecessors had lived long enough to do since Severus Alexander. It was a magnificent procession that moved along the Sacred Way and up to the Capitol, past so many memorials of Rome's greatness. On the left was the Palatine hill; at its foot a cluster of temples, dedicated to Castor and Pollux, Augustus, Julius Caesar, Vesta, Antoninus and Faustina, with vistas of the grand constructions of Trajan beyond. Into the Forum Romanum, the heart of old Rome, led the Way, between the senate-house and the rostra, on through the arch of Septimius Severus, hard by the tomb of Romulus himself. Finally, with the temple of Saturn on the left, and those of Concord and Vespasian on the right, beneath the Tabularium, in which were preserved the laws of Rome engraved on brazen tablets, the Way climbed past the portico of the Consenting Gods to the very Capitol, to the temple of great Jove himself. Two hundred milk-white oxen, decked with golden cords and silken vestures, as many snowy-fleeced lambs and ten elephants, preceded twelve hundred glistening gladiators. Matrons in golden cloaks, a parade of tame animals, a cortège of actors, buffoons and boxers, were followed by the populace, with slaves going before them bearing tapers and torches. Then came the soldiers in white uniform, the knights, the senators and finally Gallienus himself, wearing his triumphal toga and the tunic embroidered with palms. Gilded spears, banners, the standards of all the legions glistened in the autumn sun. There were, too, groups of two hundred men each, got up to represent foreign nations, over whom the emperor was presumed to have triumphed— Goths, Sarmatians, Franks and Persians. This last display was too much for the cynical Romans: some of the more daring spirits broke into the procession and started to scrutinize the faces of these "Persians" one by one. When asked what they were doing, they replied: "We're looking for the emperor's father." Gallienus, it is reported, ordered them to be burned alive, an action which infuriated the people, and made the soldiers determined to "get" Gallienus. This pitiful pageant, with its hollow pomp, its contrast of ancient glory with present misery, and its horrible end, is a macabre allegory of the age.

For both in the east and in the west pretenders still flourished. In Gaul, Postumus ruled an independent realm. Aureolus, who was himself now plotting treason, allowed the usurper to slip through his hands. Everyone said Aureolus was a guilty man—everyone except Gallienus, who was to owe his death to his stubborn leniency. Postumus set up his own senate, his own praetorian guard stationed at Trèves, and struck his own coins, from the wording on which it is clear that he saw himself as the ruler not only of the west—he had drawn Britain into his empire—but the east as well, in fact the whole world: *restitutor orbis* he called himself.

There followed four years of stalemate, during which Gallienus seems to have concentrated on the arts of peace. He was a bit of a poet himself, and a pretty little *epithalamium* of his has come down to us:

> To it, dears! with mutual heat
> Let your hearts and members beat;
> Never dove shall moan like you,
> Never ivy cling so true,
> Never clam so closely kiss:
> All night long go on like this!
> (*Leave the lights up: what they see,*
> *They'll forget immediately.*)

Gallienus, like Hadrian before him, visited Athens, became *eponymous archon*, and was initiated at Eleusis. He tolerated the Christians from policy: he encouraged their rivals, the Neoplatonists, from conviction. Under the saintly mystic Plotinus, and his pupil Porphyry, the Neoplatonists worked out a philosophy for the educated man, a vindication of polytheism as a political expedient, which would satisfy many men until the final eclipse of paganism. Ever since the days of Augustine it has excited the admiration of not a few noble Christians.

In the spring of 268, Gallienus was called to the Balkans to meet an invasion of Heruli and Goths. He had trounced them at Nish, when he received news that Aureolus had gone over to Postumus. Gallienus beat him near Milan, into which city Aureolus retired. While Gallienus was besieging him, Aureolus declared himself emperor— a piece of bravado which was soon to cost him his life. But Gallienus was the first to die, murdered by a clique of his own staff-officers.

Gallienus is a figure who seems to appeal to us across the centuries for sympathy and understanding. The Roman historian Tacitus had said of his father-in-law Agricola that he was "fortunate in dying when he did". Of Gallienus it could be said that he was unfortunate in living when he did. A good general, a sound administrator; if in some respects, such as his punishment of those who mocked his *decennalia*, he was no better than his age, in others he far surpassed it. In his treatment of the Christians, in his patronage of the Neoplatonists, in his veneration of Hellas, he was in the line of humanist emperors, such as Hadrian, the Antonines and Constantine himself. In his chivalry he foreshadows a later epoch: he proposed to Postumus that they fight in single combat, to save bloodshed, an offer which Postumus declined with the sneer "I'm not a gladiator". But not by him was the empire to be restored, nor even by his successor, Claudius, though Claudius, in his short reign of two years, did succeed in stemming the Gothic avalanche. It was to Claudius' successor, Aurelian, that the title of *Restitutor Orbis* would justly belong. To trace the steps by which he acquired it, we must turn once more to the Levant, and there survey one of the most romantic episodes in the whole of Roman history. (See Plate 27 (c) and (d).)

The city of Palmyra has already been mentioned (see page 50). Lying in an oasis of the great desert between Syria and Mesopotamia, the one-time village was destined to become, in Schlumberger's apt phrase, the Venice of the sands; that is to say, an enormously rich state, drawing its wealth from the commerce between east and west, and on the basis of that wealth founding a political hegemony which at its apogee was to rival both Rome and Persia. Already, in the second century, it was important enough to Rome for a Roman garrison to be stationed there. Petra had formerly been the great centre of the eastern trade. But with the transformation of the Nabataean kingdom into the Roman province of Arabia in 106, and the transfer of the administrative capital to Bostra, the importance of Petra (though it continued to prosper) was bound to decline. That of Palmyra amazingly increased. For one thing, it lay on a shorter and more direct route between east and west; for another, its citizens were, like those of Petra and Phoenicia, Semites, and traders of exceptional commercial enterprise. They established their agencies and counting-houses not only throughout the Levant, but even as far afield as Spain and Dacia. They became very rich, and built for themselves fine houses and sumptuous tombs, the effigies in which bear witness to a bourgeois opulence, embellished in an ostentatious style which is predominantly Parthian, with traces of Hellenic influence (see Plate 26 (a) and (b)). This is just what we should expect. Their city, in its public aspect, just like the cities of the Levant to-day, wore a western dress (see Plate 25); but, as to-day, the lives of the citizens preserved the traditional pattern, which is of the east. Parthian influence had in fact long permeated Syria, even as far as the seaboard of Phoenicia. Another asset which the Palmyrenes possessed was their army. When, in the troubled times of the third century, the Roman garrison was withdrawn, or even earlier, Palmyrene troops replaced it, a force on which the Romans, their own manpower dwindling as their commitments multiplied, came to rely more and more. The Palmyrene army consisted of a camel-corps, and of the light and heavy Persian cavalry already described on page 126.

Wealth, based on a commercial network that covered both east and west, combined with an efficient army, made Palmyra a "third force" of prime importance in the perpetual east–west struggle. And the Palmyrenes possessed that quicksilver wit which is. the key to political survival in the Levant. So far they had backed Rome, and it had paid off. But had not the time come, with Valerian's captivity and the resurgence of Sassanid Persia, to look east?

At this juncture the fortunes of Palmyra were directed by a family of outstanding ability. The city was theoretically governed by an assembly representing the commercial oligarchy; but what Pericles said of Athens was true of Palmyra: "In theory it is a democracy, but in fact the rule of the best man."

In the year of Valerian's eclipse, that man was Udheinat. It is a typical Bedu name, a diminutive such as tribesmen still bear, meaning "little ears". His grandfather, Udheinat I, was a counsellor, and on his family tomb, which he built in 230, he describes himself as son of Hairan and grandson of Wahballath, or "Gift of Allath", the moon-goddess. His son, Septimius Hairan, as we know from the dedication of a statue which a soldier put up to him in Bostra in 251, became "Illustrious senator and prince of Palmyra". Septimius' son, Udheinat II, as he is known, had by the year 258 made himself *lord* (*maran* in Aramaic, *despotes* in Greek) of Palmyra. He had been brought up in the Roman ambiance, but he now made advances to Shapur, hoping that in return for his services the free passage of the caravans on which the life of Palmyra depended would be assured. Shapur rebuffed him. And so we find Udheinat attacking and routing the forces of Shapur, as, laden with booty, they fell back upon Ctesiphon after their third attack on Antioch and Asia (see page 144). He then, as the ally of Gallienus, proceeded to capture and kill Quietus, the son of the upstart Macrianus (see page 150), and to occupy Emesa, as vital to him as it was to Rome. Udheinat now reorganized the Roman forces in the Levant, and was designated *Dux Romanorum*. In 262, at the head of his combined Roman and Palmyrene army, Udheinat once again subdued Mesopotamia, defeated the Persians in a pitched battle, and shut Shapur up in his own capital, Ctesiphon. This dazzling exploit led Gallienus, despite the fact that he had had no hand in the campaign, to assume the title *Persicus Maximus*, if only to underline the fact that he regarded Udheinat as his agent. On Udheinat he conferred the title *Imperator*, unprecedented for a vassal of Rome, who could now add the laurel crown of a Roman general to the diadem of a prince of Palmyra. "King of kings", he was styled, to show that he disputed the title with Shapur, and "corrector of the whole east", to maintain his connexion with Rome.

Udheinat's ambitions were by now no longer merely commercial: he saw Palmyra as the queen of the east, treating on equal terms with both Rome and Persia. He was not to live to realize this vision. Jealous relatives combined with suspicious Roman officials to put him out of the way, together with his eldest son and his most trusted minister. That was in 267; but those who thought that the star of Palmyra had set had reckoned without one of the most remarkable and romantic women in history. Seneca, in a famous scene, shews us Medea, at bay, bereft of all her friends and resources. "What now remains?" asks her old nurse. "Medea remains", is the answer, and Zenobia might have made the same reply.

Zenobia, or Bathzabbaï, was a woman of great beauty, a human Diana. She rode, hunted, marched at the head of her troops. She kept great state, and banqueted from gold plate and jewelled goblets. Even her helmet glittered with rare gems and golden ornaments. Zenobia would drink a bumper with her generals, yet so chaste was she that she would have no intercourse with her husband except for procreation. She spoke Greek and Egyptian fluently, and was sufficiently acquainted with Latin. She studied history, and wrote her own textbook on that of the Levant. The philosopher Longinus found a home at her court. He was a Neoplatonist, a former pupil of Ammonius Saccas and of Origen. Thither, too, journeyed Paul of Samosata, bishop of Antioch. "Thus", says Abel, "the new Julia Domna had no cause to envy the court of Rome, where Plotinus had worked on his theories under the benevolent regard of the emperor Gallienus and his wife Salonina."

Zenobia was a worthy heir of the political ambitions of Udheinat. The Palmyrene domain was bounded now on the north by the Taurus mountains, on the south by the Persian Gulf. It comprised Mesopotamia, Cilicia, Syria, Phoenicia, Palestine and Arabia. It would soon add the greater part of Asia Minor and Egypt.

When Gallienus fell in March, 268 (see page 152), Marcus Aurelius Claudius was acclaimed as his successor, not only by the troops, but by the people of Italy as well. Like Decius before him, he was an Illyrian, and had been governor of Illyria. Constantine, when he became emperor, would be proud to claim descent from Claudius' brother, Crispus, whose daughter Claudia was to be Constantine's grandmother. But, brave and capable as he was, Claudius had no time to devote to eastern affairs. He was hard put to it to restore the authority of Rome in the Balkan peninsula, which was invaded by a joint horde of Scythians and Goths. He could not even proceed against Tetricus, who had succeeded Postumus and Victorinus as independent emperor of the Gauls. When therefore Zenobia sent her general Zabdas to take control of Egypt, Claudius could only acquiesce. Zenobia for her part saw no advantage in an open breach; but in 270, when Claudius was carried off by the plague after but two years of supreme power, Zenobia felt that the time had come to cast off any pretence of subordination: Quintillus, Claudius' brother and successor, was not the man to oppose her. Quintillus was quickly supplanted by a man of a very different stamp, Lucius Domitianus Aurelianus, known as Aurelian. He, too, was an Illyrian, of obscure origin, but great ability. He was known as "hand on hilt", so ready was he always for action. He was a strong, tough character, and had been one of those who had plotted against Gallienus and rid the empire of Aureolus. Despite his limited education, he knew as if by instinct what must be done to save Rome and its dominions, and at once—"hand on hilt"—set about doing it. By a series of brilliant victories he humbled the northern invaders, and flung them back across the Danube. At the same time, he knew that Rome could no longer hold Dacia, the rich province beyond the river, originally occupied by Trajan, and retained even by the prudent Hadrian on account of its wealth. So Roman troops and civilians were withdrawn, and planted in a new settlement "within the pale" on the southern bank of the Danube, a precedent not without interest in an age when the fate of "colons" in untenable territories is once again a burning question.

But Aurelian was taking no chances: he knew how fierce, and above all how swift, the barbarian raiders had shewn themselves. If they had been able to reach Greece, and northern Italy itself, what was to prevent their raiding Rome? So the walls of Rome were rebuilt, not as an elaborate bulwark designed to resist a siege, but merely as a defence against a barbarian attack. Their full circuit was twelve miles, their height twenty feet, their width twelve. This breastwork was started in 271, and took five years to complete. It is built of brick; for despite all the vicissitudes of war and time, a large part of it survives to this day.

Meanwhile Aurelian had been compelled to continue the co-existence policy of his immediate predecessors in regard to Tetricus in Gaul and Zenobia in the east. He recognized Wahballath, Zenobia's son and titular ruler of Palmyra, as a man of consular rank, king, *imperator*, *dux Romanorum*, and the direct successor of Udheinat II. Zenobia he does not appear to have acknowledged; unlike her son, she does not figure on the coins of Syria and Alexandria, and on the milestones she is described merely as "Septimia Bathzabbaï, illustrious queen, mother of the king of kings, daughter of Antiochus". In 271 the inevitable crisis came. Urged by his mother, Wahballath declared himself independent, and assumed the title Augustus. Aurelian's effigy disappears from the coins, to be replaced by that of Zenobia; and the milestones proclaim *the emperor Caesar Lucius Julius Aurelius Septimius Uaballath Athenodorus, Persicus Maximus, Adiabenicus Maximus, pious, happy, unconquered Augustus.*

Of these names, that of most enduring interest is *Athenodorus*. It is a Greek form of *Wahballath*: "the gift of Athene" represents "the gift of Allath", just as in the syncretic Palmyrene system, Baalshamin, lord of the heavens, is assimilated to Zeus the thunderer, and Shamash the sun god to Helios—a fact which was to be of great importance in Aurelian's religious policy.

It was of the kingdom of this world that Aurelian was thinking as in the autumn of the year 271 he set out for the east. Probus, his ablest general, was despatched to Egypt, which surrendered without a blow. Aurelian meanwhile was advancing through Asia Minor. He besieged and took Tyana (which commanded the Taurus passes), sparing its inhabitants at the instance, it was said, of the venerable Apollonius (see page 120) who appeared to Aurelian in a vision, very considerately speaking in Latin, instead of his native Greek, which the Illyrian did not understand. Zenobia's relations with the occult were less encouraging: the oracles both at Seleucia and Aphaca returned damping answers to her enquiries. Nevertheless, she decided to fight on. Zabdas marched out to meet Aurelian on the banks of the Orontes. The Palmyrene army contained elements from at least two Roman legions; but it was on the armoured cavalry that Zabdas chiefly relied. Aurelian, too, was a skilled cavalry commander: he out-manoeuvred Zabdas, routed his forces, and compelled them to fall back first on Antioch, and then on Emesa. Aurelian was welcomed by the cynical and sophisticated Antiochenes, who probably regarded the rulers of Palmyra as just so many Bedu. So great was the confidence that the emperor inspired in all sections of the community, that he was called upon to arbitrate in a matter of Church discipline—a sign of the times to come. Paul of Samosata had been bishop of Antioch since 258, Eusebius says, and during his episcopate he had not only attracted the favourable regard of Zenobia, but had also caused not a little scandal by his worldly ostentation, his relations with a band of spiritual "sisters", the "*subintroductae*", or "back-door girls" as the Antiochenes called them, his love of money—he had even secured for himself a well-paid government post—and above all for his heretical ideas concerning the nature of Christ. Twice Paul contrived to out-wit councils which had been convened to arraign his views. A third council, held in 267 or 268, deposed Paul for heresy, and declared that Domnus, son of Paul's predecessor, was to be bishop in his stead. Paul refused to accept the verdict. He was Zenobia's protégé, he had a popular following such as charlatans commonly attract, and he was a civil servant. He refused to budge from the episcopal dwelling.

When the matter was put before Aurelian, he was no doubt influenced by Paul's association with his enemy Zenobia; but the reason he gave for supporting Domnus is of great significance in the development of the primacy of the Roman pontiff, namely that it was Domnus, and not Paul, who was recognized by the bishops "in Italy and Rome". Domnus thus became possessed of the see and all its temporalities, at the mandate of a pagan emperor. Pagan—but not irreligious. Aurelian's mother had been a priestess in a temple of the sun god. He himself had a devotion to this deity and, like Elagabalus, he saw in the worship of the unconquered sun the bond of empire and the pledge of unity. He was the last of the great religious pagans to rule Rome. His emotions at entering Emesa, the very hearth of the cult of the sun, may be imagined. Zabdas had rallied his forces before the city, but once again Aurelian had defeated him, aided, as was later averred, by an apparition of the sun god himself, whose shrines in Emesa he augmented and embellished with costly offerings.

Zabdas and Zenobia had meanwhile withdrawn within the walls of Palmyra, prepared to resist to the end, relying on the desert, and the raids of the Bedu, backed by Armenian and Persian reinforcements, to subdue the invaders. Once again, Aurelian proved his superiority. He intercepted the Persians, fought off some of the tribesmen, and bribed the rest into neutrality. He was thus able to re-establish his communications with Syria. Palmyra was doomed. Resolved on one last desperate, humiliating appeal to the Persians, Zenobia slipped out of her beleaguered capital, mounted a dromedary, and made off towards the Euphrates. Just as she was about to cross that fateful river, she was captured by a Roman troop that had been sent to pursue her.

Palmyra opened its gates: Shapur, now nearing his end, was awed into quiescence: Zenobia and her son Wahballath became the captives of Aurelian. Palmyra, perhaps because it too was a centre of sun worship, and its temple one of the most splendid in existence (see Plate 25), was spared. Returning to Emesa, Aurelian held a formal trial of Zenobia and her court. Alas! the queen's resolution now failed her, and she condescended to purchase her own safety by incriminating her ministers. Longinus met his death with a dignity that put his patroness to shame.

Aurelian now set out for the west, accompanied by a long train of captives, which included Zenobia and her son. After crossing the Propontis, where most of the Palmyrenes were accidentally drowned (being desert-dwellers they could not swim), Aurelian hastened north to repel yet another incursion of the Carpi. Here he received intelligence that the Palmyrenes, mistaking his clemency for weakness, had revolted. This time Aurelian was determined to make an end of the rebels once and for all. "Hand on hilt" he returned to the east by forced marches, seized Palmyra, gave it over to pillage, carried off its choicest treasures and dismantled its walls. From that day to this it has remained a poor village, overshadowed by the relics of bygone pride.

Egypt, too, was chastised: the walls of Alexandria were razed, and new levies imposed on its citizens for having dared to interrupt the Roman food supply.

The east was now "restored": only Tetricus remained to be dealt with. By the year 274, he, too, had surrendered to the invincible Aurelian.

Aurelian could now celebrate a magnificent triumph as truthfully the restorer of east and west. Two gilded chariots, encrusted with gems, once the property of the Palmyrene court, were followed by a third which Shapur had given to Aurelian. A fourth, drawn by four "stags", or more probably reindeer, had belonged to the king of the Goths, and now conveyed the victorious emperor. The usual menagerie of animals and gladiators followed, with the prisoners behind them. Then came Tetricus, though many of the senators groaned to see one of their number thus humbled. He was lucky to be alive, and still luckier when Aurelian shortly made him governor of Lucania. Zenobia was there, too, decked with jewels, and bearing golden chains, so heavy that they had to be supported by her attendants. She had hoped to enter Rome in one of those chariots, as an empress; now she ascended the citadel as a captive. To her, also, Aurelian shewed himself a kind conqueror. He settled her in a villa at Tibur, and gave her in marriage to a Roman senator. Nearly sixteen hundred years later, an Englishwoman would reverse her romantic fate: Jane Digby, once married to Lord Ellenborough who would have made her Vicereine of India, preferred to unite herself to the Sheikh of Palmyra, with whom she lived in bliss until the end of her days in 1881.

The story of Zenobia is imperishable. It sheds a sunset lustre over the bleak panorama of Roman decay. But from the princely matron of Tibur we must now return to her generous-hearted conqueror.

Chapter XXII

DESPAIR AND HOPE

TO make good his claim that he was the "Restorer of the World", it was not enough that Aurelian should stabilize the frontiers: he must also stabilize the currency, on which the economic welfare of the empire depended. Inflation, which had started under Nero, had continued ever since, until of late years the decline had become catastrophic—a phenomenon with which modern Europe is tragically familiar. Aurelian was the first emperor to try to reform the currency, instead of further debasing it. He called in the old coins and issued new, based on a single stable basis, that is the gold standard. The Rome mint was closed in 270, and only reopened in 274. Except for Alexandria, which maintained an independent mint until the days of Diocletian, colonial and municipal issues were suspended entirely, largely because the expense of minting coins was higher than the value which they could now, at face-value exchange rates, command. As from 274, all issues were under the direct control of the emperor. The gold coins varied in weight from time to time. There were no silver coins, and the Antonianus, which Caracalla had introduced as nominally worth two denarii, though even in his day it was worth only one and a half, was now stabilized at twenty, or twenty-one, denarii—in itself an indication of how disastrously the coinage had been debased. The coins were of "billon", that is an alloy in which base metal predominated. These measures, though incomplete, were at least a move in the right direction.

Aurelian also aspired to tackle the religious question. He realized that faith is the spring of action, that where people believe nothing, they will do nothing, that where faith is ardent, it will produce works. He knew, too, that religion wrought the strongest of all bonds. Was it not the one sanction that held the Jews so firmly together, scattered though they might be throughout the empire? Had he not seen for himself the power and persistence of the Christians? What an achievement it would be, to unite the whole empire in one worship, one loyalty.

For Aurelian there could be but one choice. It was the sun god that his mother had taught him to revere, it was the sun god whose intervention at the crisis of his eastern campaign had given him the victory. In Emesa he had visited one of his most august shrines, in Palmyra he had beheld his splendid temple. We have no record of his having visited Ba'albek, but he well may have—it is not far from Emesa. He must certainly have heard of its glories. So in Rome itself a temple of the Sun was now raised, enriched with the spoils of Palmyra, dignified by statues of the sun god and of Baal-Shamin, Palmyra's patron. A college of priests was established to serve the omnipotent deity, and four-yearly games instituted in his honour. Everything, in fact, was done to establish an official religion which should satisfy the demands of a movement towards monotheism which was now animating Roman paganism as much as the paganism of the orient, where, in the words of Léon Homo, "the separate divinities, Jupiter, Apollo, Mars, Sarapis, Attis, the Baals of the east, Mithras, all appeared more and more as so many incarnations, so many exact manifestations, of a higher divinity, namely, the Sun".

The establishment of the sun cult was not the least important result of Aurelian's campaign against Zenobia: she was defeated, but the cult which had formerly been honoured in her magnificent temple had become the official religion of Rome itself. Zenobia, too, may therefore be regarded as one of the agents which brought about the triumph of monotheism, even though neither she nor Aurelian could imagine or comprehend the form in which it would eventually triumph. The immediate consequence—and it was of the first importance—of the adoption of the new, universal religion was political, as Aurelian intended it to be. Whereas for the Christian politics must always be the servant of religion, for the pagan it is the other way round—religion must serve the ends of policy; and that is the fundamental cause of the opposition of Christian and pagan polities. For Aurelian, to proclaim himself *deus et dominus natus*, god and lord born, was but a corollary of declaring that the sun was *dominus imperi romani*, lord of the Roman empire: to the Christians it was blasphemy. Aurelian adopted the trappings of monarchy: the diadem, the jewelled robe, the servile protocol. He did this not from personal inclination—he was an austere man—but for what he regarded as reasons of state. His reign marks the final end of the old conception of the *princeps* as the best citizen, and the beginning of the autocracy which Diocletian and Constantine were to perfect. (The process had in fact begun before Aurelian, but it was he who, as it were, brought the new picture into focus.)

It seems inevitable that such a concept should bring Aurelian into conflict with the Christians. His domestic policy, it is true, was as salutary as his military triumphs: he abolished debts, he reorganized the guilds, encouraged viticulture, carried out public works, and increased the inland water-transport on both Nile and Tiber. Nevertheless his assumption of deity and his patronage of the cult of the sun must in Christian eyes annul all these material benefits. He never proceeded against the Christians. He had intended to do so, says Eusebius, but he did not live to issue the edict. Aurelian was on his way to the east, "hand on hilt", for yet another Persian campaign, when he was assassinated on the European shore of the Dardanelles. A dishonest servant, fearing punishment, persuaded a group of Aurelian's staff-officers that they were, with him, destined for execution; and so to protect themselves they struck first—such were the standards of the time.

The violent death of this clement and capable soldier after only five years of rule threw the empire back into the competitive anarchy from which he had sought to rescue it. After an interregnum of three weeks, the senate prevailed on one of their number, a seventy-five-year-old consul, called Tacitus, to succeed. He did not last long. He punished Aurelian's murderers and committed military affairs to Probus. In April, 276, Tacitus was killed by the soldiers, after a reign of six months. His brother Florianus, who regarded himself as the natural heir, survived for three. Probus was emperor at last.

"Of few reigns of such note as that of Probus have we so slight and unsatisfactory a record", says the *Cambridge Ancient History*. His *Life* in the *Augustan History* is, indeed, little more than a windy panegyric. There is evidence that Probus did concede to the senate the right to hear appeals, rather as the privy council in this respect deputizes for the English sovereign, and also allowed it to nominate provincial governors. This latter privilege extended only to civil affairs, for now in every province which might be the scene of military action there was an independent *dux* in charge of the troops and answerable to the emperor—in theory: Probus had to cope with no less than four rebellions, and was finally carried off by a revolt of the soldiers who resented his employing them on useful but pacific tasks such as the increase of vineyards, and feared that he might really make good his prophecy that so peaceful had he made the world that there would soon be no need for soldiers. That he really had established the right to be called *pacator orbis*, the pacifier of the world, there is evidence in Eusebius, who now, be it remembered, is writing as a contemporary. Looking back on these good and tranquil days, he says, at the beginning of the eighth book of his *Church History*: "It is beyond our powers worthily to describe the extent and the nature of the honour, the freedom, which everybody shewed,

Greeks and non-Greeks alike, to that word of worship of the God of the universe which had been proclaimed through Christ to the world —before the persecution in our day, that is. Proof would be available in the favours granted by the rulers to us and ours. They even entrusted the government of provinces to them, freeing them from mental agony on the sacrifice question, because of the great friendliness they had for their doctrine." Christians were, Eusebius goes on, to be found in the palaces of the emperors and in their secretariats, and they were permitted complete and open freedom to practise their religion. They were particularly esteemed, more than their pagan fellow-servants, by their masters. The bishops were treated with universal deference by procurators and governors. So large had Christian congregations become, that the old conventicles, the house-churches, could no longer hold them, and so completely new ones, on new sites, were erected in every city.

Concurrently with this remarkable expansion in the cities, there occurred—so broad and bountiful is the spirit of Grace—a development of a diametrically opposite sort, which was to be of the greatest value to the life of the Catholic Church, and still is, namely monasticism.

Recluses there had been before, such as the Jewish *Therapeutae* in Egypt, a contemplative order of great antiquity, whose doctrine and practice as described by Philo so impressed Eusebius that he succeeded in persuading himself and others that they were really Christians, converted by St Mark, and that their "ancient writings" were the Gospels and Epistles, none of which had yet been written.

The Essenes of Palestine have acquired much fame in our own day not only from the writings of Josephus and Pliny, but from the excavation by the French Dominican École Biblique of the "monastery" of Qumrān, on the Dead Sea, and the publication of the documents which its inmates produced, now preserved in myriads of fragments in the Museum in Old (Jordan) Jerusalem.

It was natural that the first Christians should in this as in so much else follow Jewish precedent, though the desire for solitude as a means of spiritual refreshment and growth is not confined to any one religion—it is nourished by one of man's strongest instincts. It was inevitable that as pagan society became more and more unsympathetic to the Christian ethic, the faithful should retire from the world. Persecution stimulated the movement. In the days of Decius, we read of a young Christian in Egypt, called Paul, who fled to the Thebaïd to avoid persecution, and liked the experience so much that he stayed there until he died. And it was in Egypt that the monastic movement as such really had its origin. The first "monks" (that is "solitaries") were what we should now call hermits, living in caves, or tombs, such as may still be seen in the *wadis* of the wilderness between Jerusalem and the Jordan, with evidences of habitation at no distant period. The first Egyptian recluses were similarly housed. (It was only in the fourth century that the *communal*, what we should now call the monastic, life was organized by Pachomius.) The founder of the Christian hermetic discipline was St Anthony, who as a young man of twenty sold all his considerable property, and went to live in the desert, in an old fort. He stayed there for twenty years, leaving his retreat only to visit Alexandria during the final persecutions, to comfort those who were in prison or condemned to the mines. His reputation spread far and wide, and he soon found himself the director of a large group of hermits. Finally, he sought even greater solitude near Thebes, where he lived for another forty years, dying in 356 at the age of 105. St Anthony can with propriety be called "the first monk".

Probus had been killed in the early autumn of 282, in the "Iron Tower" near Sirmium. He was contemplating a campaign against Vahram II of Persia, who had broken the truce which he and Probus had agreed on but a short while before, after Probus had rejected Vahram's presents with the message that when he wanted any of the riches of Persia, he would come and help himself. The campaign was now entrusted to Carus, the praetorian prefect, who had been created Augustus by the army and approved as such by the senate. The new emperor crossed the Euphrates early in 283, and inflicted severe defeats on the Persians. Having captured Seleucia and Ctesiphon, he died mysteriously during a thunderstorm at the end of July. Was he struck by lightning? Did he die of an illness which had confined him to his tent? Was he killed by his successor as praetorian prefect, Arrius Aper, the father-in-law of Carus' younger son, Numerian? The last seems the most likely, in view of the treacherous way in which he undoubtedly did kill his son-in-law. Numerian suffered from inflammation of the eyes, and so was carried in a litter which Aper forbade anyone to approach, telling enquirers that Numerian was too ill to appear, and must be protected from the wind and the sun. It was only when the stench from the litter became overpowering, near Nicomedia, that the troops realized the truth. They held a council, arraigned Aper for the murder of Numerian, and laid upon the commander of the bodyguard, whom they hailed as their new Augustus, the task of avenging Numerian. This man's name was Diocles, known to history and fame as Diocletian, the Romanized form of his name which he adopted on his elevation. Long ago, a Druidess in what is now Belgium had told him that one day he would be emperor, when he had slain a boar—in latin, *aper*. Now at last he understood what the seer had meant. In front of the assembled army, "he pointed his sword at Aper, and drove it through him", and then shouted out a verse from the *Aeneid* (x, 830): "Well may you boast, Aper, it is by the hand of mighty Aeneas himself that you fall."

That was on the 17th November, 284. Early next spring, Diocletian moved west to meet the challenge of Carus' elder son, Carinus, who as senior Caesar had there assumed the supreme power without opposition. Diocletian, if he felt in honour bound to avenge the death of the younger brother, saw nothing dishonourable in trying to rid himself of the elder. Carinus was a vicious brute, and an officer whose wife he had seduced did Diocletian's work for him. Diocletian was to be the last emperor of the old Roman, pagan, empire, as his successor Constantine was to be the first of the new Byzantine, Christian, empire. As a cadenza may recapitulate the themes of a concerto, so it is possible to recognize in Diocletian the characteristics of many of his predecessors. Every trait that we associate with the word "Roman"—the organizing ability, the sense of discipline, the love of hard work, of erecting magnificent public monuments, of military glory—all these are present in the character of Diocletian, and made him an object of intense admiration to his contemporaries. Unfortunately he was also a victim of the barren conservatism and corroding superstition which were all too often, in the latter days of Rome, the foil of great talents. Diocletian's attitude to the tasks that lay before him is well put by Abel (II, 239):

"The obscure officer born into the *clientèle* of the senator Anullinus in Dalmatia, who, after serving in Gaul under Aurelian, governing Moesia under Carus and commanding the bodyguard during the Persian campaign, now found himself at the head of the empire, would merit general approbation by his organizing talent even more than by his military gifts. Conscious of the reforms which the exercise of the supreme power demanded, such as the redistribution of the troops both in the interior and on the periphery, and of the lack of proportion between the provinces, he was to prove himself of sufficient stature to carry out the great task envisaged and entered upon by Claudius Gothicus, Aurelian and Probus. Only in the realm of religion was he to shew himself the enemy of all reform, even enlarging upon the cleverness and violence with which his predecessors has assailed Christianity. His thoroughly reactionary attitude would find its sanction in this principle: that it was not permissible to claim that a new religion could reform the old religion. To desire, in that sphere, to change ancestral institutions was the greatest of crimes. Although he was astute enough to lay on the shoulders of his colleagues the odium of certain enactments, Diocletian has bequeathed his name to the most savage of the persecutions."

The cardinal and most permanent achievement of Diocletian was his complete reorganization of the administration of the empire—so cardinal and so permanent that to this day the Christian Church uses the very terms which Diocletian devised for his new structure. The provinces were reduced in size, large ones being split into two or more, a process which Septimius Severus had started (see page 74). The remodelled provinces were then grouped in twelve *dioceses*, over each of which was set a *vicar*, at first regarded as the *deputy* of the praetorian prefect, but in fact an officer responsible to the emperor. The second fundamental reform of Diocletian was the creation of the *tetrarchy*, or rule of four. A tetrarch had originally been a ruler of a fourth part of a state, but just as our word "quarter" has come to mean any district or region, so the word tetrarch came to be used of any subordinate ruler, in which sense it occurs in the New Testament. Diocletian now revived the word in its literal sense. He saw that so long as there was only one emperor, the odds between him and a would-be usurper were at the best even—as recent history had shewn with depressing and disastrous frequency. If there were four rulers, any upstart, even if he succeeded in doing away with one, would still have the other three to reckon with. Diocletian therefore decided to associate with himself a colleague, as Augustus, and to each of the two Augusti a Caesar, as adjutant and eventual successor. He chose his men well. As his brother Augustus he chose Maximian, an old comrade-in-arms, loyal and brave. As the two Caesars, he appointed, as his own, a soldier called Galerius, and for Maximian a nobleman called Constantius Chlorus, a man of high merit, and the father of Constantine. This arrangement, in its final form, was not arrived at until the year 293; but the principle which underlay it had been evolving over the years, Maximian having been made Augustus the year after Diocletian's accession. Besides remodelling the provincial administration and instituting the tetrarchy, Diocletian also adopted an openly monarchical style. He dressed as a king (though it was left for Constantine to assume the diadem), and lived surrounded by pomp and mystery. Only a privileged few were admitted to the presence, and they must greet their emperor by kneeling and kissing the hem of his garment.

The new organization worked well. The frontiers were restored, by Maximian and Constantius in the west, by Diocletian and Galerius in the east. Persia was forced to make peace on Diocletian's terms, to surrender Mesopotamia, and to forgo all claim to Armenia. A revolt in Egypt was suppressed. The coinage was once more overhauled, and taxation in kind was introduced, largely to furnish provisions for the armies. These, too, were reorganized, and the cavalry made an independent arm. There was, in fact, no part of the machinery of government which Diocletian did not review, and improve. The introduction of taxation in kind involved the assessment of each district at an annual quota. To produce this it was necessary that the land should be regularly and efficiently tilled, that is, that its labour force should be settled and constant. Thus, in an enactment which was originally designed to overcome inflation may be discerned the primaeval germs of the feudal system.

It could hardly be expected that the author of this new unity of empire, this uniformity under a supreme despot, could view with favour an organization like the Church, which claimed to be directed not by Caesar but by God. Nevertheless, Diocletian was too shrewd to abrogate the toleration that Gallienus had proclaimed. He saw Christians holding high office, faithful, intelligent and trustworthy. In Nicomedia, his own capital, the Christian church was immediately opposite his own palace. He himself claimed Jupiter as his patron, and Hercules as that of Maximian: the Christian God was a competitor, but it seemed that more was to be lost than gained by provoking a clash.

Unfortunately, this "wise and salutary neglect" was not to last. It was Galerius who took the first step towards its reversal. In the year 297 Galerius had won a brilliant victory over the Persians, and this greatly strengthened his authority: he was now in a position to dictate to Diocletian, and it appears that he did. First of all, the army was to be purged of Christians: officers who refused to sacrifice were dismissed, ordinary soldiers discharged with ignominy. One or two Christian soldiers were executed; but there was as yet no general anti-Christian campaign. In the winter of 302–3 Galerius was with Diocletian at Nicomedia, and here, Lactantius tells us, the Caesar urged his Augustus to take stronger measures against the Christians. Diocletian continued to resist: for nearly twenty years now he had been emperor, his policy had been successful, his arms victorious. Why should he make war on a section of his own subjects? To what end?

Galerius was bent on persecution, and he had powerful allies, not only in his army, but among a group of Neoplatonist philosophers, one of them the governor of Bithynia, who had inherited Porphyry's anti-Christian spirit. Diocletian, not wishing to precipitate an open breach with his Caesar, agreed to refer the question to the oracle of the Milesian Apollo, who in his reply shewed himself to be the enemy of the Church. Pressed by Galerius, urged by his friends, and now exhorted by a god, Diocletian at last gave in—but even now, only on condition that no blood was shed. His final consent may have been influenced by an incident which had occurred shortly before in Antioch. The emperor himself was offering a sacrifice: Galerius was present. The augurs could find no trace of anything significant in the entrails of the victim, whereupon their chief declared that it was the Christians in the emperor's suite who had nullified the proceedings by making the sign of the cross. Diocletian had on that occasion ordered that the whole palace staff must be made to sacrifice on pain of flogging, and that any officer of the army who failed to offer sacrifice should be dismissed. In this atmosphere, it was less hard for Galerius, whom both Eusebius and Lactantius hold to be the author of the persecution, to have his way.

The 23rd February was celebrated as the festival of the Terminalia, the feast of the old Roman god *Terminus*; and so that day in the year 303 was appointed as that on which the Christian Church was to be *terminated*. Without waiting for the prescribed day agents of the government at Nicomedia entered the Christian church opposite the palace on the 22nd, and started to demolish the building.

We have no copy of the actual edict; but its general provisions are known to us. All churches and all houses used as churches were to be destroyed. All bibles and service-books were to be surrendered and publicly burnt. Christians in high positions were deprived of their privileges, such as immunity from torture in judicial proceedings, and all Christians were outlawed. Christians employed in the imperial domains were to be reduced to slavery, just as they had been in Valerian's day (see page 145).

The fact that the church at Nicomedia could be demolished in a matter of hours suggests that it was not a large or solidly constructed building. Unfortunately we have no record of what a Christian church was like at this period. The earliest description we possess is that given by Eusebius (CH, X, iv) of a basilica built at Tyre, in the days of Constantine. This was a splendid edifice, approached by way of a courtyard furnished with fountains, and entered by a magnificent triple doorway, through which the rays of the rising sun penetrated to light up the richly adorned interior. The altar was placed "in the middle", and surrounded with rails. There were thrones for the "presidents" and benches for the congregation. The roof was of Lebanon cedar. The general plan of this church is not unlike that which may still be descried in the Church of the Nativity at Bethlehem; but to what extent it reproduced earlier Christian churches it is not possible to say. It seems probable that its internal arrangements were traditional, but that its extent and splendour were the fruit of victory and peace.

"No bloodshed", Diocletian had said. Galerius thought overwise: he was out for blood, and plenty of it. Twice mysterious fires broke out in the palace at Nicomedia, after the second of which Galerius ostentatiously left the town: he was not going to be burnt alive by the Christians, he said. As in later times, a charge of arson was a useful political weapon. Diocletian, now in the most uncomfortable of all political predicaments, that of the moderate who has been proved wrong, lost his head. Those who confessed Christ were punished as incendiaries, the Christian chamberlains were strangled, the bishop of Nicomedia and his flock were killed, Prisca, Diocletian's Christian wife, and her daughter, the wife of Galerius, apostatized.

A *second* edict soon followed—"it will have blood, they say; blood will have blood": Galerius and his like, and in that brutal age there were many of them, were determined to annihilate the Christians. This time it was against the clergy that the state proceeded. They were to be imprisoned, and so, in Eusebius' words, "everywhere a countless throng were shut up, and on all sides prisons built long ago for murderers and grave-robbers were filled with bishops, presbyters and deacons, readers and exorcists, so that there was no space left for condemned criminals". Baynes comments: "In the days of Elizabeth the Catholics similarly filled the prisons of England. 'The prisons are so full of Catholics (1583) that there is no room for thieves.' "

In the summer of 303 Diocletian went to Rome to celebrate the twentieth anniversary of his reign. The customary amnesty was proclaimed; but what was to be done with the imprisoned clergy? A *third* edict announced that they were to be compelled to sacrifice and then freed. Every sort of subterfuge was resorted to to make it appear that they had sacrificed, so anxious were the authorities now to win, rather than to lose, these valuable citizens. But Galerius' thirst for blood was still unslaked. Diocletian fell ill during his visit to the west, and when he got back to Nicomedia he was a wreck. Galerius seized his opportunity: while his master was incapacitated, he issued a *fourth* edict, which enjoined that every man, woman and child in the empire was to sacrifice and pour a libation to the gods of Rome, on pain of death.

Diocletian realized that Galerius had, for the time being, won: twenty years of good rule, of success, of moderation, was not that enough for one man to have bestowed upon Rome? Diocletian decided that it was, that he did not choose to see it all undone by a quarrel between himself and Galerius which, by the custom of that day and age, would certainly have rekindled civil war. Diocletian found another solution: he abdicated, the first emperor ever to do so, though, as we have seen, Philip the Arab contemplated the same step (see page 136). With him, he compelled Maximian to retire as well. That left Galerius and Constantius as Augusti, for whom two new Caesars had now to be found. It was generally thought that Diocletian would have appointed Constantius' son, Constantine, as one of them; but now it fell to Galerius to select his own men. He chose as his own Caesar a nephew called Maximin Daia, and allotted to Constantius a certain Severus. These four, Constantius, Galerius, Daia and Severus formed the second tetrarchy. Maximian withdrew to his estate in Italy, Diocletian to his native Illyria, where he built the palace at Split which still dominates the town. It was to have an influence which Diocletian could not have foreseen, any more than he could have known that the Church would adopt his administrative nomenclature. Nearly fifteen centuries after he had built it, an English architect, Robert Adam, visited Split and was so impressed by the monumental scale and style of Diocletian's palace, that he modelled his own London Adelphi on it, and so set a pattern which was to be copied by Nash and other Regency architects in the still surviving terraces. For Diocletian, the original was just his country villa, where he spent the last decade of his life—it was in 305 that he abdicated— growing vegetables.

Galerius could now continue his persecution without opposition. In the west, under the mild Constantius, the edict does not appear to have been widely enforced. In the east, Galerius and Daia worked like savages. Every sort of torture was employed to induce the Christians to recant. Some were burned, some roasted or smoked to death. Others were hacked to pieces, or thrown to wild beasts, or drowned. Hot irons, molten lead, the rack, bludgeons and flails were all pressed into service, besides the more ordinary punishments such as crucifixion or beheading. Tongues and eyes were torn out, tendons were severed and, thus mutilated, men were packed off to the mines, women to the brothels. There were many apostates; but there were numberless martyrs, too. When it is a struggle between those who are out to kill, and those who are ready to die for what they hold to be true, it is always the latter who win. The heroism of the Christians who faced death calmly, confidently, and with prayers of forgiveness on their lips, deeply impressed their pagan brethren. And then in 311 the unbelievable occurred: Galerius himself recanted. He was smitten with a horrible disease, and issued a decree of toleration. Galerius was soon to die, whereupon Daia tried to restart the persecution. He put into circulation forged *Acts of Pilate* which were full of blasphemies against Christ, arrested and executed bishops and other leading churchmen, and urged the inhabitants of Syria to expel the enemies from their towns. Daia lived until 313; but before then his persecution had been brought to an end, at the instance of a young man from Britain, called Constantine.

Chapter XXIII

DAYSPRING

THE theme of this, the final, chapter of this study is twofold: the rise of Constantine to supreme power, and the liberation and establishment of the Christian Church.

In his influence upon the fortunes of mankind, Constantine stands in the very first rank, comparable with such figures as Alexander the Great, Cromwell and Napoleon. The steps by which he attained to the sole rule over the Roman empire were complicated and protracted. Just as it took a generation to distil, as it were, the authority of the old Roman republic, by way of two triumvirates and prolonged civil strife, into the principate of Augustus; so now, at the beginning of a new era, it was by way of the tetrarchies, and again war between the rival dynasts, that Constantine was to emerge as sole sovereign. Simultaneously with this process, he was to shine as the champion and liberator of Christianity. It is an achievement without parallel in the recorded history of man.

Constantine was born at Nish, about the year 280, the son of Constantius Chlorus (see page 166) and a simple Balkan serving-maid called Helena, a name she was to make revered and loved throughout Christendom. When in 292 Constantius was appointed Caesar, Diocletian compelled him to put away Helena and to marry Theodora the daughter of Maximian, by whom he had six other children. Constantius was despatched to the north, to rule Gaul, Spain and Britain: Constantine remained behind with Diocletian, a hostage to guarantee his father's loyalty to Diocletian and the tetrarchy. As a governor, Constantius was conspicuously successful. In Britain, one of Maximian's officers, a low-born Menapian called Carausius, had revolted and set himself up as an independent ruler, with his own fleet and his own coinage (see Plate 29(d)). In 293 Carausius' chief minister killed him. In 296, after careful preparation, Constantius invaded Britain, defeated the rebel, and sailed victoriously up the Thames to London. Constantine, meanwhile, had accompanied Diocletian and Galerius on their travels to the east. In 295 he was in Palestine, where Eusebius, who was afterwards to become his close friend, saw him for the first time. The boy made a deep impression on his future biographer. Everyone admired his noble carriage, his air of authority, his look of spirituality. Already he gave proof of his love of literature, and of his moderation and wisdom. He spoke Greek, but preferred to compose his letters and speeches in his native Latin, and then have them translated. His military training was thorough, and he saw service not only in Persia and Egypt, but in Asia and on the Danube.

His residence at the centre of world politics, and his travels, also enabled him to see that in persecuting the Christians, men such as Galerius were not only behaving with unpardonable cruelty, but were ruining the state by alienating an ever-increasing proportion of its citizens, and depriving it of the services of some of its most steadfast and capable servants.

As already recorded (see page 170), when Diocletian and Maximian abdicated, Constantine was passed over in the selection of the new Caesars. So was Maxentius, son of Maximian. Constantine at once realized what had happened: Galerius was out for the supreme power, and was jealous of rivals such as Constantius Chlorus, now Augustus, and his son. When Constantius asked that his son be sent to help him, Galerius could not refuse without openly insulting his brother Augustus; but he could easily arrange with his Caesar, Severus, that Constantine be delayed, or even killed, on the way. He reckoned without Constantine's energy: the young man simply left the palace as though he were a fugitive prisoner, and rode hell for leather right across Severus' dominions, killing the post-horses behind him to avoid pursuit. He joined his father at Boulogne. That was in the spring of 306. In the summer, he accompanied his father on a campaign against the Picts, after which father and son withdrew to their headquarters at York. Here, on the 23rd July, Constantius died; and that very same day, largely at the instance of a German prince with the delightful name of Crocus, the troops hailed Constantine as emperor.

When the portrait of Constantine, wreathed in laurel, was shewn to Galerius, he flew into a rage. He at once elevated Severus to the rank of Augustus, which meant that Constantine was only to be a Caesar. Meanwhile, Maxentius, son of Maximian, not wishing to be outdone by Constantine, had himself proclaimed Augustus by the praetorians. That meant that there were now *four* Augusti in the west (Constantine, Maxentius, Severus, and Maximian, who, at his son's request, had emerged from his retirement to bring over the army to his son's support) and *two* in the east, Galerius and Daia.

Clearly, this overcrowded chaos could not last. The first to go was Severus, who was killed by Maximian. Galerius replaced him by

Licinius, an old comrade-in-arms. In the struggles to come, the support of the Christians would be more valuable than ever. Even Maxentius "at the beginning counterfeited our faith", says Eusebius; but it was only an interlude in the persecution, which, as carried on by Galerius and his associates, lasted in all no less than ten years. When Galerius did issue his edict of toleration, in 311, it bore also the signatures of Licinius and Constantine.

Constantine had been studiously ignored both by Galerius and by his creatures; but fortunately for him, Maximian fell out with his son, and took refuge with Constantine, who was then in Gaul. The former emperor rewarded Constantine's hospitality by declaring him to be an Augustus, and giving him in marriage his daughter Flavia. A little later, having failed to unseat his son Maxentius, the now ridiculous old man tried to engage his daughter in a plot against Constantine. The plot was discovered, and Maximian was constrained to commit suicide. How much wiser was Diocletian, growing his cabbages in Illyria.

It was Maxentius who provoked the next round in the struggle. He rashly decided to march against both Constantine and Licinius. This gave Constantine the opportunity for which he had been longing. On the 24th September, 312, after crossing the Alps, he arrived in Italy. Having stormed Susa, he pressed on to Turin. Milan and Verona capitulated to him. Everywhere his moderation was blessed, and he was hailed as a liberator. Modena surrendered, and the road to Rome, the great Flaminian Way, lay open.

Constantine's one fear was that Maxentius might not quit the city, relying upon Aurelian's walls to exclude Constantine as on a former occasion they had thwarted Galerius and Severus. It was the Sybilline books that proved Constantine's first ally: they assured Maxentius that in the ensuing engagement "the enemy of the Romans would perish", and so he moved out for the fatal battle at the Milvian Bridge over the Tiber.

Constantine had another ally, of far greater power, namely the God of the Christians.

That Constantine was a spiritually-minded man there is no doubt. He had long been an adherent of monotheism, first as a worshipper of the sun god, and then with a more elevated belief in the divine spirit which governs the world, and of which the sun is but the symbol. During the march on Rome, Constantine appears to have twice undergone what would now be called a religious experience. The first occasion is recorded by Eusebius, in his *Life of Constantine*, as follows:

"He besought his father's god in prayer, beseeching and imploring him to tell him who he was and to stretch out his right hand to help him in his present difficulties. And while he was thus praying with fervent entreaty, a most incredible sign appeared to him from heaven, the account of which it might have been hard to believe if it had been related by any other person. But since the victorious emperor himself long afterwards declared it to the writer of this history, when he was honoured with his acquaintance and society, and confirmed his statement by an oath, who could hesitate to accredit the relation, especially since the testimony of aftertime has established its truth?

"He said that about noon, when the day was already beginning to decline, he saw with his own eyes the trophy of a cross of light in the heavens, above the sun, and an inscription, CONQUER BY THIS, attached to it. At this sight he himself was struck with amazement, and his whole army also, which followed him on an expedition, and witnessed the miracle.

"He said, moreover, that he doubted within himself what the import of this portent could be. And while he continued to ponder and reason on its meaning, night overtook him; then in his sleep the Christ of God appeared to him with the sign which he had seen in the heavens, and commanded him to make a likeness of that sign which he had seen in the heavens, and to use it as a safeguard in all engagements with his enemies."

This experience had taken place "on an expedition", before the march on Rome. The second experience occurred while Constantine was encamped in the neighbourhood of the Milvian Bridge. It is described by Lactantius, in his *Deaths of the Persecutors*, which was written within six years of the event:

"The anniversary of Maxentius' accession, the 27th October, was near, and his first five years of rule were drawing to a close. Constantine was directed in a dream to mark the heavenly sign of God on the shields of his soldiers and thus to join battle. He did as he was ordered, and with the cross-shaped letter X, with its top bent over, he marked Christ on the shields." This is the origin of the Christian use of the symbol ☧, which denotes the first two letters of the Greek word Christ. Like other Christian symbolism, this sign had long had a secular signification, because the two letters are also the two first of the Greek word for "useful", or "serviceable".

At the battle of the Milvian Bridge Constantine won a complete victory. To accelerate what he confidently expected to be a victorious advance, Maxentius had constructed a bridge of boats over the Tiber, to supplement the ancient and historic stone bridge which spans the

175

river at the beginning of the Flaminian Way, then as now the trunk road leading north from Rome. When Maxentius was routed, the bridge of boats collapsed, and he and a large part of his army were drowned.

Constantine had in fact shewn conspicuous generalship. He had made the best possible use both of terrain and of the possibility of surprise which it gave him, comparable to, say, the brilliance with which Wellington was to employ the same two factors at Salamanca. Constantine fixed his headquarters at the Saxa Rubra, the tawny cliff which is to-day known as Grotta Rossa, on the Via Flaminia about four miles north of the Milvian Bridge. He was thus able to station his army on the plateau, below whose escarpment ran the swift-flowing Tiber, out of sight of Maxentius, whose approach, once he had made the fatal decision to leave Rome, led along a dead straight highway, across a dead flat plain, for two whole miles beneath the eyes of Constantine's pickets. Constantine allowed Maxentius' army to cross the river, and to weary itself by scaling the height beneath the autumn sun. Then like a thunderbolt his own troops, untired and ardent, burst from their cover to hurl the enemy back down the fatal slope, where they met destruction by sword or drowning at the wreckage of the bridge below.

Constantine might well have claimed this action as a great feat of arms. But he never did: he was perfectly conscious to whom he owed this crowning mercy: it was to the Christian God. In Baynes' words:

"Against the advice of the augurs, in spite of his military counsellors, unsupported by the troops of Licinius, with incredible audacity Constantine had risked everything on a single hazard—and won. How shall that success be explained? Constantine himself knew well the reason for his victory: it had been won 'instinctu divinitatis', by a 'virtus' which was no mere human valour, but was a mysterious force which had its origin in God ... Victory had been promised him by the God of the Christians; he had challenged the Christian God to an Ordeal by Battle and that God had kept his pledge. This belief of Constantine remains of fundamental significance for the understanding of the policy of the reign."

The reign belongs to a new epoch: this study must close where that begins. In and through Constantine, the Church had triumphed. The very next year, 313, Constantine and Licinius met at Milan. Licinius married Constantine's half-sister, and the two emperors jointly issued what is known as the Edict of Milan (though it is strictly speaking not an edict but a letter addressed to certain governors), which grants complete religious toleration to one and all, Christian or pagan. It is no grudging concession, but a declaration of toleration *"given freely and unreservedly"*. Confiscated Christian property both personal and corporate was to be restored, "setting aside all delay and doubtfulness", bona fide purchasers of such property to be compensated by the exchequer.

The long strife was over, the battle won. Licinius was to turn against Constantine and against the Christians: there were internal troubles to be faced with heretics. Constantine was not to be sole emperor until the year 324. But the old age perished at the Milvian Bridge, ar.d a new Christian age began. The empire was still largely, perhaps predominantly, pagan. But its ruler, even if he postponed his baptism until his last hours, was a convinced and sincere Christian. This inadequate study of the process which had brought about this wonder may fittingly close with the words with which Eusebius ends his *Church History*:

"Constantine the most mighty victor, resplendent with every virtue that godliness bestows, together with his son Crispus, an emperor most dear to God and in all respects like his father, recovered the East that belonged to them, and formed the Roman Empire, as in the days of old, into a single united whole, bringing under their peaceful rule all of it, from the rising sun round about in both directions, north as well as south, even to the utmost limits of the declining day. So then there was taken away from men all fear of those who formerly oppressed them; they celebrated brilliant festivals; all things were filled with light, and men formerly downcast, looked at each other with smiling faces and beaming eyes; with dancing and hymns in city and country alike they gave honour first of all to God the universal king, as they had been instructed to, and then to the pious Emperor with his sons beloved of God. Old ills were forgotten, and oblivion cast on every deed of impiety; present good things were enjoyed, with the further hope of those which were yet to come. In short, there were promulgated in every place ordinances of the victorious emperor full of love for humanity, and laws that betokened munificence and true piety. Thus verily when all tyranny had been purged away, the kingdom that belonged to them was preserved steadfast and undisputed for Constantine and his sons alone, who when they had made it their very first action to cleanse the world from the hatred of God, conscious of the good things that he had bestowed upon them, displayed their love of virtue and of God, their piety and gratitude towards the Deity, by their manifest deeds in sight of all men."

THE END

Table I

THE ROMAN EMPERORS
27 BC–AD 324

BC
27 Augustus
AD
14 Tiberius
37 Caius (Caligula)
41 Claudius
54 Nero
68, ⎧ Galba
  ⎨ Otho
69 ⎪ Vitellius
  ⎩ Vespasian
79 Titus
81 Domitian
96 Nerva
98 Trajan
117 Hadrian
138 Antoninus Pius
161 Marcus Aurelius
180 Commodus
   ⎧ Pertinax
193 ⎨ Didius Julianus
   ⎩ Septimius Severus
211 Caracalla
217 Macrinus
218 Elagabalus
222 Severus Alexander
235 Maximinus
238 Pupienus and the Gordians
244 Philip the Arab
249 Decius
251 Gallus and Volusianus
253 Valerian and Gallienus
260 Gallienus
268 Claudius "Gothicus"

270 Aurelian
275 Tacitus
276 Probus
282 Carus
283 Carinus and Numerian
284 Diocletian
286 Diocletian with Maximian
293 Diocletian with Maximian, with Constantius and Galerius as Caesars: *the First Tetrarchy*
305 *Abdication of Diocletian and Maximian* Galerius and Constantius emperors, with Maximin and Severus Daia Caesars: *the Second Tetrarchy*
306 *Death of Constantius*; Constantine acclaimed emperor at York
307 Maxentius acknowledged as emperor by Constantine *Death of Severus*
308 Licinius proclaimed emperor by Galerius
310 *Death of Maximian*
311 *Death of Galerius*
312 *Death of Maxentius*
313 *Death of Maximin Daia*
315? *Death of Diocletian*
324 Licinius defeated and banished: CONSTANTINE SOLE EMPEROR

Table II

THE SYRIAN DYNASTY

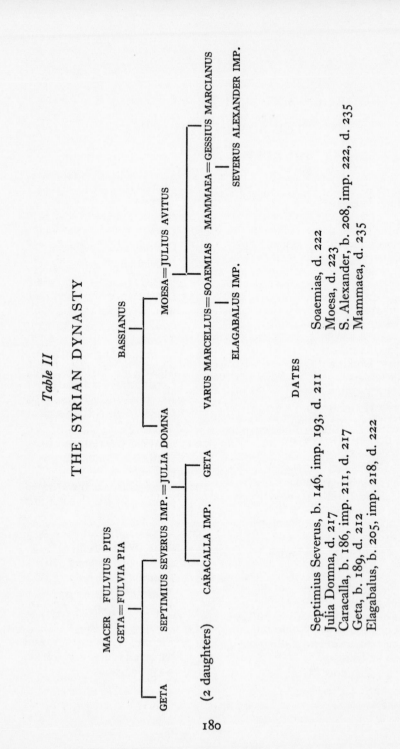

DATES

Septimius Severus, b. 146, imp. 193, d. 211
Julia Domna, d. 217
Caracalla, b. 186, imp. 211, d. 217
Geta, b. 189, d. 212
Elagabalus, b. 205, imp. 218, d. 222

Soaemias, d. 222
Moesa, d. 223
S. Alexander, b. 208, imp. 222, d. 235
Mammaea, d. 235

SOURCES AND ACKNOWLEDGEMENTS:
SCOPE OF THIS STUDY

A. ANCIENT SOURCES

I. *Pagan.* These are nearly all late and tenuous, becoming ever thinner as the third century progresses. The following table cites them in order of importance:

(1) *Up to AD 229:* CASSIUS DIO COCCEIANUS, a Bithynian who held official posts in the provinces and in Rome, and was twice consul, the second time with the emperor Severus Alexander in 229. He wrote a history of Rome down to that year in eighty books. For the years 180–229 he is an eye-witness. He is therefore able to be much more detailed, but inevitably writes with less perspective. The narrative of the last ten years is an afterthought. Observations on Dio's attitude and character will be found in the text. We do not possess the original of his work, but only a compendium made in the twelfth century.

(2) *AD 180–238.* HERODIAN, a Syrian Greek, wrote his history in eight books, for the latter years as a contemporary observer. He supplements Dio, whose work he did not use. His Syrian origin and outlook make him a valuable source for the Severan dynasty, despite his florid style and the dreary speeches with which he peppers his narrative.

(3) *AD 117–284,* with a gap between *244 and 253.* The AUGUSTAN HISTORY is a collection of *Lives,* written ostensibly by six authors, and dedicated to Diocletian and Constantine. It may be a later compilation, based on material of the third century. It is a much disputed work, which is, in Rand's words, "generally damned and generally used".

(4) *Up to AD 306.* SEXTUS AURELIUS VICTOR, an African, wrote a history of the empire about the year 360. We possess his work only in a late epitome, which is nevertheless, amid the general poverty of our sources, of considerable use.

Apart from these historians, for particular incidents or persons mentioned in the text, we are able to cite MARCUS CORNELIUS FRONTO, a native of Numidia; AELIUS ARISTIDES, of Athens, the panegyrist (not to be confused with his Christian namesake); and their younger contemporaries, AULUS GELLIUS whose *Attic Nights* is as delightful as its name: a miscellany of anecdotes and comments in the style of a modern literary "columnist", and APULEIUS, another Numidian, whose *Metamorphoses* (*The Golden Ass*) are still read. So, in a very different genre, are the famous *Meditations* of the emperor MARCUS AURELIUS, of whom the four authors just named were contemporaries. The philosophers LONGINUS, PLOTINUS and PORPHYRY who lived in the latter half of the third century, will be mentioned in their place.

II. *Christian.* It is impossible to cite here more than a few, the more outstanding, of a very great company. First there are the *Apologists,* men who wrote to commend their Faith to pagans. Of these the most important during the second century is JUSTIN, of Nablus in Palestine, who died as a martyr in Rome in 165. TERTULLIAN, of Carthage, born about 150, is so bountiful and compelling a writer that, although his *Apology* is one of the most famous and fascinating books of its kind ever written, it would be gravely underestimating Tertullian to regard him solely as an apologist. MINUCIUS FELIX, who flourished about 200, wrote an apology called *Octavius* which is among the most charming productions of the early Church. The prince of apologists is ORIGEN, of Alexandria, who taught and wrote during the first half of the third century. Chadwick, in the Introduction to his translation of the *Against Celsus* (Cambridge 1953) writes: "There are perhaps few works of the early Christian Church which compare in interest or importance with that which is here translated. The *contra Celsum* stands out as the culmination of the whole apologetic movement of the second and third centuries." Origen, like Tertullian, was a writer of great scope and multiplicity of interest.

Of *Theological and Pastoral* writers there are many, of whom special mention must be made of IRENAEUS, the great bishop of Lyons in the last quarter of the second century; CLEMENT, of Alexandria, who flourished about the same time; and CYPRIAN, of Carthage, who suffered martyrdom in 258. There are a host of others. I am humbly aware that I have not even mentioned many whose faith and merit still command veneration. In so wide a sea, an inexpert navigator must sail from cape to cape.

Finally come the *Historians*. For our period there are two of the first importance: EUSEBIUS, of Caesarea in Palestine, and LACTANTIUS, an African. Both these men lived through the final persecutions of the end of the third and beginning of the fourth centuries, both became the trusted friends of Constantine. Their works have therefore a double value. In the text of this book, Eusebius' *Church History* is cited in the abbreviation CH.

The preponderance, indeed the near-monopoly, of Africans and Asians, both pagan and Christian, in the above list is of great significance. In literature as in politics, it was the eastern provincials who increasingly took the initiative.

III. Special mention must be made of the *papyri*, those precious scraps of writing that come to us from the sands of Egypt. These may be either such a rarity as the Bodmer Gospel of St John, shewn in Plate 1 (*a*), or, more ordinarily, pages from domestic correspondence and accounts, or, like those cited on page 138, from official files. They are always "best evidence" of the events they concern.

IV. *Inscriptions and coins* furnish us with valuable and authentic material. In a period when pagan *literary* material is so scarce, the evidence of inscriptions, official and unofficial, is of great importance. The same applies to coins, both from the images they bear, and the "slogans" that explain them—sometimes even from the metal of which they are made (e.g., see page 160). For certain events modern scholars have to rely solely on these two authentic and contemporary sources.

V. Finally, for early Christian ideas and motives, we have *gems, sculpture* and *frescoes*, examples of each of which will be found among the Plates.

B. MODERN WRITERS

Modern literature on the period is very extensive. The Eldorado is the *Cambridge Ancient History*, specially Volumes XI and XII. Whatever may be the shortcomings of the last Volume as a narrative (see Introduction), as a mine of scholarship it is extremely rich; and the *Bibliographies* are an excellent guide to the politics, art, religion and commerce of the age. Intending students of the period, after savouring Gibbon, cannot do better than start with the *Cambridge Ancient History*, cited in this book by its abbreviation CAH.

In the evaluation of the progress of the Christian Faith, I can only name here certain works which I have found of particular help.

First comes Monsignor Louis Duchesne's *Histoire Ancienne de l'Église* (Paris 1906), or in its English translation, *Early History of the Christian Church*. The English version of Volume I appeared in 1909, and the work has been reprinted seven times: what was once controversial has now become a classic. Even so, it has been supplemented by other French scholars. H. Daniel-Rops has written a work entitled *Histoire de l'Église du Christ*, covering the period from the Apostolic age to the year 1350. All three volumes of this history are available in English. The first of them, covering the period AD 36-397, was published last under the title *The Church of Apostles and Martyrs*. A truly monumental work is the *Histoire de L'Église depuis les origines jusqu'à nos jours*, prepared, in twenty-four volumes, under the direction of Augustin Fliche and Victor Martin, of which Volume II, by Jules Lebreton and Jacques Zeiller, covers the period from the end of the second century to the Peace of Constantine. This appeared in 1948. It is now available in English and is one of the best products of the modern French school of theologians and Church historians, who are *hors concours* in their field. For the pagan religious background Franz Cumont's *Réligions orientales dans le paganisme romain* (Ed. 4, 1929) may be supplemented by Legge's *Forerunners and Rivals of Christianity* (repr. New York 1950). On Conversion two standard works are, in English, A. D. Nock's *Conversion* (Oxford 1933), and in French, Gustave Bardy's *La conversion au Christianisme durant les premiers siècles* (Paris 1949).

In a class by itself is *L'Histoire de Palestine depuis la conquête d'Alexandre jusqu'à l'invasion arabe*, by the great Dominican scholar, the late Père F-M. Abel (Paris 1952). Père Abel spent more than half a century in the Levant as archaeologist and scholar. He knew every site, every inscription, every coin that bears upon the story. Quotations in this study are taken from Volume II.

For individual emperors, the *Life and Reign of the Emperor Lucius Septimius Severus*, by M. Platnauer (Oxford 1918); and the *Life of Alexander Severus*, by R. V. N. Hopkins (Cambridge 1907), will be of help to English readers.

On the catacombs the best and most balanced recent work is that of the Jesuits Ludwig Herthing and Engelbert Kirschbaum. It is now available in an American translation published in Milwaukee under the title *The Roman Catacombs and their Martyrs*. For the study of a typical early church building in Rome, *Les Origines du Titre de Saint Martin aux Monts à Rome*, by René Viellard (Paris 1931), is a good guide.

Of those who have helped me the list is long. Once again I thank the Master and Fellows of Corpus Christi College, Cambridge, for allowing me to reside in the College during the summer of 1960, and so to get the book started. Among others to whom my thanks are due I mention with special gratitude the Government of the United Kingdom of Libya, and Contessa Cicogna, for forwarding my researches in Libya; Mr Peter Parr, of the British School in Jerusalem; M. Henri Seyrig, Directeur des Musées de France, Professor C. H. O. Scaife, of the American University of Beirut, Dr Selim 'Adil 'Abdulhaq, Director General of Antiquities and Museums in Syria, and his staff, and Mr and Mrs G. de la P. Cassels, for the same kind offices in Jordan, Lebanon and Syria. In Rome, I have been continually assisted and encouraged by the Director of the British School, Mr J. Ward Perkins, and his staff, and by Professor Kirschbaum, S.J.

In conclusion I wish to say that the general view of Constantine which I have adopted is that put forward by the late Professor N. H. Baynes in CAH, Volume XII, because it seems to me to be the only one that makes sense of all the recorded facts. In this view I am fortified by the endorsement independently given to it by two of the most eminent English scholars in this field. I cannot write as a scholar, nor for scholars: they are familiar with all that I have attempted to describe, and with the multitudinous controversies that surround nearly every issue. The intention of this study is a modest one. It is my hope, only, that it may serve as a guide, not a preceptor, to those ordinary folk who may be wondering how to start their study of the period, a period which was to have an abiding influence on all future epochs, including that in which we now live.

S. H. P.

INDEX

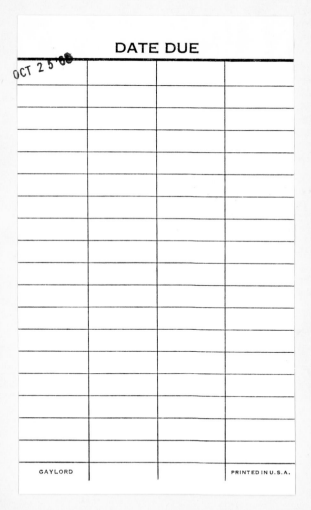

DATE DUE

OCT 25'66

GAYLORD   PRINTED IN U.S.A.

NOTES

1. This map does not pretend to be complete. It has been kept as simple as possible; and only those names have been inserted which are necessary for understanding the narrative.

2. No attempt has been made to maintain consistency in the use of ancient or modern names; they are used, whether ancient or modern, either because they are the most familiar, or because they accord with the text.